T0047293

The Complete Guide to Chakras

THE COMPLETE GUIDE TO

Chakras

Activating the **12-CHAKRA** Energy System for Balance and Healing

APRIL PFENDER

Illustrations by Enya Todd

ROCKRIDGE PRESS

Copyright © 2020 by Rockridge Press, Emeryville, California

No part of this publication may be reproduced, stored in a retrieval system, or transmitted in any form or by any means, electronic, mechanical, photocopying, recording, scanning, or otherwise, except as permitted under Sections 107 or 108 of the 1976 United States Copyright Act, without the prior written permission of the Publisher. Requests to the Publisher for permission should be addressed to the Permissions Department, Rockridge Press, 6005 Shellmound Street, Suite 175, Emeryville, CA 94608.

Limit of Liability/Disclaimer of Warranty: The Publisher and the author make no representations or warranties with respect to the accuracy or completeness of the contents of this work and specifically disclaim all warranties, including without limitation warranties of fitness for a particular purpose. No warranty may be created or extended by sales or promotional materials. The advice and strategies contained herein may not be suitable for every situation. This work is sold with the understanding that the Publisher is not engaged in rendering medical, legal, or other professional advice or services. If professional assistance is required, the services of a competent professional person should be sought. Neither the Publisher nor the author shall be liable for damages arising herefrom. The fact that an individual, organization, or website is referred to in this work as a citation and/or potential source of further information does not mean that the author or the Publisher endorses the information the individual, organization, or website may provide or recommendations they/it may make. Further, readers should be aware that websites listed in this work may have changed or disappeared between when this work was written and when it is read.

For general information on our other products and services or to obtain technical support, please contact our Customer Care Department within the United States at (866) 744-2665, or outside the United States at (510) 253-0500.

Rockridge Press publishes its books in a variety of electronic and print formats. Some content that appears in print may not be available in electronic books, and vice versa.

TRADEMARKS: Rockridge Press and the Rockridge Press logo are trademarks or registered trademarks of Callisto Media Inc. and/or its affiliates, in the United States and other countries, and may not be used without written permission. All other trademarks are the property of their respective owners. Rockridge Press is not associated with any product or vendor mentioned in this book.

Interior and Cover Designer: Erik Jacobsen
Art Producer: Megan Baggott
Editor: Sean Newcott
Production Editor: Matt Burnett
Illustrations © 2020 Enya Todd
Author photograph courtesy of Unplug Meditation © 2019

ISBN: Print 978-1-64739-060-0 | eBook 978-1-64739-061-7
R0

To all my teachers who blazed a path so bright I had no choice but to stand in the light. Mary Magdalene and Kali Ma (possibly my greatest teachers)—you always arrive with perfect timing. To Thoth—without you, this book wouldn't have happened. And finally, to the Andromedans, Mantis, and Pleiadians, thank you for helping this material find a voice through you.

Contents

Introduction

AS A REIKI MASTER TEACHER, sound healer, and meditation instructor, I have had thousands of patients and students come to me over the years to receive advice, treatments, and coaching on their own energy systems. I have given a countless number of chakra readings at the educational trainings, retreats, and workshops I host. I let people know where they are holding energy and how they can work to correct their imbalances. I have the benefit and privilege of seeing the collective commonalities that tie us all together with a golden thread, weaving the story of our energy bodies as individuals and as part of the greater whole. I have seen the stories changing and evolving, and now I invite you, starshine, to embrace your personal ascension journey so that you may discover the truth for yourself of who and what you really are.

While my previous books, *Chakra Balance* and *Essential Chakra Meditation,* have had their own successes, this more advanced, complete volume has been gestating in the background for some time. I'm excited to present an updated look at the traditional chakra system—a more comprehensive view that focuses on the ascension journey in this template of New Earth, our current paradigm. The first three chakras primarily address earthly concerns like safety, sexuality, and power. As you climb the ascension ladder, these worldly preoccupations lighten, and you'll begin to uncover new layers of consciousness that will be integrated through massive collective shifts, such as the one we are in right now: the Age of Aquarius, ushering in the rise of the Divine Feminine.

Here we will begin to peel back the layers of this eternal story so that you can get a clear picture of how the chakras influence your body's energy systems and how you can work with them on a deeper level to achieve ultimate healing and balance. We will touch on how the chakras are historically viewed, what it means when you experience blockages or stagnancy, and different techniques you can work into your life to help clear and manage these precious energy sites. We will peer into each chakra in depth, examining its location on or outside the body, its governing principles and functions, as well as the planets, deities, archetypes, and personalities associated with each.

There are moments when it seems the Universe gives you a glimpse behind the scenes. The legged, winged, and scaled creatures of the land show themselves as they move about, circling, slithering, and slinking. The song of the cool wind whips through the trees, and the plants echo waves of agreement on the swaying breeze. The sound of water streaming nearby soothes the soul, as the benevolent cosmic dance reveals a night sky—a sky in which your royal legacy is written in clear, shining lights. It is the same canopy that your ancestors gazed upon, and it is embedded deep in the helixes of your DNA.

This moment whispers that you are a spark of pure consciousness, participating in physicality. You instantly feel your connection to all that is and all that ever was. You are but a breath away from the infinite, yet this ancient truth is also contained within every single cell that makes up your being. This now moment is a merging of light particles, transmitting your Divine blueprint into the embodiment of all your expressions. And through this union of the physical, mental, emotional, and spiritual, your experiences will be a reflection of what is possible. Your life will be a contribution to all humanity, as you inspire others to live less in fear and more in love with each step.

Like the twinkling stars in the sky scattered into clusters, your chakras are pure light and energy points that create a map on, above, and below your body. Together, your 12 chakras form a rainbow constellation that corresponds with regions on and around your physical body and acts as a celestial bridge as it flows from above your crown and spirals up into the cosmos. This book is an invitation to lean in and take an intimate look at how these energy portals guide all aspects of your life. From how you engage with the world to how the Universe is managed and contained within you, your chakras hold the key to your health and vital well-being. The seven main traditional chakras are the foundational elements of life itself. Your complete chakra system houses 12 energetic vortexes with a great number of smaller energy inlays (for example, your meridian system and nadis).

This book covers the 12-chakra ascension model, illuminating exactly what these centers are, how they work independently and together, and how you can use them to direct your energy to higher ends. This book focuses on how the constellation of your energy creates a Divine blueprint, tying you back to the stars and celestial bodies, universal and Source energy, using this ascension model. This model reminds you that your chakras encompass all layers of your being. They contribute to raising, restoring, and maintaining higher levels of consciousness from the micro to the macro, within your body, humanity, Earth, the solar system, and beyond.

The energies currently entering Earth are remarkably different from what they have ever been in that they contain higher frequencies and bandwidths of light, which must be integrated into your personal energy field so that you can experience all the physical, energetic, and subtle upgrades available to you through these transmissions. This updated look at the chakras considers the new powerful energetic shift that we are all experiencing. When you claim this ascended energy in your life, it sets a foundation of light for humanity to follow collectively.

PART ONE

Understanding the Chakras

In this part of the book, I'll cover what chakras are and how they function in the body. We will review regulating and balancing chakra health, therapeutic techniques you can use to remove blockages, and the mystical benefits of chakra healing. This section will give you a broader context of how the chakras function both independently and together to create transformational and evolutionary change.

1

Chapter One
The Body's Energy System

Let's begin with a general discussion of chakras and energy. Then we'll take a peek at the chakras in a more historical context, spanning timelines and continents, and complete this chapter with a look at subtle energy and energy healing.

The Chakras

Traditionally, we think of chakras as energetic gateways between our physical bodies and the world around us. They allow the currents of energy to flow between you and the world at large. Energy can be thought of as both the power it takes to make something move and the moving information. Your body actively generates frequencies in the form of electric and magnetic currents, which radiate inside, outside, and around your physical body. These currents overlap, forming vertical-oriented gateways. That's lots of moving energy! Chakras can be described as spinning, whirlpool-like wheels of light on both the front and back sides of your being, and when balanced, they channel energy optimally to keep your body at peak performance. In addition, everything we know has a chakra system—humans, plants, animals, the planet, and beyond.

It is well known in energy medicine and holistic healing that everything is energy. This energy originates within your auric field. The frequencies that generate optimal health as well as potential illness first arrive and live outside your physical body and, with enough accumulation, are later internalized, presenting as symptoms or physical effects. Your spiritual body (or subtle body) contains this energetic information and optimizes it as you move about your daily activities. The chakras have a profound influence over everything you do, including all your vital systems, inside and out. They process all the energy you come into contact with, including psychic energy (which is very fast), sensory energy (which is very slow), and everything in between.

Your higher chakra centers are continually projecting the hologram of your physical body into existence as it pours from the etheric template of your higher self into form. In this sense, you are an eternal energetic reflection, mirroring back the harmonics of your Divine radiance as an Earth being. To change your hologram, you must begin to work with and master your own energy. In other words, if you want to see change in your physical body, you must alter your chakra frequencies. Sometimes this starts with thoughts and feelings, which can affect the mental and material plane. Oftentimes, you can alter your energy field directly. We'll get into detail on how to work with your energy in chapter 3.

In this modern ascension chakra system, your chakras are associated with specific rainbow, metallic, and pastel colors (or frequencies), which are represented by spinning, colored lights that help connect cosmic energy through your physical body and into the heart of Gaia, or Mother Earth. Thinking of colors as frequencies may help illuminate their energetic nature as it relates to what's covered in this book. If you were to see the chakras spinning, they would appear as a blur because of how fast they spin. And if you were able to see the color spectrum on the body, you'd see the seven main chakras in a bandwidth from red to white. The expanded chakra system has more colors, or bandwidths of light, in which it operates. Chakras also have a shape, a speed and direction of spin, and the ability to open and close as necessary to regulate the energy coming and going from the physical body and all the subtle body layers (your aura, the biomagnetic wrapper that surrounds you).

We'll dive into chakra health in the upcoming chapters, but for now, it's important to recognize these energy centers as a complete system, responsible for your mental, physical, emotional, and spiritual well-being. These sensitive gateways, or portals, are adept at managing your energy along with physical issues. Each portal is generally associated with organs, glands, systems, body parts, and other characteristics within its relative resonance frequency, with the exception of some systemic crossover between chakras. Chakras are organic and fluid and, most importantly, highly characterized by the individual. That means that the chakras may be slightly different from person to person, as each one of us is a unique expression and frequency. Each chakra functions on a vibratory plane of its own that most closely correlates to locations on the body, but it's more accurate to say that the chakras flow like liquid, just like energy itself. If your chakra is vibrating at a certain frequency, energies outside that frequency cannot exist there for long.

Chakras throughout History

You are likely familiar with the Sanskrit word *chakra*, meaning "wheel," but where did it originate? Scholars have discussed this worldwide, and studies suggest the word and concept of chakras, originally denoted as *cakras*, originated in the Vedas. Unarguably, this collection of philosophical and metaphysical writings offers teachings that date back to between 1700 and 1100 BCE as the oldest written texts of the East. Since the Vedas house four main texts, each written in different time periods ranging from between 2200 and 900 BCE, it's hard to pinpoint exactly when discussions of the chakras arrived on the scene. The four main Vedic texts are the *Yajur Veda, Sama Veda, Rig Veda,* and *Atharva Veda*; they were passed down orally for thousands of years before being formally transcribed. Estimates suggest the information contained in these Hindu texts was likely shared verbally long before it was written, which dates it to between 12,000 BCE and 1000 BCE (a staggering 11,000-year stretch). The word *cakra* is also found in the Upanishads, part of Vedic scripture, which are Sanskrit texts shared by other religious traditions like Jainism and Buddhism.

To really begin to understand these writings, we must look to the authors. Many of these sacred Hindu texts sprang up in the Indus Valley around 1500 BCE, with the arrival of the Avestan-speaking people and the Aryans, who descended from Indo-European and Russian civilizations. The Aryans brought Sanskrit to the region, and both cultures believed in the existence of an invisible force that lived both inside and outside themselves. These ideas are thought to have been cultivated within their respective cultures and generally blended with the indigenous cultures that were already living in the local Indus Valley (the Harappans). Historians believe that the Vedic scriptures reflect both philosophies and may even allude to authorship contributions from more ancient cultures like the early eastern Indians or Dravidians.

While we would expect the texts to describe the chakras as spiritual organs, this compilation of literature does no such thing, mostly describing chakras, oddly enough, as representing the wheel of a chariot. In addition, the chakra was a symbol for dynamism and for the dawn. Since creation rotates on an axis, the word often appears as a symbol for this movement. Vishnu—the Hindu god said to hold Earth, space, and the atomic realm together—is also often mentioned in relation to chakras. He carries what is known as the *sudarshana chakra*, a disk-like weapon of ancient myth with 108 serrated edges, used to eliminate obstacles opposing his Divine plan.

Depending on the lineage and texts, many countries and cultures across the world offer conflicting information about chakras. While the West tends to compare chakras to organs in the physical body, chakras are not a static reality; they are a fluid reality due to their flowing, energetic nature. Chakras are also relatively prescriptive in nature, meaning they can point to recommendations to achieve specific goals by mystical means. For example, the original Vedas may have you visualize a white thousand-petaled lotus at a specific focal point on the body (in this case, the crown), and then activate its symbols through chant, mantra, or another means. Most of the ancient cultures attempted to install deity energies and mantras at chosen points on the body through *nyāsa* (meaning "to place"). In other words, the original chakras were not much more than inception portals for deities to enter the body. Our modern system of chakras developed over time, as these portal placements grew into energy centers, reflecting the energy of the deities invoked at those sites. This body template of the lotus chakra system was associated with three things: mystical sounds (found in the petals), specific elements (earth, wind, water, fire, and ethers), and a specific Hindu deity.

In addition, the psychological states that we in the West typically associate with the chakras happen to have sprung up as an historical innovation derived from Carl Jung's archetypal theories and aren't typically represented within the Sanskrit context. For example, the solar plexus is associated with power and purpose in modern chakra systems, while the ancient context would associate each lotus petal chakra with a distinct emotional state. An important cross-cultural takeaway here is that the chakras can be used as general tools to heal and balance the energetic, physical, spiritual, and emotional bodies. Things shake up a bit when we're comparing systems, and it varies across cultures, so let's take a deeper look into how this translates in different ancient cultures across the world. After that, we'll take a look at how the ancient Sanskrit roots evolved into the modern system we have today.

CHAKRAS ACROSS THE WORLD

Chakras themselves, energy medicine philosophies, and cosmologies have historically and contemporarily existed everywhere, woven into the international fabric of our world across a diverse spectrum of representation and application. India, Africa, the Middle East, Europe, and America all have similar or equivalent traditions that highlight the modern relevancy of chakras as energy centers. Intertwined in the teachings are the basic tenets of awareness, consciousness, energy bodies, and doorways to Spirit. Let's take a closer look, starting with the Hermetic mystery traditions (Egypt, India, and Persia), almost all of whose philosophies embrace beliefs in intangible energy.

In Africa, the Kemetic Tree of Life sprang up with the Egyptians, who practiced magic and mystery teachings as part of their daily life. They primarily focused on the energy body called the *ka* and worked with the Tree of Life as a pathway from Earth to the heavens. The circles in the tree represented the locations of the chakras. Jewish mystics likely adopted the Kabbalah from Egyptian influence, tracing back to when Moses, a Hebrew, led the exodus of the Israelites out of Egypt. Early Egyptian energetics contain a goldmine of concepts analogous to the chakras and subtle energy we know today, like that of *sekhem*, or life-force energy. The *ba*, or soul, represents nonphysical energies. The Yoruba tribe of Africa, who also practiced mysticism and magic, had *orishas*, or spirits, that dwell within the body, correlating to Hindu chakra sites. The Dogon were another tribe that worked with sacred geometry and information received directly from their home-star, Sirius, to help control living conditions and heal tribe members. The information they received from the stars was extremely mathematically accurate, far surpassing their technological abilities. Some say these ancient cultures were always connected to galactic gateways, which allowed this transfer of universal knowledge.

In Hinduism, the energy of the *ka* body would be considered *prana* (breath, or life-giving force) or *kundalini* (energy coiled at the base of the spine). The Hindu text *Bhagavata-purana* lists six locations for the chakras; two other spiritual centers were added later for performing higher spiritual practices. Moving into Tibet with Buddhist philosophy and a continuation of Tantric and yogic ideas, chakras are most commonly thought of as channel wheels or doors that would aid in achieving emptiness, or enlightenment. There are sometimes 4, 5, 7, or 10 wheels, which vary, but in general, they all rely on *tummo*, or kundalini, for ultimate awakening and integration of the full chakra system.

The Middle East, with its diverse religious history, is replete with variations of the chakra system. Zoroastrians, authors of the scripture Avesta, had the holy system Amesha Spentas, or Divine emanations, which most closely translated to a six-chakra system. The Sufis and Jewish people were rich in mystical cosmology, and both talk about vital energy bodies throughout their sacred texts and teachings, relating the realms of the metaphysical to that eternal creation that lies within each one of us.

In North and South America and Mesoamerica, the ancient Mayans, Incans, Andeans of Peru, and Huicholes, as well as other native cultures, worked with the elements and physical locations of chakras on the body. Their shamanic teachings and temple iconography indicate inclusive knowledge of energy bodies and spirits (energy) from the land and sky. In North America, tribes like the Cherokee had mystical connections to the Pleiades and highlight body and Earth matrices, meridians, and various interconnecting points on the body in their cosmology. It would seem that across the world, all of these cultures were mysteriously able to access very similar technological, mathematical, and mystical information.

Stepping into Europe, the Vikings held an understanding of the chakras, evocatively symbolized by a tree with nine Norse worlds. The Yggdrasil tree was a bridge connecting the human realm to Asgard, the place of the gods. The Celts of Neolithic Britain had many myths and lore of gods and goddesses, too, which contained the concept of *arganto-rota*, or "silver wheel." It is said that in Avalon, which is a sacred chakra of Earth, the chakras were framed as seven points of consciousness, with the top point of consciousness (the crown) being a house for the rest of the energies and not an actual chakra itself.

Subtle Energy, Healing Energy

Early on in human history, our ancestors figured out that more subtle dimensions of energy existed within and outside of their own physical bodies. They worked with this subtle energy to heal the body directly, and this type of energy can be found referenced across many civilizations and ancient cultures. Subtle energy is also called *qi* or *chi* in Chinese. It is the vital life-force energy that moves through and animates all things. This energy is also referred to as *ki* in Japanese or *prana* in Sanskrit.

The body meridians, auric layers, and chakra system are the three main subtle energy systems of the body. We cannot see or touch these systems, as they are intangible. If we were to compare subtle energy to physical energy, subtle energy would feel delicate like the wind, and physical energy would feel solid like the earth. Subtle energy is present everywhere, and it can be harnessed and channeled, just like powering a windmill. Although subtle energies are to be felt and experienced, there are modern ways to map and measure them. These energies can be identified and classified as localized, meaning they exist where we expect to find them and can be relatively measured with contemporary technology. Subtle energy manipulation is employed to bring about physical and energetic change. Let's look at the three subtle energy systems.

The meridian system is used in traditional Chinese medicine. This system is like a river or highway that runs through the inside of the body and channels energy throughout the entire physical body. Ancient medicine practices such as acupuncture work by adjusting your qi to more easily move through this intricate web of channels so that it may service the interconnecting areas of the body. For example, specific points can address things like allergies, digestive issues, and lung or kidney deficiencies. There are more than 400 points in the body that are connected with the meridian system, and they all tie in to these superhighways. By clearing stagnancy at these points, your body frees up and improves the flow of qi, creating a ripple that benefits the entire system.

The auric field, which is made up of layers, exists outside the body and has a profound effect on your evolution and state of consciousness. Anything that is happening in your mind, body, or soul is directly reflected within your aura. The seven subtle aura layers are (1) the etheric body, (2) emotional body, (3) mental body, (4) astral body, (5) etheric template, (6) celestial body, and (7) casual body, or ketheric template. These bands of light energy wrap the body like a bubble, and each layer moves progressively away from the physical body. These layers start at about one to three inches away from the physical body and extend up to six feet or more, depending on the individual. It is thought that each layer corresponds to one of the seven main chakras. You can also think of these layers as similar to your electromagnetic field, although these layers are actually a step up in vibration. They hold a variety of information and are most easily accessed during states of deep meditation, where the ability to foster healing and balancing exist.

Finally, the chakras are your subtle energy system that act as energetic exchange points, organizing the energy your body intakes and discharges. These vortexes are the primary focus of this book, and you can think of them as the most important because they are responsible for enabling you to convert nonphysical energy to physical energy and vice versa. They step energy up and down in frequency and determine what to let in and out. The chakras allow you to access universal energy in all its forms and efficiently process the energy you receive from other people, places, and occurrences.

Regulating this precious energy is a big job, and if done well, it can keep you healthy and healed. Let us think of healing as less of a static, fixed term and more of a liquid, flexible term. Healing comes to us when we need it, and you are always in various stages of resonance. The frequencies in your multidimensional self are constantly shifting, creating new versions of you and new ways of being. Working with your chakras and knowing how to identify optimal functioning will build your awareness and healing toolkit.

The Chakra System

In my book *Chakra Balance*, I discuss the seven main chakras in depth and provide insight on how they function and operate, as well as information on how to bring balance and healing to your entire system. The information presented in that book is an easy-to-understand, modern approach to learning about these energy vortexes as we know them today. This book takes our journey a step further as we dive deeper into the chakra system, incorporating and remodeling a vast array of divergent information into a much more detailed and comprehensive updated look.

Let's take a peek at the 12 chakras we'll be discussing, which include five chakras outside the seven commonly known energy vortexes. These chakras make up a more complete picture of the intersecting energy gateways atop and around your body to reveal how these relatively untethered portals express the totality of who you really are. Outside the physical body exist additional meeting points for further-reaching energy centers. These are your etheric, or transpersonal, chakras. When you connect to the infinite rays of Divine energy available from gateways above your crown space, you can more intimately know your oversoul (the main umbrella of your soul) and start to tap into the collective consciousness to access different insights and wisdom for this time of increased evolutionary energies on Earth.

Lesser known and even less commonly understood because of the conflicting published misinformation on the matter, these etheric portals put us in touch with a whole array of dimensions within and beyond our human purview. The 12-chakra ascension system outlined in this book offers a holistic picture of health and wellness beyond the localized physical senses. When you draw on energies and outside cosmic forces within an extended system of your own energy body, you begin to personally relate to the Universe as an individual part of a vast expanse of oneness. This unification provides a holistic model that is more adapted to the current increasing changes happening within our energy fields.

The traditional chakra system follows a rainbow spectrum of light frequencies; the 12 chakras trail this spectrum and broaden as they extend out from your being. In addition to extending below your physical form into the heart of the earth, the etheric chakras (which are entirely disembodied in that they do not physically touch the body) flow out from above you and reach upward toward the cosmos. They connect thousands of minor energetic centers that weave like rivers in a dance with your mind, body, and spirit. The 12 chakras form a pillar of light, or ascension column, which bridges your body between Divine Source and the core of Gaia.

The 12 chakras begin with ground zero, your Earth star chakra below your feet, and travel all the way up through your seven main chakras, which flow into purely etheric chakras above your crown space. The higher chakras connect you outside your physical being to the collective, as well as to your own unlimited vastness of consciousness and higher realms. In general, the frequencies of your soul star, stellar gateway, universal gateway, and Divine gateway make up your four highest etheric chakra centers. Your mental energies live in the crown space, while your vision and clarity live in your third eye. Your expression lives in the throat, energies of acceptance and loving frequencies in the heart space, motivation and confidence in the solar plexus, sensuality and balance in your sacral region, and stabilizing energy in your root chakra. I'll be covering these in much greater detail throughout the book, as each chapter in part 2 is dedicated to exploring each energy portal in depth.

Remember, there are many different systems throughout the world; this book follows the 12-chakra ascension model. As mentioned, many ancient writings and sacred texts disagree on the number, location, and specific functions of the chakras. This book clarifies the 12 chakras in detail according to bodies of historical research as they apply to our world today. Calling upon ascended realms and specific channels, as well as my own channeled information, I'll present a new way to look at the chakras at this time. It is my highest hope that this information will be a great benefit to your spiritual growth so that we can reach the next tiers of higher collective consciousness together.

Alternative Chakra Systems

As discussed, there are a myriad of translations and interpretations of the chakra systems compiled from across the world. The chakras as we know them are mostly Western derived at this point, in terms of their physiological, localized, and functional associations, and this book presents one viewpoint and model for our current page of planetary existence. Looking back at the rich cultural diversity and history of how our modern system came to be, it's important to take away a few key points so that you can better understand the fluidity of what we are going to be working with.

When you compare all the far-reaching systems of the world, there is no standard chakra system. Rather, these concepts are endlessly varied, extensively divergent, and colossal in nature. As touched on, the variations in the Hindu and other Tantric systems alone can recognize as few as three and as many as 12 chakras. Apart from these, there is a medley of differing ideas between original scripts across and between cultures. In a six-deities Hindu system, for example, you use a six-chakra system. Tantric Buddhism (from Tibet) preserves an older five-chakra system, while Pranic Healing (as developed by Master Choa Kok Sui) uses an 11-chakra system that includes the knees and spleen, which we traditionally see in traditional Chinese medicine.

Your Personal Aura and Merkaba Body

Inside your body, billions of molecules act as their own cosmos, swirling and sparking together and apart. If we start to zoom out, past the physical layers of the body, we come to the next cosmic stratum, your auric layers, or simply your aura. These etheric blankets, which wrap the body, are made of light-energy particles and create your subtle body.

Beyond your aura is your *merkaba* (*mer* means "light," *ka* means "soul," and *ba* means "body"). This is an Egyptian term for the light-body technology that surrounds your outer aura. The merkaba is generally thought to be an electromagnetic sacred geometry space/time/dimensional vehicle, which, once activated, allows the traveler to cross multidimensional boundaries. This is not a new concept; in fact, it is as old as time. The concept of a light vehicle pops up in the Torah (*merkavah*), the Bible (Ezekiel and the wheels of light in which he ascended to heaven), *The Egyptian Book of the Dead* (merkaba), and the Zulu tribe in Africa, whose legend has it that this is how their tribe originally arrived on Earth.

Drunvalo Melchizedek, a well-known ascension leader of our time, teaches this concept as an ascension technology that can carry us to different realms through the mind. The merkaba can be visualized and activated through specific meditation, sometimes spontaneously, and can be considered a jump in consciousness. This field of light is a living field and thus responds to human thoughts and feelings, which can grow or shrink the field. Within the field, we can achieve and sustain unconditional loving thoughts and ecstatic frequencies, helping us ascend back to Divine Source energy. In chapter 14, you'll find a merkaba meditation to practice. Also, in my book *Essential Chakra Meditation,* I offer a complete merkaba field activator for your crown chakra. You can use either of these meditations to help visualize and bring your merkaba to life!

However, three centers remain relatively common across all the systems: the head, the heart, and below the belly (sexual centers). Humans experience emotional and spiritual occurrences here, and for the most part, these are included across the board in many of the cultural descriptions and depictions. They likely developed to match an evolutionary blueprint of creation that showcased the culture's particular beliefs, religions, and cosmologies.

Some of the information presented in this book may surprise you, as this chakra format is somewhat nontraditional to modern Western eyes. And, in reality, all systems outside the one we know and love can be considered "alternative." Here, we follow an ascension process that specifically belongs to Earth at this time. We are all in this together, holding the frequencies for New Earth and new ways of being, which will set the templates for future generations to heal this reality while creating heaven on Earth. As the planet vibrates higher, so do we—and that changes the name of the chakraology game for us as we know it.

Chapter Two
Regulating the Energy Centers

I n this chapter, we'll discuss what it means to have a healthy and functioning chakra system. You'll also learn what it may look like when you're experiencing a block and how to restore function and flow back to your chakra system for better health and well-being.

Everything Is Energy

To touch back on chapter 1, absolutely everything in the world (and outside of it) exists as energy. Your pets, the sounds coming from your TV, the water running from the sink, and the thought forms you used to think about all these things—all energy. Let's turn our attention to how this applies to your personal energy. Since all living beings are composed of this sacred cosmic stuff, the chakra system is essential to wellness, balance, and living a thriving life through higher levels of consciousness. Any living (and, some would argue, nonliving) thing has a consciousness, and all of it is interlaced into a Divine multidimensional tapestry that creates your reality and your participation with it.

We can think of this connection like covalent bonds: it holds us to one another just like covalent bonds bind electrons to other atomic particles, allowing them to spin within their own orbits but still touch others in an influential way. In a holographic reality of the multiverse, everything can be considered to house these layers of shared energy, and it goes on into infinity.

Each chakra has an approximate resonant vibration, which translates to a light frequency range. This range creates the colors associated with the chakras—but remember, it's merely a general approximation. As we peer higher up into layers of consciousness that have been previously inaccessible on this planet due to our level of evolution, we begin to access new frequencies and alternate bandwidths of light energy. When we look at the body systems and functions, everything can be relatively placed within a certain vibration, which loosely corresponds with color bands. For example, your stomach vibrates with a hue of yellow as it is in the solar plexus bandwidth, while the organs in your chest (like your lungs, heart, and thymus) resonate with a green or pink energy. Green and pink are associated with different dimensions and aspects corresponding to similar bandwidths that are contained in the heart chakra (as well as the high heart chakra), which we'll delve into in chapter 9.

When each chakra functions properly, the entire holistic system is kept in check. Since the health of these sensitive energy centers has a profound effect on the body systems and your emotional state, the chakras greatly impact the way you give and reserve energy for yourself. For example, if you are experiencing grief or loss or have just come through some massive changes in your life, you may have a root chakra blockage. With this chakra stopped up, it will be harder for grounding energy to move from Earth to stabilize your system and bring you relief. When you have a crown chakra blockage, universal energy isn't flowing in the way it should, and therefore your spiritual centers aren't able to pass you higher streams of consciousness or information. Specifically, when these caps, or poles, are closed, it becomes difficult to move energy in and out of your system, which can be extremely disruptive to your overall flow of life. In general, I rarely see crown chakra blockages, but I do see root space issues more and more increasingly in over half my patients. Also, if there's a block in the heart chakra, I like to focus on opening it right away, as this portal is involved in transmitting higher dimensional light frequencies directly from the etheric chakras.

All energy centers are intrinsically linked, and they need to create and maintain a certain vibration to stay healthy. When one chakra entrains to a lower vibration, the others become compromised—first in small ways and then building up over time. The chakras play vital roles and functions within the physical, psychological, emotional, and spiritual layers of your being. Understanding how to work with your own energy is crucial to maintaining optimal health. We'll be intimately exploring the ins and outs of your whole system in this book, so you'll be getting a close and personal look at it as well as a new mastery in energy medicine. I'm so excited to be sharing this adventure with you!

Healthy Chakras

It is a Buddhist belief that nothing is good or bad—it simply is. But we sure do notice when something is going well as it allows us to spiral up into positive feelings like happiness, cheer, gratitude, contentment, euphoria, and excitement. When you experience positivity, grace, ease, and flow in your life, this is a sign you are moving into higher bandwidths of energy. Your physical body will experience rejuvenation and restored health and healing, and your spiritual body will be nourished as it experiences accelerated synchronicities along with heightened states of consciousness on a more regular basis. When your chakras are balanced, clear, open, and healthy, they will optimally conduct energy in a grand symphony, in and out, between your body, all its layers, and the world around you.

Healthy chakras can be described in a number of ways. We can best define them as being free from debris and lower-vibrational energy while maintaining physical and subtle body function at a high level of homeostasis.

Debris consists of environmental entanglements that can interact with your subtle energy field, causing distortion. Debris can include biomagnetic particles like free radicals (which are unstable molecules), density (such as interdimensional interference), or even spirits (ancestral or etheric beings). Your energy generally needs to be pretty low to be susceptible to such negative energetic influences. Debris may also include energy imprints stored in your body or aura from past or, perhaps, parallel lives. Energy imprints are magnetic charges that are left behind, for example, from a strong memory or recollection you've experienced.

Besides debris, lower energy can hold a chakra back from opening to full health. Lower energies are represented by lower-vibrating emotional, mental, and spiritual energies. The waves these energies ride on are literally slower and longer and therefore denser than those of higher bandwidths. Anger, fear, grief, guilt, shame, doubts, and worries constitute some of the heavier emotional frequencies, while gratitude, passion, joy, enthusiasm, optimism, happiness, and empowerment make up some of the higher-vibrational ones. For healthy chakras to exist, you'll want to stay in the higher bandwidths, which attract and magnetize more of the same through the Law of Attraction. You can only manifest that which you are already the vibration of, so being healthy will create more of the same for you.

A healthy chakra is also free from energy leaks. One way we might experience energy leakage is when an energetic cord is formed that creates an attachment to a person, place, or thing outside the self. During meditation, this cord, although invisible to the naked eye, may resemble a string of light energy coming off the body and connecting to another party or object, which siphons energy away from you to the other source. A cord is formed through consistently diverting energy away from yourself to the other source. For example, placing focused energy for a prolonged period of time on anything creates an energy flow in that direction. If that energy flow is not reciprocal, it can become unhealthy.

Releasing cords can be as simple as calling outstanding cords into your vision within a meditation. Ask to be shown the cords and say, "Let all that is needed be known, especially any unhealthy energetic attachments that are no longer serving me or my highest good." The cords may appear to be strings, strands, ropes, bars, or beams running through your body, connecting to a specific area on the body or in the aura. You can ask your guides for assistance removing these cords and watch the cords sever, with one end returning to you and the other returning from where it came.

In general, a healthy chakra will have symmetry and uniform consistency and shape and will be free from holes, deficiencies, and blotches in color or areas of energy. It will radiate in a specific bandwidth, or a range of frequencies, specialized for each energy center and will help alchemize energies within and without to regulate, revitalize, and stabilize your physical, mental, emotional, and spiritual body.

Healthy chakras also interact with your auric layers and release trapped energy that shouldn't be in your system. Ideally, healthy chakras function as perceptual filters that provide impetus for spiritual change, growth, and expansion. If you're questioning the health of your chakras, I'll review everything you need to know to identify and fix these issues in the coming sections and chapters.

Blocked Chakras

Your chakras may get blocked from time to time. When energy becomes congested, it is unable to flow freely through the energetic vortexes of your chakra system. The blockage may manifest physically, emotionally, or spiritually and show up in the form of illness or *dis-ease,* which is the state of being out of ease. Illness or dis-ease denotes a dysfunction in your energetic blueprint that needs to be corrected through balancing, cleansing, purifying, and restoring. Think of blockages in terms of knots in your system. These knots close off your chakra flow and can inhibit subtle and physical energy exchanges between your body and the world around you.

In my experience, the chakra vortexes can slow down (due to low energy), close off, speed up (if they're too open), or warble, which could mean you aren't taking in enough energy or you've taken on too much—perhaps a burden activated from input you received from another source outside yourself, like an ex, your boss, or a stressed colleague. We all manage our energy in different ways. As creatures of habit, humans tend to place energy back into the same spots time and time again. Eventually, when enough energy accumulates, it can cause a blockage that will need to be discharged to invite movement back through the chakra.

In my practice, when I'm giving a chakra reading to assess chakra centers, I'm able to tell if the chakras are changing speed, atypically shaped, too open, or too closed. If I notice any of the aforementioned and it looks abnormal compared to the rest of the system, I investigate further. Usually, I perform an intuitive body scan to read the energy of the person and feel for the differences in the auric field. The differences may simply show up as temperature differences (warm or cool), an electric or tingling feeling over the blocked area, or energy radiating from the source of the block. You can assess your chakra centers for yourself by working with a pendulum (see page 29). You can also review the chakra chart in the appendix to determine which chakras to focus on for healing and review the entries in part two of this book to get a better understanding of the qualities of overactive and underactive chakras and their associated illnesses. For now, know that a blocked chakra isn't a reason to panic. It is simply a nice marker for you to focus on during your self-healing journey.

Chakra blockages may occur for a variety of reasons (usually a combination of several). You can experience emotional, physical, mental, and spiritual blockages, and they may show up in one or more of your chakras. Let's begin with emotional blockages. Your feelings are emotional reactions to events, and your emotions point to your natural intuition and instinct-based beliefs. Emotional blockages usually occur because triggering inputs cause tension and stress, which can then build up. Humans experience 10 main emotions: joy, sadness, fear, disgust, anger, excitement, surprise, contempt, shame, and guilt. Each of these feelings presents you with messages, and, generally, the more accepting you can be of yourself when these feelings come up, the more easily they'll be able to pass through without getting held up. Consequently, when you experience an emotion and are unable to acknowledge it or express it properly, a blockage can occur.

Mental blockages are up next. Identifying these can be trickier because they challenge your negative thought patterns, or in this case, the limiting beliefs and conditioning of the mind. Limiting beliefs may include feelings of being unworthy, powerless, unwanted, "wrong," or ashamed. Conditioning shows up as unhealthy programs that have been established for you to fit into. Not being aligned with social, personal, or familial conditioning tends to create tension in the body. You can think of feeling tension as moving through alternating frequencies. Healing for this type of thinking comes through raising your vibration to one of unity consciousness or, in other words, love. Life becomes a quest of unlearning all the programs you have been fed since birth that keep you down, playing small, and not living up to your fullest potential.

Let's address physical blockages next. These are perhaps the easiest to identify in the body as they are sensory in nature, and you can notice their presentation within your own body as something that just doesn't feel right. These types of blocks include pain from injuries or wounds and illness. Phantom pain shows up as an energetic imprint, a reminder of the frequency your body (usually) held when you were processing a trauma. For example, if you have been moving through heartbreak, even if it seems cleared in the physical system, occasionally you may still receive energy zaps around the heart chakra (depending on where you store the trauma). These phantom pains serve as a reminder that the energy of your past will need to either resolve on its own or be completely cleared through energy work, meditation, or other therapeutic methods. Phantom pains typically present themselves when the original emotional scar hasn't been entirely healed or addressed.

Lastly, spiritual blockages may pop up in the subtle body and psyche and need to be addressed to be cleared. Spiritual blockages can include energetic imprints from aspects of your soul or another's that have been affecting your field. These can range from mild to more severe in nature. Spiritual blockages can also occur due to interdimensional interference.

It is a common misconception that we take on other people's energy. We are sovereign beings with our own unique paths, and each of us operates within our own level of consciousness. After you've had a negative experience like a breakup or clash with a colleague, it can certainly *feel* like you've taken on energy from outside yourself. In reality, we don't take on another's energy for them unless we agree to it. Yes, you actually have to agree—either consciously or by your higher self's choice—to directly take on energy from another person. Taking on another's energy can happen when you willingly give your power away, but in general, it's uncommon to absorb energy from someone else directly into your field.

The fact is, energetically, we alter our frequency often. It is our energetic frequency that changes when we feel as though we're absorbing negative energy from others. When we stay in toxic relationships far beyond their expiration date or have negative interactions or experiences, these energies can leave imprints in our energetic fields. That is why it's important to clear your body and space after you've had an argument or after any traumatic event has occurred. A quick clearing can be done through smudging (burning sacred herbs), placing Himalayan salt in bowls around your home, or taking a cleansing shower or salt bath.

REMOVING BLOCKAGES

Energy wants to naturally flow freely through the body, and your body has lots of ways of telling you when it's in distress and needs a clearing. Luckily, purification is possible when you begin to listen closely and become intimate with the signs that a blockage may be present. Once you determine there is an energy block, you can get to work removing it.

It's important to remember that every physically manifested blockage (in the form of illness, injury, physical change, or symptoms) begins in the energy field. It can take up to two years until the physical issue appears (although changes can occasionally come around quicker), so it's logical to assume that it also takes time for the body to heal and recover. There are many ways you can speed up the process, but overall, it may take some time, especially if you are handling things on your own without the help of a healer.

Once you've identified which chakra needs some work, explore your options to find out what the most effective form of removal might be. Everyone who comes into my healing office knows that I am a huge proponent of natural energy medicine when possible, paired with meditation for energy maintenance. When your energy is off, you'll need to do two things quickly to turn it around: remove the lower-vibrating frequencies that are keeping your blockage in place and replace them with higher vibrations. I suggest starting with guided meditation to create the spaciousness required to begin your healing journey. Although Reiki healing is my personal go-to, I always recommend energy work as a first attempt at removing the blocks yourself, as an alternative to invasive procedures or pharmaceutical solutions, which only address the physical level of the problem. If you address the energetic issues first, the physical ripples will self-correct in time.

To address the body holistically, you'll want to address all the levels, which include physical, mental, emotional, and spiritual layers of your being. All of these can be covered within the scope of energy medicine and holistic modalities because these types of treatments address the primary cause of all blockages. They help by raising your vibration and tweaking the body so that energy can flow freely. In the next chapter, we'll explore different modalities like Reiki, yoga, meditation, acupuncture, acupressure, reflexology, essential oils, crystals, breath work, nutrition, and more to get you started on your self-healing journey. Chakras respond well to cleansing through natural elements, hot herbal baths, smudging, and placing Himalayan salt lamps (or bowls of Himalayan salt) throughout your home. These practices can also aid in creating a healing environment for you to encourage the releasing process. Remember, all things take time, and the natural path is no exception.

UNDERACTIVE CHAKRAS

Fatigue, malaise, denial of feelings, poor memory, disconnection, and low energy are all symptoms that you may have an underactive chakra. Underactive chakras can sometimes be mistaken for blocked chakras, but many times, actual blockages will display noticeable physical symptoms and manifestations, whereas underactive chakras will tend to have less of an effect or manifest as more mental/emotional in nature. I like to describe underactivity to clients like dust on a bookshelf. The dust collects, and there is a need to clean it, but you still have access to the books—you're able to pick them up and read them, but they need a gentle cleansing. In this case, the lack of energy creates an energy gap, which you'll want to correct through energy replacement or adding energy to the deficient areas.

Energy leaks are rips, holes, tears, or thin areas within the auric space, which can sometimes, but not always, be felt. Rips are normally present as the aftermath of abuse (mental or physical) or severe trauma. This trauma can be from this lifetime or even a past or parallel lifetime. It can also be caused by neglect. Thin areas in the chakra system can mean energy is traveling away from the area. An energetic cord might be present, or the system may need to compensate by prioritizing sending its energy from one chakra to another to bolster an area in need. Holes indicate missing chakra energy and can imply an attachment cord was recently removed and hasn't evened out yet or that a portion of energy repeatedly leaves the body. We see this in the case of addictions and abuse when the soul chooses to exit or eject from the body. This exiting is slightly different from astral travel, which is a phenomenon that can happen consciously and deliberately during deep meditation or while in the dream state. Leaving the body is not ideal, as our whole human experience is based on being able to integrate new energies and embody them in a physical experience.

Examining your chakras with divination tools like a pendulum (see page 29) or by using muscle testing will help you determine if you have an underactive chakra. For example, when using a pendulum, the spin will be slower instead of a *yes* or *no* response.

(For me, a back-and-forth tick-tock swing represents a *no*.) Muscle testing is a kinesiology tool of energy medicine that relies on muscle weakness or strength to reasonably determine the root cause of someone's imbalance. During muscle testing, you might get a weak pushback response from your testing arm, indicating that the chakra you are inquiring about is underactive. You can also review the chakra chart in the appendix as well as the descriptions of underactive (and overactive) chakras in part 2 for signs and symptoms. Follow up with meditation to clarify your results by asking your higher self. In this way, you'll be able to confirm your results far better than you would by relying on someone else's opinion.

OVERACTIVE CHAKRAS

An overactive chakra presents as a heightened spin within the energy center. It can occur when too much energy or attention goes to one specific area and that area absorbs so much energy that it widens the chakra too much, letting in too much outside energy. Although everyone's chakra width is unique to them, ideally chakras shouldn't be too narrow or too wide—either state can indicate improper energy distribution within the system and may need to be corrected. You can get an approximate feel for the width of your chakras by assessing them with a pendulum or by consulting a Reiki Master who can measure them for you.

Difficulty concentrating, pleasure addiction, jitters, poor or rigid boundaries, obesity/overeating, material fixation, confusion, disassociation, inability to listen to others, and codependency are all signs of chakras that may be experiencing overactivity. Of course, symptoms vary depending on which chakras are being affected at any given time. You may not experience these specific symptoms, but very much like a blocked chakra, you'll be able to identify that something is amiss because too much energy is being channeled to one place, typically at the cost of energetic depletion in other areas.

As discussed in chapter 1, the chakras above your crown are higher vibrational in nature and are therefore related to your consciousness. You'll want those chakras to be open wide; they serve as portals to higher realms, so overactivity is not a consideration. In general, your etheric gateways, as well as your mental and visionary energies in the third eye and crown space, will tend to correlate less with your physical being. Therefore, identification of overactivity in your third eye or crown space can be more of a challenge. Your chakras from your throat down will more closely engage with your physical layers of embodiment. It should be fairly easy to determine when these body-based chakras are overactive, underactive, or expressing balance. Just start by asking yourself how you are feeling and then tune in. It's that simple—and it's all you need to do to start locating any issues.

Sometimes it's necessary for your body to reallocate your energy resources to serve vital functions. For example, if you need to stand up for yourself to a boss, colleague, or client, you'll need to summon extra energy to your solar plexus to harness your confidence. In the case of overactive chakras, the energy doesn't dissipate and instead tends to build in one area, causing the imbalance. Redistribution of energy can be more closely managed through various tools, many of which you can also use to remove blockages. Meditation is always one of my choice picks since it allows for the greatest freedom of usage and convenience.

Activating the Chakras

Activational energy is essentially powerful, charged energy that carries potential. Moving a lower vibration into a higher vibration is activational in nature. Activating the chakras may include moving a chakra up in vibration by adding in higher frequencies. In essence, to stimulate a chakra is to activate it, especially after it has been blocked. While activated chakras are on the path to clearing, they may not be totally cleansed or open yet. Activational energy within a chakra signals that this energy center is on the pathway to holistic restoration.

When you place your attention on healing, several things are possible. Usually, you start to remove negative energies by removing lower-vibrating frequencies around them, which can include limiting beliefs, patterns, toxic ties, and social conditioning. Once you have begun the process of removing what no longer serves you and isn't a vibrational match, you're on your way to unblocking a chakra. But activational energy is more than simply removing what doesn't belong. Even the word *activation* implies its root concept—activity, or to take action.

Activating a chakra requires that you *add* energy by taking steps to grow the energy that is already there to bring your frequencies more into natural alignment with where your system wants to be vibrationally. Focused attention *is* energy. For example, let's say you are trying to get a new job, heal a broken heart, or become pregnant. When you put your attention into a visualization meditation, yoga posture, vision board, or even have an intense discussion around this topic, you'll find your attention, or energy, goes to this chakra. The medicine of healing begins as activational energy.

My favorite way to activate a chakra is to place my hands on the intended space and visualize healing white or golden liquid crystalline light pouring into the space. You can allow the healing streams to begin dissolving anything that might be keeping you stuck (you don't need to label it, by the way, but rather just set an intention to feel it so it can be released). If that sounds a little like a self-Reiki technique, you're not wrong. We'll talk more about Reiki channeling in the next chapter. The good news is that you don't have to be Reiki attuned to channel energy to yourself (although it is a good idea to become attuned if you'll be healing or working on others so that you don't deplete your valuable energy resources).

Next, try to envision the color of the chakra frequency you want to come into your chakra (for example, green for the heart chakra). Spend some time with this activation. If you're able to see the color clearly, you have activated the chakra. Most of the time, if your frequency doesn't match, it will be more difficult for you to summon the color vibration on demand.

Another way to activate the chakras is to work with your kundalini energy. Kundalini is the essence of pure shakti waves, or personal life-force energy (different from qi). You can use kundalini yogic practice to begin the awakening process and then perform various postures and visualizations that move this special energy up the spine. As it moves up the spine, it will add a cleansing and activational force to each energetic portal. Although uncommon, you can awaken this energy within yourself and, with time, begin to see its life-enhancing properties at work within your chakras. For more on awakening kundalini, see page 43.

Balancing the Chakras

Chakra balancing, also known as chakra alignment, involves an adjustment that corrects equilibrium within all the layers of your chakra system. Balance is an ideal state for your chakras to be in at any given time as it optimizes the energy you're able to access. Balance is important, because too much or too little of this concentrated energy can throw your system off. Practicing the techniques in the next chapter can help you regain this essential state. But what does balance mean? Since the chakras are essentially spiritual centers that are formed as spiraling wheels of light, they have a spin, a color, a frequency or vibration, a general shape, and a connection to the nerve centers on your physical body. When these are all functioning optimally, balance can be achieved.

These characteristics can be hard to identify if your third eye vision isn't open, so use a pendulum to get a reading (see page 29) or consult an energy worker like a Reiki Master who will be able to help you determine these more fine-tuned aspects of balance. (If you wish, you can work on opening your third eye through meditation; there are a few meditations for this in my book *Essential Chakra Meditation*.)

A balanced chakra will look as though the front and back are mirroring each other. The shape of the front should be similar to that of the back. Chakras are normally circular, so a different shape would indicate imbalance. Also, each chakra should be spinning at a similar speed to the others. A spin that is a lot slower could indicate underactivity and vice versa. There's no standard to measure this against, and every day your body could be slightly different. The spin should be in a clockwise direction. In general, most chakras will spin clockwise unless they are releasing energy, which can happen naturally or under special circumstances. I have seen chakras spin counterclockwise when they are dispelling or dispensing energy. For example, during Reiki or when you are actively working on clearing your chakra, the chakra should spin counterclockwise.

A balanced chakra will also be in line with the vertical stack, which is what is referred to as alignment. Alignment denotes a vertical connection that reflects its highest spiritual potential. Since your chakra energies contribute to your overall functioning, they all have to work independently and together in alignment for your optimal flow to be achieved. With regard to color, balanced chakras will generally vibrate at their associated colors. A chakra's vibration can be difficult to assess without clairvoyance or a very open third eye. You can give visualization a whirl during meditation and simply ask, "Show me the vibration and frequency of my chakra," and tune in to your body's response.

Divination with a Pendulum

A pendulum is a divination tool used to answer yes or no questions. Anything can be a pendulum, as long as it is free to swing from side to side (long necklaces or chains with a weighted pendant work well). You may have tried working with a pendulum without fully knowing how or trusting in the response you received. Know this: It takes practice! You control the movement by surrendering and channeling a response. It's best to first find a baseline for your responses by asking the pendulum to show you a *yes* or *no*. A *yes* might look like a circular motion (clockwise or counterclockwise). A *no* might look like a back-and-forth swing or stuck position.

To read your chakras, begin by placing your nondominant, or feeling, hand face up to the sky and hold the pendulum loosely with your dominant hand. Be sure to connect with your spirit guides to ask for assistance. Move your hand over each chakra you want to check, asking, "Is this chakra healthy and clear?" In general, the speed and intensity of your response correlate to the health of the chakra, and you'll be able to distinguish between a *yes* or *no* with some practice. If your circular *yes* is large and fast, the chakra is open and healthy. If the *yes* is smaller with a weaker range of motion, your chakra may have some stagnant energy to clear.

You may also use the pendulum to ask any closed question (one that can be answered with a *yes* or *no*). I like to ask around current health-related topics and stay away from asking questions I feel too personal an attachment to or questions about future-related items. In general, when you're practicing this in connection with a Reiki treatment, you are consulting with your angels and Reiki guides.

Chapter Three
Restoring Balance
to the Chakras

This chapter takes a close look at the techniques and therapies you can use to initiate a healing response in your body. When you are working on clearing and rebalancing your chakras, each of these modalities has the potential to yield incredible relief and results. It's just a matter of choosing which one or combination you feel the most in line with at the time. In fact, you can try any number of these techniques and therapies until you find one that works for you. Healing is so personal and should be more about listening to your body than following someone else's recommendation. There is a real benefit to tuning in to the ancient wisdom of your body as a sovereign, informed source.

Chakra Cleansing and Rebalancing

If you've been feeling the need to rebalance your chakra system, it's likely that your body has been attempting to convey some important information to you. The time for clearing has come. Cleansing and rebalancing can be simple—a multitude of tools and methods are at your disposal, and experienced practitioners are available to aid you in your journey to chakra health. Meditation, yoga, Reiki, reflexology, breath work, crystals, essential oils, aromatherapy, and nutritional or lifestyle changes are all amazing, enjoyable modalities that are relatively easy to employ. Cleansing the chakras helps restore optimal health so that your chakra is back in balance and all blockages, knots, stagnant energy, and debris are removed, ensuring it is purified and able to receive more energy.

You will likely be able to tell right away if something is off. Many of my clients express some degree of various injuries, ailments, emotional issues, physical pains, mental stresses, and spiritual blocks every day. In general, it's normal for your body's energy to be different from one day to the next, but you shouldn't be frequently oscillating between blocked and unblocked chakras unless there is a great imbalance. Our feelings correlate to certain chakras and point us to where we are experiencing deep imbalances. For example, you might seek chakra cleansing if you are experiencing grief or holding on to sadness in your heart chakra following the loss of a loved one. Or you may feel over your day job, in which case, your disconnection to your purpose and lack of motivation could indicate a block in your solar plexus chakra. When your chakras are underactive, overactive, or blocked, chances are you will feel like something is slightly wrong and that you need to do a bit of course correction. As we've discussed, you can help identify where you are off by tuning in during meditation or reading your own chakras with a pendulum (see page 29).

When deciding whether to work on one chakra at a time, only the seven major chakras, or all 12, my suggestion is to tackle what you know first. If you have a crown or heart blockage, start with these primary energy centers. These spaces directly correlate to your ability to access Divine wisdom and information, so they should be open to fully connect to your higher self.

Let's walk through the different methods you can use to purify and rebalance your system. Each of the following techniques aims at easing stress, treating numerous health conditions, downregulating negative gene expression, decreasing inflammation, and alleviating physical pain. These techniques are becoming increasingly popular because many Western doctors are now acknowledging their efficacy in treating chronic pain and nausea. What's more, ongoing research is looking to illuminate the effectiveness of these techniques in treating anxiety, depression, and even different forms of cancer!

MEDITATION

Contrary to popular belief, meditation is more about cultivating awareness than quieting a busy mind. By focusing your consciousness (or awareness) on the present moment, you can master the simple yet artful technique of mindfulness while cutting to the core of most of your mental and emotional issues. Many people get worried when I suggest meditation to them as a healing therapy. They hold common misconceptions that this practice is only for people who can sit still and is intended to stop racing thoughts. However, nothing could be further from the truth. Meditation is used to maintain, adjust, or heal your energy system and is probably the most valuable (and simplest) tool I recommend. You can begin to tap into your infinite potential and break through endless limitations just by sitting with what is present for you each time you practice.

At a leading meditation studio in Los Angeles, California, I've explained to thousands of students throughout the years that there really is no right way to meditate. Meditation doesn't have to be long and complicated, and you can start with a simple five-minute practice each day. Whenever you practice, you'll have the chance to develop and deepen a stronger mind-body connection. By training the mind to come back to your breath time and time again and by attending to your thoughts with gentle observation, the mindfulness practice you cultivate on the mat will slowly blend into your waking life, building spaciousness in your mind and allowing more of you to show up in each moment. What better gift can you give than to simply be present with others and with yourself?

In my experience both as an instructor and a life-long student, meditation is an incredibly accessible tool for energy maintenance. There is no cost other than time. Making the time each day for meditation can be a challenge, especially for those who are parenting, have full-time jobs, or managing both. Dedication and willingness here will get you far, and commitment pays off if you can stick with it. There will most certainly be days you'll want to skip meditation or feel as though you don't have the time, and for those times, you may want to switch it up and change your approach. There are a multitude of meditations you can try.

For beginners, I suggest a simple awareness practice, which you can cultivate over time on your own. A way to do this is to set an alarm on your phone to go off a few times a day. When you receive a notification, stop and focus on your breath for 30 seconds, in and out. This attention to your breath will help slow your breathing, calm your nervous system, and put you back in the present moment. Over time, you can build upon this practice as you increase the length of your timed breathing.

Another option is guided meditation. In this practice, an instructor leads the narrative with anchors and teaching moments threaded in to move you through the entire process. If you are seeking to dive deeper with guided meditation, I present various meditations that take you through a journey of healing your chakras in *Essential Chakra Meditation*. The meditations are timed so that you can select the container, or time frame, you'd like to work in each time you sit.

You can also lead a guided meditation yourself, like object meditation or a body scan, giving yourself anchor points on which to meditate. Mantra meditation and Transcendental Meditation use repeated phrases throughout a meditation to carry you through the vehicle of the mind into a trancelike state so that you might access greater consciousness. Try adding a mantra to your meditation to see if it helps focus your attention and awareness. There is also movement meditation, which you can do anytime on your own. Tai chi, yoga, dance, and walks in nature all fall into this category. As you begin to explore, try them on to see which flow suits you best—by the merit of your effort, you can't go wrong!

YOGA

One of the greatest practices that sprang from Eastern tradition, yoga has roots in northern India, originating more than 5,000 years ago. First mentioned in the Vedas (one of the oldest sacred texts), yoga was originally included in this collection of mantras, rituals, and songs so that the Vedic priests, or Brahmans, could use it to attain spiritual evolution. Yoga is celebrated in three major religions that sprang up around the time—Hinduism, Jainism, and Buddhism.

This physical, mental, and spiritual practice quietly yet profoundly expands awareness of the mind-body connection. By anchoring your awareness to your physical body, yoga asanas (or postures) help you remove blockages through balance, inversions, and twists, as well as by standing, sitting, and lying down. The beauty of yoga is that it gives you the opportunity to train your mind to release attachment and judgment around people, situations, and outcomes. Constantly pushing you to the edge of your comfort zone and beyond, the poses of yoga create feedback that you then expand upon and take into your life to put to the ultimate test. Is it perfection you're after or comfort? Is it best to bring balance to a situation through active pushing or complete surrender?

The eight limbs of yoga, deriving from *The Yoga Sutras of Patanjali*, describe the path to ultimate liberation. These limbs are meant to decondition us as well as help us achieve enlightenment. By practicing and integrating these pillars, you use your energy in a worthwhile way to benefit yourself and the world around you. It's strongly encouraged to incorporate as many of these tenets as possible, but even if you follow just a few, you can still receive many of the chakra-related benefits yoga practice offers. The following are the eight limbs of yoga:

YAMA: RESTRAINTS, MORAL DISCIPLINES. These are social ethics, including as kindness (*ahimsa*), truthfulness (*satya*), nonstealing (*asteya*), moderation (*brahmacharya*), and generosity (*aparigraha*).

NIYAMA: POSITIVE DUTIES, OBSERVANCES. These are personal practices including purity (*saucha*), contentment (*santosha*), austerity (*tapas*), self-study (*svadhyaya*), and surrender (*ishvara pranidhana*).

ASANA: POSTURES. These are the traditional positions in yoga to help you better connect your mind, body, and spirit through movement.

PRANAYAMA: BREATH. Mindful breathing helps you purify and reach deeper layers of stillness within.

PRATYAHARA: SENSORY WITHDRAWAL. This is the art of turning inward to honor yourself in silence.

DHARANA: FOCUSED CONCENTRATION. This is full attention to yourself and to all things.

DHYANA: MEDITATIVE ABSORPTION. Dropping all your efforts and just letting go is the intention of this practice.

SAMADHI: ENLIGHTENMENT. A state of pure bliss and complete harmony with the Self and the Universe.

There are a number of yoga systems, including hatha yoga (aligning/calming), ashtanga vinyasa yoga (repeating sequenced flow), kundalini yoga (shakti activating), yin yoga (restorative), Iyengar Yoga (alignment-focused), hot yoga (heated), and acroyoga (aerial/partner work). Each style has its own flavor and concentration that is best experienced directly if you're trying to figure out which style is right for you.

Yoga will challenge you to focus your mind, body, and breath, and it will increase your flexibility, muscle strength, and respiration. Yoga can also improve your cardiovascular and circulatory health, balance your mind, and stabilize or reduce your weight. Use your breath, identify your limits, come back to an attitude of positivity, and have faith in your practice. As your practice grows, so will you.

REIKI

Directly translated, *Reiki* breaks down into two words: *rei,* which means "universal," and *ki,* which means "energy." Its first recorded origins date back to the ancient Egyptians. Examining the hieroglyphs on the pyramid and temple walls, you can see that energy and magic were very much a part of this ancient culture's lifestyle. The more traditional Japanese practice that we are familiar with today was a tradition formally developed much later by Dr. Mikao Usui in the early 1900s. The practice has three or four levels, depending on how it is taught. These include Reiki I and II and Reiki III (master practitioner level), which is either combined or split into personal mastery and professional mastery (Reiki Master Teacher, RMT).

Reiki is a gentle, hands-on healing modality that involves channeling positive, high-vibrational energy to the recipient for healing. This high-vibrational frequency can be transmitted through an in-person session or performed remotely via long-distance healing. This energy treatment is so gentle that it can safely be used on fetuses *in utero*, babies, children, the elderly, and pets. Reiki rejuvenates your whole mind-body system, accelerates healing, bolsters your immune system, and promotes good health.

A typical Reiki session takes about 45 to 60 minutes, as it is intuitively led. Each session will remove layers of blocks and work on moving stuck energy through the system. In my practice, I begin Reiki treatments with a chakra reading, which assesses my patient's energy in each one of their chakras and gives an accurate idea of where they are holding stuck energy. The time before your session is a beautiful opportunity to connect with your practitioner and let them know about any diagnosis or physical issues you might be experiencing that you wish to work through during your session. Remember that energy work is not a substitute for doctor's orders, but your Reiki practitioner may work alongside your doctor to come up with a healing schedule or treatment plan for you if your level of treatment requires it. Normally, it takes about 48 hours to fully integrate the Reiki energy, with lots of water and rest afterward to feel optimal, reenergized, and aligned. The lasting positive effects can be felt for weeks or months afterward and are often life changing.

As mentioned, Reiki can be performed locally in person or sent remotely anywhere in the world. During a distance healing, you can send healing energy backward and forward in time. This type of energy can be considered quantum, since softening effects can be achieved through timeline healing. When we begin to heal our past, we soften and rewrite our stories around traumas, dramas, suffering, and painful memories. Reiki energy can also be sent to a future timeline to create positive flowing energy around an upcoming opportunity, like a job interview, birth, or big exam. This level of distance transmission requires at least a second-level Reiki degree.

Most people are natural healers and were born with access to their own healing abilities and often appear to intuitively channel the most beneficial energy for someone in need. But any form of healing requires training and experience. Reiki attunements are different from treatments in that they open and begin to clear the body channels, giving the recipient the ability to perform Reiki on themselves and others (depending on the level of attunement). Mastery-level attunements pass the ability to channel the Reiki energy to others through the crown chakra and out through the palms of the hands.

Advanced techniques such as cord cutting, soul retrievals, programming grids, and holding space for large groups (such as a meditation class or Reiki circle) are typically left to third-level Reiki practitioners, or Reiki Masters. There are various practices that can certify you for personal mastery and then separately for Reiki Master Teacher. Typically, Reiki degrees of this level are considered a spiritual consciousness shift and are offered to students who are absolutely ready and have shown their proficiency in all lower levels. If you are searching for a Reiki practitioner, take a look in your network and select some-one with excellent referrals who has preferably practiced up to the Master level.

REFLEXOLOGY

The hands and feet have incredibly powerful gateways that greatly impact your entire physical body and energetic system. Home to thousands of nerve endings, temperature and pressure sensors, and meridian lines, these small portals also contain a number of secondary chakras that allow energy to release from the body. In reflexology, pressure is applied to specific points on the hands and feet to clear qi, or vital energy, cleansing the corresponding organs and parts of the body.

The pressure sensors in these areas directly link to zones on the body and, when stimulated, create waves of relaxation and detoxification that affect the intended areas. Reflexology is used to prevent disease, remove energetic blockages, reduce pain and inflammation, improve health and well-being, and enhance vitality.

The hands and feet process an enormous amount of environmental information. For example, the pressure sensory information sent from your feet lets your body know whether you are sitting, standing, lying down, running, or walking, which, in turn, lets your body know if its needs are being met with enough circulation, oxygen, blood sugar, muscle contraction, and such. Applying pressure to the middle of the big toe (which cor-responds to the pituitary gland), for example, will induce a revival response in the body because it activates a single nerve that controls respiration, movement, and heart rate.

Evidence suggests that the practice of reflexology dates back to the ancient Egyp-tians as well as ancient Chinese medicine. The modern practice developed in the nineteenth century and matured during the 1930s when reflex zones were mapped and charts were devised to reflect healing zones relating directly to the body's anatomy.

Zone theory is a facet of modern reflexology that focuses on 10 longitudinal zones that run from your head to your toes. These zones are all interconnected and imply that tension in one area can affect all other parts within that zone. Therefore, working within a zone can relieve pressure and restore equilibrium to that whole zone. The body is divided into three zones, with dissection lines at the shoulders, belly, and waist. The feet and hands are also divided into zones accordingly.

Modern practice can include applying pressure to the hands, the feet, and even the ears. Although some of the techniques are simple enough to do on your own at home, a visit to a trained reflexologist is advisable for accomplishing advanced techniques or in the case of a serious illness. Looking after your own health is important, and the benefits can leave you with improved immunity, elevated mood, reduced pain, recovery from illness and injuries, healthy digestion, increased fertility, and reduction of illness-related symptoms. This practice is generally easily accessible, noninvasive, safe, natural, effective, and popular because it is a treatment option for a variety of health concerns and can be conducted almost anywhere, anytime.

ACUPUNCTURE AND ACUPRESSURE

Another set of popular alternative Chinese medicine modalities, acupuncture and acupressure are very closely related. For healing, I really value acupuncture and have found practitioners who are gentle-handed, knowledgeable, and incredibly intuitive. Some practitioners you find may be doctors of Eastern medicine, and some may be licensed to practice acupuncture and herbalism. These two tend to go hand in hand, as many prescriptions from your acupuncturist will tend to be along the lines of Chinese herbs, diet, and moxibustion (the therapeutic use of heat).

Originating in China around 6000 BCE, acupuncture treatments involve inserting very small, thin needles into the skin on specific points on a person's body following mapped meridian lines. The meridian lines in the body form an energetic network that channel qi through the body. This transport system is composed of 14 pathways—the yin, yang, and central mid-meridians (the Governing Vessel and Conception Vessel). The stomach, spleen, heart, small and large intestines, kidney, bladder, gallbladder, liver, lungs, pericardium, and triple warmer form pairs with one another that balance the feminine and masculine energies within. Because your acupuncturist will be selecting the sites to place the needles in your body for your desired results, it's important to connect on a vibrational level with the right practitioner.

Acupressure treatments also use points along the meridian lines with the intention of releasing qi to flow freely, but acupressure work is massage-based for optimal stimulation. While this may sound similar to reflexology, the primary difference is that reflexology mainly uses finger-pressure techniques on the feet, hands, and ears, and it works within zones rather than the meridians. Acupressure is a larger field of practice in general and is used to treat internal disease, toxic energy patterns, and musculoskeletal disorders.

BREATH WORK

Connecting your breath to your body is a basic concept for refreshing your energy. Your breath is a form of pulling in your spirit, and many spiritual teachers, especially breath work and meditation facilitators, suggest deep breathing as a tool to self-soothe and regulate when the system is off. Breathing is usually done automatically, but breath work is a concentrated practice. Breath work is a powerful method of focusing your breathing practice with conscious control to attain mental clarity, physical well-being, release from stress, and improved emotional connection.

Most people tend to be shallow breathers, breathing only into the top of their lungs. Although there is no wrong way to breathe, there are optimal ways to breathe to improve the exchange of oxygen and help restore and reset the parasympathetic nervous system. The secret to optimal breathing is breathing into the belly. Guiding the breath to the diaphragm, the dome-shaped muscle below the rib cage, helps create a healing response in the body. In particular, deep breathing activates your vagus nerve, which is an essential part of the parasympathetic nervous system. This system governs your ability to calm yourself after a fight-or-flight response. Developing this system over time promotes better sleep, more stable blood sugar levels, less chronic inflammation, and improved digestion, as well as a reduced risk of diabetes, cardiovascular disease, and stroke.

Breath work classes are offered at most meditation studios, where an instructor will guide you, but you can do a simple three-minute practice with diaphragmatic breathing at home on your own. In a relaxed seated position, start by placing a hand on your belly. Begin to descend your breath as you inhale, expanding the belly as you take in a new breath. You'll notice there are organs within the belly that also expand with your inhale. Imagine the breath filling your belly entirely. Take your time breathing in a slow and steady manner and then release a long, slow exhalation. As you exhale, you might imagine breathing out anything that no longer serves you as you completely empty your breath. For a full detoxification effect, make sure you're breathing in through your nose and out through your mouth, as the nose is a natural filter for anything that doesn't belong in the body in the first place.

As you breathe, notice all the sensations arising and see if you can practice being in the moment with each breath. This tool creates instant transformation, even if it's done for only a few minutes. Practicing deep breathing, especially in the morning, will benefit you for several hours. Let your breath guide your day to an enhanced state of being.

HEALING STONES

Gemstones, crystals, and rocks are all types of healing stones that have unique healing properties; they honor the earth element as they are natural gifts from Gaia. Crystals selected for healing can be polished, raw, tumbled, dipped, dyed, or treated. Beautiful to look at, these gems are also master healers, as they carry specific frequencies within their crystalline structure that can aid in healing, promote health and well-being, and invite you to go deeper within yourself as you uncover and connect with the feelings they bring to the surface. You can harness the stones' power simply by having them near you, as their frequencies start to entrain to yours—in other words, you will effortlessly sync up to their naturally higher vibrations.

Although I've rarely ever met a healing stone I didn't like, selecting your healing stone is such a personal experience that it's best to tune in to yourself for the answer rather than seek help from outside sources. I encourage you to select stones that resonate with you the most. The one you are initially attracted to is likely going to be the stone that your system most needs to balance itself. For instance, if you are gravitating toward a citrine crystal, your chakra reading will likely show a small dip in energy or a blockage around your solar plexus, the center for motivation and connection to purpose. You can test this theory out yourself with a pendulum (see page 29).

You can shop for crystals at a meditation or spiritual store, or you can collect natural stones outside. I love to travel to energy vortexes and planetary sacred sites such as Peru, Mount Shasta, Joshua Tree, and Sedona, and it has become part of my personal ritual to ask the land for permission to bring a special stone home with me. I like to leave a small offering such as a rose or piece of fruit in its place to show my gratitude and to honor the land.

I recommend starting with a basic chakra set that has an array of crystals reflecting the colors of the rainbow, or all seven primary chakras. This could include a nice black tourmaline for the root, sacred sacral carnelian, honey calcite or citrine for the solar plexus, rose quartz or amazonite for the heart, kyanite for the throat, lapis or amethyst for the third eye, and clear quartz for the crown space.

Once you've selected your stones, align them on top of your body during meditation or Reiki, or place them in a grid on your altar space. You can alternatively place the crystals under your pillow at night to improve your dream state or at your bedside while you sleep to protect and infuse your space with love, or put them in your workspace to increase productivity and communication. Sometimes I carry my stones in my purse or pocket, and you can always find them placed strategically around my house. I love to place my special natural crystals from energy vortexes in a grid beside my plants or directly in the soil to promote growth and vitality. Animals love crystals, too; just be sure not to place any crystals directly on your pets as they are normally much too sensitive for the strong effects crystals can generate on and outside the body.

ESSENTIALS OILS, AROMATHERAPY, AND FLOWERS

Botanicals help form a vital branch of holistic health treatments, delivering natural solutions to everyday problems while improving well-being and instantly lifting vibrations. Frequencies from plants can be some of the most potent homeopathic medicine; they have a natural symbiosis with the human body.

Essential oils directly affect your limbic system, which governs memories, emotions, and arousal or stimulation. This part of your brain deals with both high and low functions. These powerful and pure oils are derived not only from flowers but also from leaves, fruits, roots, stems, and other parts of the plant. The distillation process carefully extracts the fragrant portion of the plant so that it can be bottled. Aromatherapy is basically another term for essential oil therapy. Essential oils can be used aromatically, topically, or, in some cases, internally, depending on the quality of the product and the manufacturer, so it's beneficial to do your research on a few reliable companies that have dependable and positive testing.

Since essential oils can be so potent, most of the time you'll want to dilute them with a carrier oil, such as jojoba oil, fractionated coconut oil, grapeseed oil, or almond oil. If you have sensitive skin or are using a "hot" oil like cinnamon, clove, lemongrass, or oregano, make sure to dilute them! In the crystals and aromatherapy meditation I teach, I encourage students to apply essential oil roll-ons to their wrists, palms, and back of their hands as these areas are generally less sensitive than other parts of the body with proper application. You can get creative with essential oils, but be sure to check for any contraindications before using them to prevent any potential reactions.

In my healing office and at home, I use an aromatherapy diffuser to diffuse essential oils, which creates a lovely ambiance and calming effect throughout the space. Essential oils like lavender, vanilla-bean (derived from the resin), geranium, ylang-ylang, jasmine, clary sage, and neroli are all wonderful on their own, or you can mix them to create complex blends.

In addition to creating fragrant healing notes for essential oils, flowers can be used in other ways for optimal healing. Herbalism, for example, includes medicinal treatment through plants (including flowers) for illness, allergies, skin conditions, anxiety, and much more. Various healing flowers can also be made into tinctures and salves. Dried petals and leaves can be enjoyed as a tea or tucked into fragrant, uplifting sachets.

NUTRITION

As with any holistic program, lifestyle changes may be necessary to implement core changes you wish to see in your body, mind, and spirit. What you embody in the physical is always a direct reflection of the energetic vibration you are holding. Your power lies in your ability to make healthy choices for yourself each day, based on the frequency and vibration you wish to maintain. Certain food groups may work really well for you, and you may need to steer clear from others entirely. At the end of the day, your health relies on your energy levels and frequency. For chakra balancing, it's ideal to let your intuition guide you to the highest vibrational matches.

Many food and dietary protocols are available these days—low-FODMAP, keto, paleo, macrobiotic, gluten- and grain-free, vegetarian, vegan, Ayurvedic, and more. If you pay attention to what your body needs and one of these protocols is working for you, then you've got it figured out! But sometimes we eat foods that don't match our frequency and experience uncomfortable side effects like bloating, constipation, irritable bowel syndrome (IBS), chronic irritability, weight gain, skin issues, kidney stones, urinary tract issues, or depression. It's also important to note that cancer cells, as well as fungi, viruses, and bacteria, thrive in acidic environments.

With the science of epigenetics coming to the foreground in food research, we also know that our gut and microbiome (the colony of microbes that live in our bodies) play critical roles in our health. Gut bacteria, we now know, is primarily responsible for our mood and emotional state, and it's extremely responsive to vibration. Fueling yourself with high-frequency foods helps you activate not only higher frequencies in yourself but also the higher resonance in everyone you interact with. Your higher frequency works through entrainment, which is the scientific principle that a lower-vibrating object tends to sync up with a higher-vibrating object nearby. Your body might demand new ways and types of consumption to produce these higher frequencies, so pay attention.

To nourish your physical body with higher frequencies, add fresh, organic whole foods that are not genetically modified and have been treated humanely with love and respect or grown in natural environments, and eliminate any processed lower-vibrational foods (which have less nutritional value and poor energetic quality). Aim for an alkaline system to keep the highest frequency possible. This means avoiding or reducing your intake of acid-forming foods like coffee, dairy, soy, alcohol, sugar, MSG, and artificial sweeteners. Even certain healthy foods like kombucha, eggs, honey, and cashews are moderately acid-forming, so do your research when striving for alkalinity.

Awakening Kundalini

Shakti energy is the most seductive, sensual, Tantric, juicy, and feminine of energies, and believe it or not, this energy lives within all of us. In Hinduism, kundalini is otherwise known as the "coiled serpent," which lies dormant at the base of your spine when you come into this Earth plane. Many seekers spend lifetimes attempting to awaken this special energy, which is said to travel up the spine, or *sushumna*.

As potent kundalini serpentine energy is awakened, it undulates up the spine, clearing through lifetimes of karmic records, which are stored in the Brahmic knots at each chakra portal. Brahmic knots are tiny centers that house your karmic records, which in turn, store all the imprints (good and bad) of your soul's journey. These are considered spiritual blockages that accumulate over the course of many lifetimes throughout various incarnations. The moment your kundalini energy reaches the top of your spine, it unites with your crown chakra, illuminating your mind and etheric chakras with enlightenment. Awakening this energy represents the next evolutionary jump for humankind and the next higher level of consciousness that is available for integration now in this timeline.

I experienced my kundalini awakening many years ago through an activation process called *shaktipat*, which is another term for this type of awakening. I was receiving Reiki while this was performed, so it was a beautiful, safe, and gentle experience. (If a person were to experience kundalini awakening outside the safety of a space like this, the effects could shock the nervous system; it is typically an electrifying process.) Shaktipat activates the nervous system and heightens emotional, physical, and spiritual sensitivities. In my experience, this held to be true. In addition, I was energized as I tuned into higher levels of being and thinking. I slowly started to resonate with and attract people into my vibrational field who shared similar viewpoints and served as expanders for me on my path. This awakening initiated a chain reaction of purification throughout my entire life.

Until this special time on Earth, spontaneous kundalini awakening was relatively uncommon, but the energies are different now, and it is critical for the collective to begin to awaken to new levels of consciousness. During Reiki attunements as part of my Reiki training programs, students, especially those with a specific intention, also now spontaneously awaken to different degrees. Their perception heightens their own sensitivity within their chakra system because kundalini awakening gives rise to new energy levels in the body while purifying it of physical and emotional blockages. New levels of awareness, abilities, and consciousness begin to stream in as senses heighten.

A full awakening would include a total resolution of the knots and issues of one's psyche, which is rare to have spontaneously. With everything opening up at once, kundalini awakening can also be an extremely intense and unnerving experience, and it traditionally takes years of practice to control it. When you experience energy moving, it is likely the initial stirrings of kundalini as it begins its journey up your spine. If you're interested in feeling your kundalini begin to move, you might join a kundalini yoga class or kundalini Reiki group, which aims to activate and move this energy. You can also use specific stones during meditation, like serpentine or carnelian, to enhance movement and sensitivity. The stones can simply be placed on or around the body to amplify your vibrational experience.

Sound Healing

Sound therapy—the use of sound and music to improve health and well-being—is a beautiful complement to any healing modality and can be applied on its own or alongside any of the techniques discussed in this chapter. Sound healing can reduce pain, stress, and anxiety, improve memory and sleep patterns, and reduce blood pressure. In fact, sound healing therapies have many mental, emotional, and social benefits.

This ancient practice has been used across the world and is recorded in the first sacred texts of the Vedas. Civilizations from India, Greece, and Africa used this primordial healing medicine across their cultures, and written history documents that plenty of ancient temples were built specifically to harness the power of sound (along with magnetics, light, and sacred geometry).

Sound, which travels four times faster through water than through air, is particularly useful in raising your vibration since, in adulthood, your body is made up of 50 to 60 percent water. Tuning your physical body, then, is an easy, natural fit. You can think of this as giving yourself a tune-up, just like you would tune a guitar.

Sound therapy can be applied through a number of means. Sacred instruments like tuning forks, crystal singing bowls, gongs, and chimes are typically used in sound baths. A sound bath is a meditative experience in which a sound-healing practitioner provides music, tones, and sounds for the listener. Sound baths are relaxing and soothing and work by delivering healing tones that adjust the listener's frequency gradually by harmonizing the vibrations on and around the body. During my Reiki treatments, I use the solfeggio frequency tracks, which contain special brain entrainment waves that produce delta and theta waves in the listener's brain. Delta and theta waves occur most often in sleep and are present during deep meditation and dreamlike states, bringing the body and mind into a beautiful state of relaxation. During a session, I also cycle through a number of frequencies that heal the chakras.

Rife frequency is another sound therapy based on technology that delivers a specific frequency to the body to increase one's resonant vibration. The hertz frequencies of various conditions, diseases, and disorders are mapped, and thus, the healthy sound frequency that is set disables the dysfunctional target areas or brings them into resonance through vibration.

Chapter Four
The Mystical Benefits of Chakras

Working with these fascinating energy centers can create a positive space for healing many different human conditions, including stress, trauma, negative thinking, and more. In this chapter, we'll discuss these healing benefits, and I'll provide some suggestions for how you can set your sights on new ways of being.

Health and Harmony

States of health and harmony are natural; our bodies want to create balance and achieve a state of flow. Where your mind goes, your energy flows, so you must look within to understand how you can use your energy for your highest benefit. Addressing the state of your chakras can illuminate what is going on in you on a physical, emotional, psychological, and spiritual level. By understanding your energy on an intimate level and learning how to work with it, health and healing will be your new natural vibratory state, keeping illness, injuries, anxiety, and other lower-vibrating conditions at bay.

It's easy to become dysregulated when we lead busy, distracting, and stressful lives. We can become increasingly disengaged, depressed, or anxious when we are in a downward spiraling cycle because that energy produces more of the same. The same effect applies to joy, creativity, and loving energy. We give more, and we get more of the same or greater. It's how the Law of Attraction works. Vibrations attract like vibrations into the same unified field. The good news is that healing is only as hard as we make it. From the thought forms you generate (mental energy) to the cells floating around in your bloodstream (physical energy), virtually every energetic action contributes to your overall well-being.

Your chakras are always regulating these vibrations with an acute intuitive biological sensitivity. They are constantly upshifting and downshifting between higher-vibrational and lower-vibrational energies. Because all energy and matter vibrate at a specific rate, we create our realities through our vibrations. When the body downshifts energy, it's creating slower energy, or matter. Although you aren't able to perceive it through your physical senses, this matter generally contains electric impulses as molecular, biological, or hormonal energy. If you want to change your physical form to become healthier and stronger, you must first address the energetics within your energy field, beginning with chakra healing.

Identifying and discerning your issues is the first step to finding the solution you need. From there, you can work to troubleshoot your own healing. Balancing the chakras will help, as will cleansing negative thoughts and feelings from your body and energy field. It's easy to think of these intangible items as stuck in your energy or body. The reality is the energetic imprint needs to be addressed, either through a clearing so the imprint or blockage can move or through adding higher-vibrational energy to dissolve it away and rewrite the painful memory or toxicity. By working on changing your narratives, you will see the possibility of healing trauma. Letting go becomes easier, and this helps release unwanted stories that stockpile in the body. You gain clarity on your direction and vision, as well as expand spiritually. Through all the growth, it would be impossible *not* to become a more whole version of yourself.

When my patients put effort into healing the root cause of their suffering, they enjoy relief on many levels. For example, if you came in for digestive issues, we would look for the energetic cause. In many cases, it would lead back to general anxiety, which is held at the solar plexus. Healing the root cause will have a ripple effect throughout your entire energetic landscape, allowing other higher levels of energy to stream into your body. The energies that exist in higher planes of reality are that of unconditional love and light frequencies, which aid in removing any fear that keeps you in the fight-or-flight response or in an illusion of separation or duality.

Balancing the Chakras

To keep everything functioning smoothly, the framework of the chakra system, along with each individual chakra, needs to stay balanced. Achieving equilibrium is imperative. As we've discussed, the chakras can alter your physical, psychological, emotional, and spiritual state in a number of ways, contributing to your development, maturation, and the energy you emanate around you.

The chakras help manage the crucial flow of masculine and feminine energy, or your yin-yang balance. They allow these energies to flow to the left and to the right sides of your body. The left side is your feminine side, controlled by your right brain, and the right side is your masculine side, controlled by your left brain. It is thought that the feminine side of your being receives or allows energy, and the masculine side transmits or commits that energy into action. Your meridian system and chakras process these energies and then project them back into your energetic field. In this way, when your system is in good working order, your body maintains vital balance.

If you've ever felt like you were trying too hard or struggling with control issues, you were probably experiencing an imbalance on your right side. Likewise, if you haven't been filling your cup or you have not taken the time to slow down, process, and integrate, you're likely imbalanced on your left side. Imbalances can throw off the whole chakra system. This also applies to vertically stacked energies within your chakra portals. For example, if your sacral chakra is super wide and more open than the rest of your chakras (an indication that it might be overcompensating), the balancing chakra, or counterpart vortex, is probably not receiving adequate energy.

Aside from the heart chakra, each of the seven main chakras has a balancing chakra. The pairs are crown and root, third eye and sacral, and throat and solar plexus. It's important that your chakras aren't overcompensating, as this can lead to physical abnormalities or manifestations down the road. When performing a Reiki session, I may do a chakra balancing for the patient, giving equal energy to the analogous pairs of chakra centers for about five minutes each to balance the entire system. If you choose to work with a Reiki practitioner, this may be something they do as well.

Each chakra can also be thought of as taking in energy on the left side and expelling it on the right side. With the whirlpool-like vortex forming from the top center of the chakra portal, in combination with the motion of the left and right energy swirl, your chakras are propelled to spin. They are in balance when they are spinning, open equally, and sharing uniformity with the other chakras in your system.

The front and back sides of the chakras also need to be considered. In some systems, it is thought that the back of the chakras receives energy and the front presents that animated energy into the world. In other words, the back represents the subconscious and the front represents the conscious manifestation. When your entire system is stabilized, you can do the work required to master your own energy.

CLEANSE NEGATIVE FEELINGS AND THOUGHTS

Seeking balance among the chakras can help end the negative energy spirals and cycles you experience from heavy emotions, pain, and suffering. Balancing the chakras helps relieve and cleanse negative thoughts, feelings, and beliefs. Sometimes, these types of emotions or responses can be good to have. The body shifts energy for survival, but once you understand it, you can make it your friend. Usually, acknowledging the pain in your body is a good place to start.

In this case, you'll want to investigate by asking a few questions around the unwanted emotions. What is causing the pain? Where did the source originate? What core wounding (if any) created the situation, and how can this be worked through? Heavy emotions are sometimes a necessary inconvenience to receive the valuable lessons they carry. Otherwise, the Universe will simply serve you the lesson again through different means later. Your stories, narratives, and conditioning all contribute to your overall feelings of emotional well-being, but they are all malleable. Usually, it's best to start there to really begin to rewrite your version the way it will benefit you best. Remember that a change of mind will bring a change in your energy.

Sometimes the negative feelings you are experiencing persist, especially through trauma bonds and repeated reinforcement. These can show up as obsessive-compulsive disorder or as a lighter version of that: dwelling on things. When you want to start to dispel these hardened negative feelings, it's important to remember that everything is energy. Energy moves, forms, and transforms. Since thought forms are essentially energy waves, you must try to upshift the vibratory state of the waves to begin to feel positive effects. You can accomplish all this through a chakra cleansing.

Looking at the energy spectrum of varying emotions, there is a range of voltage vibration for our different feelings. We call it a bandwidth. Gratitude, joy, peace, love, acceptance, and willingness sit at the top of the frequency scale. Courage and pride are vibrationally pretty neutral, while anger, fear, grief, blame, guilt, and shame are on the lower end of the scale. If you're experiencing anger or fear, there is a good chance you are experiencing a lack of self-love. It's good to identify where you are on the emotional frequency scale so that you can repattern your internal dialogue (stories/narratives), mind, behavior, and overall energetic signature. The higher you and your emotions vibrate, the healthier and happier you'll be. Practice raising your vibrations through awareness and releasing any judgment that comes up. This practice will allow more love to flow and cleanse your energy spectrum. My books *Chakra Balance* and *Essential Chakra Meditation* go deeply into awareness practice, should you want to explore meditation, yoga, and other elements of mindfulness intention practice.

FIND RELIEF FROM STRESS

Your body's natural desire is to be stress-free. A long time ago, the fight-or-flight stress response was vital for the survival of our primitive ancestors. When you were under a direct attack from a predator or when your body was craving warmth or sustenance, the brain indicated to the body that it needed immediate attention. Cortisol, the stress chemical, would be released into the bloodstream and brain signals would pick that up, triggering thoughts and behaviors to respond to the emergency at hand. Of course, the stress response is still vital for survival in threatening situations, and the body is still incredibly adept at letting us know when we need to pay attention. However, our tendency to overlook the body's warning signals is becoming increasingly problematic. Without proper attention to the stress response, we tend to miss vital markers of health decline, ultimately undermining our well-being and causing needless suffering.

Since we know through experience that dealing with the effects of stress are simply not enough, we need to look at the underlying core issues to resolve the stress response. If you suffer from the following, you may be experiencing a body stressor: pain (especially in the back, neck, and shoulders), spasms, numbness, discomfort, illness, fatigue, listlessness, or dizziness. These symptoms usually appear in succession (for example, someone first feels tired and then later feels pain) and tend to build gradually, presenting as a slow decline in physical health. With repeated exposure to stress, it's likely your vagus nerve has been compromised. As mentioned earlier, the vagus nerve is the part of your parasympathetic nervous system that is most responsible for involuntary actions, like breathing, metabolic rate, blood pressure, and digestion, and for producing a feeling of calm. When the vagus nerve is balanced, we are able to take ourselves safely out of the fight-or-flight response. The problem is we're so conditioned to dealing with stress-inducing situations that this cycle can feel like a tricky loop, keeping us stuck in stress much longer than we actually need to be.

Since you know that your physical body is created from the energetic blueprint you hold within your auric field and chakra system, you know that you must change the blueprint frequencies to experience physical changes. I like to think of these as upgrades, especially when dealing with stress. A huge component of clearing up tension in your physical body lies within your energy field.

HEAL TRAUMA

Traumatic stress is a basic response to a trauma, tension, or stressful event that has occurred in your life. These may include an accident, a near-death experience, physical or psychological abuse, childhood abandonment, death of a loved one, a violent crime, and so on. There are plenty of examples that highlight the pain and suffering one goes through during these dire times.

Traumatic stress response, also known as post-traumatic stress (PTS), occurs when the danger around the event has passed, but the threat to you remains heightened. Triggers can reinitiate feelings of fear, anxiety, shock, or helplessness. More often than not, symptoms begin within three months of the traumatic event, and they can have long-term effects, whether the event directly or indirectly occurred (for example, witnessing a violent crime but not being directly affected). Avoidance, difficulty sleeping, hypersensitivity, nightmares, flashbacks, irritability, anger, anxiety, stomach problems, weakened immune system, sleep disturbances, difficulty concentrating, and feelings of guilt or blame are all strong indicators that you have experienced a traumatic stress response. For a diagnosis of PTS or traumatic response, you must experience two or more of these symptoms that lead to distress or difficulty coping, and these symptoms must not be substance or medication induced (or due to another health condition).

By addressing your chakra's needs head-on, you can find relief from trauma and have a high chance of returning to a normal life. Although chakra work isn't a replacement for medical treatment, there are many tools you can use on your own to complement any therapy that may be necessary. When you lift your overall vibration through chakra work, the old toxic programs, including traumatic memories and energetic imprints, start to flush themselves out. There is simply no room for any lower-vibrating energy pattern to exist when you clear your energetic programming. If you give special attention to your solar plexus by altering your diet, focusing on your core during meditation, nourishing yourself with high-vibrational foods, and using healing stones that bring you calm, your anxiety can diminish, and your connection to your purpose will increase. This will boost not only your solar plexus chakra but also the core of your entire chakra system so that real healing can take place.

STRENGTHEN PROTECTIVE ENERGY

Think about your body as a sacred vessel. It holds emotions, personal energy, and medicine for healing. It also separates out what is not meant to be inside the container, like a whirlwind of negativity from other people, disease, or energy vampires (people who consciously or subconsciously suck your energy away for their own benefit). Your sacred vessel separates you from the rest of the energies circulating on the planet at any given time.

The vessel of your body exchanges energy with the outside world and the Universe through your chakras. Balanced and clear energy strengthens your whole system and builds immunity against outside forces that threaten to bring down your overall vibrations. When your chakras carry lower energy, debris, or blockages, they are more energetically susceptible since they are already in a decreased energy state. It's the same principle as a downward spiral. For example, when you experience states of worry, you can easily slip into deep sadness, which could eventually turn into depression because when you're upset, you're already in a dysregulated state. Adding to an already overwhelmed state creates an additive effect and brings your vibrations down.

Next, let's talk about what chakra cleansing can do for strengthening your personal boundaries. When you are empathic or intuitive, it can be easy to pick up on other people's energy—it's contagious. It's important to develop healthy boundaries to be able to tell what belongs to you and what isn't yours to hold on to. This way, you will be less affected by the media or someone's negative words or bad behavior.

It is your sovereign birthright to live a life free of manipulation and control from others. We know this on a basic level, but many adults who seek chakra healing may need help and guidance setting proper boundaries. Setting appropriate boundaries isn't something we necessarily grow up learning how to do. There are a few things you can do to improve your boundaries on your own, like working on compassionately saying no, setting an intention to protect your energy before going into a situation, or restoring your energy after a negative encounter. When your chakra system is strong, your boundary-setting skills will increase naturally and feel organic, leading to a healthier and happier mental well-being.

RELEASE UNWANTED ENERGY

Chakra cleansing is the perfect way to clear away energetic imprints after an unwanted or negative encounter. Since so much of our lives is spent dealing with other people, this can be a real challenge, especially when you know you'll need to deal with the same people again, day after day. For this, it's best to seek out an energy healer, like a Reiki Master, pranic healer, herbalist, or shaman to provide therapy or treatment. These healing modalities (Reiki, Pranic Healing, herbalism, shamanic sessions like retrievals and extractions) all specialize not only in energy boosting but also in energy removal.

In some traditional shamanic cultures (for example, in Peru), other people's negative energy, or *wetiko,* is considered a virus or psychic pathogen that infects the mind. It is contracted through energetic exposure, just like one might contract the flu. This spiritual disease spreads when one's energy is contaminated by another's infected energy. An infection might present in the form of selfishness, anger, or other malignant psychosis that disturbs the peace of humanity. In the West, we believe this condition to be a state of the psyche that is created internally and reinforced externally. But, as we know, we can only view that which we are the vibration of already, and energetic balancing creates a new vibratory state where wetiko cannot exist. Or it may exist, but you won't be able to interact with it anymore or absorb it since the vibration range is outside of what exists inside you.

I like to think of other people's energy as a bug that we can catch and release back into the wild whenever we want. You can briefly touch it, but it ultimately won't stick to you or integrate with your body if you do not ingest it and willingly take it on as your own. Since we are all so connected, it's easy and natural for our energy to intertwine within our partnerships, families, and community. This interaction affects the way we feel and view ourselves and others and our general participation in the world.

Emotions create vibrational magnetic waves that your energy body connects to as soon as someone walks into a room or even calls you on the phone. We are becoming more sensitive to outside energy, and that is a real gift. Yet for those of us unwilling to take on outside influences, there are options. Perhaps your higher self will seek self-healing or the help of an outside practitioner. Perhaps your consciousness will choose to shift to a different resonance and, therefore, won't be as affected by what others say. It's always a sovereign choice to reject outside influences, and you get to make that choice at any time. Chakra cleansing can help, so give one of the techniques in the previous chapter a try—you may surprise yourself!

GAIN CLARITY

Your higher etheric energy portals, or transpersonal chakras, form a bridge between you and the Divine. This pillar of light is an information superhighway that is conducted by your oversoul (see page 170) and your higher self. It is linked to your soul's blueprint, higher vision, ability to connect with and discern your path, and elevated levels of consciousness. All your chakras directly affect how much light you can hold within your system at any given time. The more light you can hold, the more your consciousness can expand and the closer you can come to your true self. This is the self that exists beyond your egoic self; it is your true essence. When you begin to access your true self, barriers you once thought were walls turn into doorways to other dimensions of understanding.

Your thoughts, beliefs, feelings, and needs weave a beautiful multidimensional tapestry that you get to create for yourself. Once the fog of illusion, known as *maya* (a Hindu word that means "great illusion"), begins to lift, you will experience this loving Divine cocreation. Remember, everything within your experience is first created in your energy field. What does it mean to cocreate our physical reality? When we start to access higher energy light streams, the inner critic with its stories and judgments begins to fall away, leaving a pure vibration of truth and simplicity. We gain access to truth and higher perception instead of viewing things through a distorted lens. Anything outside of love is distortion and illusion. When you allow and give permission for love to integrate, you move into higher levels of consciousness where these truths are readily accessible and distortion can no longer exist.

EXPAND SPIRITUALLY

There will be many stages and layers of awakening during your life. Luckily for us, this lifetime is an extraordinarily special one. We are moving at an accelerated rate that this planet has not seen since the ancient times of Atlantis and Lemuria. We are discovering our inherent intuitive gifts, and psychic skillsets are being turned on. In Hinduism, the word *siddhis* refers to the supernatural gifts we store in each of our chakras. This extrasensory information consists of abilities that expand our range of hearing, seeing, feeling, sensing, and knowing. As the chakras become aligned into a balanced state, these siddhis start to reveal themselves and guide you down an ever-expanding spiritual path.

You have the ability to tune in to discover your psychic style. Whether you are new to a spiritual path or well on your way down the dharmic road, you may discover that your ability to access new insights develops as you open and expand energetically. After all, intuition is a form of accessing your subtle body energies.

Intuitive styles can be broken down into two categories: kinesthetic (body sense or empathy) and mental (visual and verbal information). Physical intuitives can actually feel metaphysical information as physical energy. We call these people empaths. Empaths might specialize in one of the following gifts of empathy: physical, feeling, mental, relational, natural, or supernatural (mediums). They may cognitively know or intuitively sense by using taste, touch, smell, or other physical means. Then we have spiritual intuitives, which include the empath who accesses prophecies or channels insight through visual symbolism or clairvoyance. The main difference between the two types of styles is that spiritual intuitives gain intuition through transcending various levels of consciousness rather than through the physical senses.

The more you spend time with yourself, the more your gifts will make themselves known. They can always be developed, and you'll see progress through plenty of consistent practice.

Ascension through the Third, Fourth, and Fifth Dimensions

Dimensions can be best described as levels of consciousness that exist within different realms in the Universe. In this version of Earth, we primarily work with three dimensions available to us—the third, fourth, and fifth. We are living in all three at once, as they are layered on top of one another.

The three-dimensional (3D) reality we know is comprised of all the things in our physical world. Energy creates form as its reflection, and this three-dimensional reality is constantly being fed by higher level consciousness. Third-dimensional beings have physical body density and participate in the world of form.

The fifth-dimension (5D) reality shift is currently taking place on this planet, and it's an entirely new wavelength for humanity. The fifth dimension can be thought of as a heart-centered consciousness that is comprised of nonphysical light frequencies. Fifth-dimensional beings are generally not physically embodied and do not experience the density that we do here on Earth. This is the consciousness level that we are integrating right now. It's why so many of us are waking up and discovering new ways of being and participating in the New Earth.

The fourth dimension (4D) is the transitional layer of consciousness that bridges the gap between the third and fifth dimensions. Many of us believe that the fourth dimension is time, and in fact, this level is necessary to step the energy down from the fifth to the third dimension so that we humans can fully integrate the higher levels of consciousness streaming into our bodies from solar energies, our sun. The process of moving up in consciousness is called ascension, and although in this lifetime we won't become astral (beings made of pure light), we are well on our way! We retain our physical bodies while pulling in more energy for our light body. It's likely that anyone alive now is functioning already within a fourth- to fifth-dimensional consciousness or higher—and the same goes for future generations. What an exciting time to be alive! We have front-row seats to the entire ascension process, and it's going to be the ride of a lifetime.

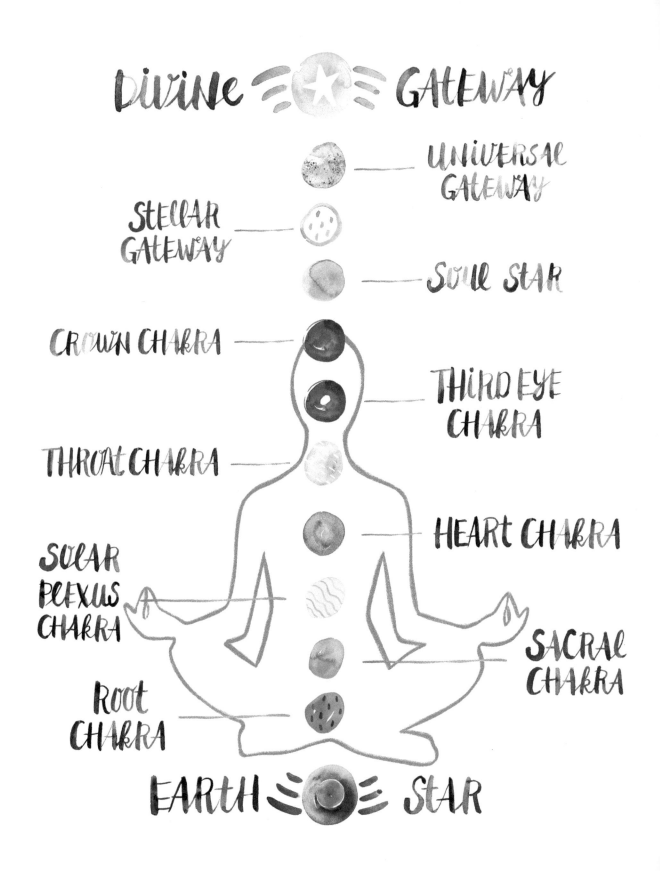

DiVine GATEWAY

UNIVERSAL GATEWAY

STELLAR GATEWAY

SOUL STAR

CROWN CHAKRA

THIRD EYE CHAKRA

THROAT CHAKRA

HEART CHAKRA

SOLAR PLEXUS CHAKRA

SACRAL CHAKRA

ROOT CHAKRA

EARTH STAR

PART TWO

The 12 Chakras

In this part, we move into the finer details of the
mystical world of energy, chakra by chakra. We'll begin
from the ground up, ascending through all 12 chakras.
As we escalate through the familiar energy centers,
I will also introduce several new transpersonal chakras.
Together, we'll dive into what and where they
are and how they function.

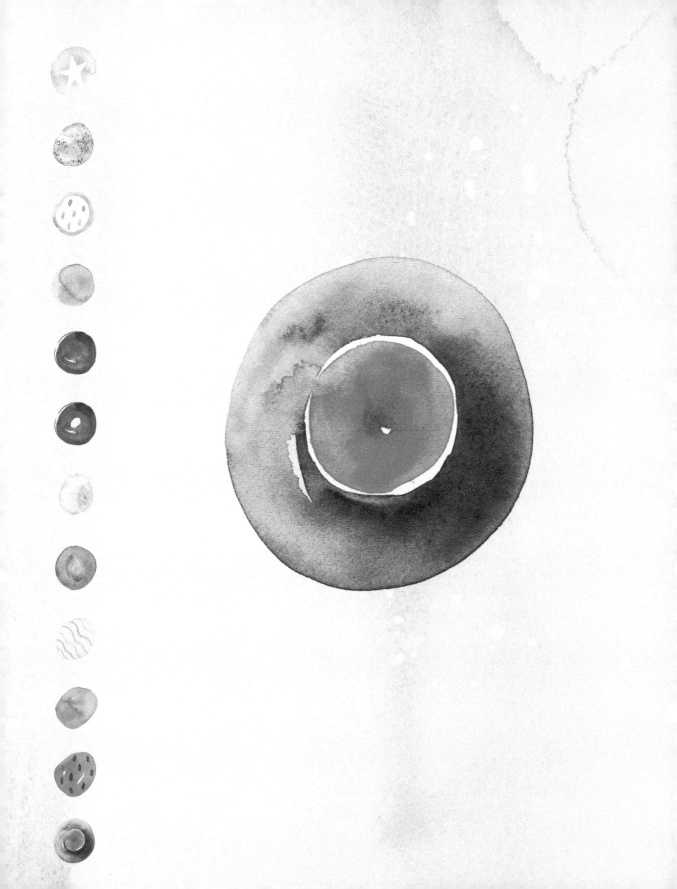

Chapter Five
The Zero Chakra: Earth Star

I f you haven't worked with the 12-chakra system before, you may be used to seeing the root space, your first chakra, addressed first. But to gain the deepest understanding of ourselves, we are called to first look below ground level, at the gateway to Inner Earth, our Earth star chakra. This portal connects us to the heart of Gaia and her crystalline iron core. The ground spirits, as well as the gem, microbial, and mineral kingdom, hold the wisdom of our ancestors and collective consciousness in this layer. When you drop into your Earth star connection, you access the Akashic records of all of Earth and its inhabitants as well as their timelines (see "Akashic Records" on page 71). Personally and collectively speaking, this connection strengthens intuition and builds a greater awareness within of the harmonics of the natural world, including the entire Earth.

Think of this chakra as a deep-rooted anchor. Since we are moving into an ascension period on Earth, our pillar of light stretches tall as it rises through the dimensions of consciousness into the celestial realms. And, as the ancient saying goes, "As above, so below." We must create a strong mooring to our home star to expand our upward-reaching consciousness range and move beyond the third-dimension density we experience. We can think of the dimensions as becoming less dense with each higher dimension. The particles that move within each higher plane become more spacious, accelerated, and expanded. To remember our connection to the Earth star chakra, we must start by looking at Earth's iron core and understanding that this is the most incredibly dense material in existence—outside of whatever material exists in a black hole.

The particles of the Earth star chakra connect us to many layers of Earth, and the chakra's entire purpose is to connect us to the wisdom of Mother Earth as a whole. We are just beginning to remember our powerful influence and kinship with Gaia. The more this connection is integrated into humanity, the closer we get to creating a New Earth vision of harmony for all beings. Legend has it, in ancient times (more than 26,000 years ago), Atlantis and Lemuria were the historic civilizations that held fifth-dimensional consciousness gateways on Earth. These ancient people were far more advanced and possessed higher consciousness because they harnessed the healing capacity Earth naturally provided. They lived in unity with all of Gaia's minerals, plants, elements, and creatures. We are now reopening the gates of remembrance as we foster, care, and tend to Earth's needs once again. We must protect Earth, her resources, and precious wildlife so that we can thrive again in harmonious rapture with our environment.

We can think of the Earth star chakra as being a little like dirt. Dirt is dense, full of life-giving nutrients and microbes, and pulses at a lower frequency than our physical being (which is made up of breath, thoughts, and body). It is the source of most of our vitality as we know it. When you consciously work with your Earth star chakra, you allow yourself to be tethered to your center of grounding while simultaneously holding an enlightened state. The Divine gateway and Earth star chakras are essentially bookends to our being. Through the activation of your Earth star chakra, you create a gateway of knowledge that streams information from all of Earth to you. Think of yourself as accessing a living library of codes, which will greatly serve you in your personal evolution.

Names & Meaning

The Sanskrit word *vasundhara* translates to "daughter of the earth," and, thus, is another name for the Earth star chakra. The Earth star chakra, although existing energetically for millennia, is only now making a comeback in the Age of Aquarius because humans are reconnecting to Earth. We are being inspired by the ancient cultures of our ancestors who knew the land and how to live and play symbiotically with the Great Mother. We are learning how to reconnect, protect, and heal our oldest spiritual home, along with all the creatures, plants, animals, and other forms of life that reside within her.

Color

When we think of velvety, fertile soil, we imagine a rich dark brown. Natural and earthy, brown is the color of your Earth star chakra. This energy center is said to turn magenta when fully activated. So, if we were to view the Earth star chakra of someone who is on an awakening path, it would first appear brown and then magenta, or brown with a magenta core. Its vibrational frequency is low and intense.

Location

The Earth star chakra center is located anywhere from 6 to 12 inches below the feet. Since this chakra is a subpersonal energy center, it is located outside and underneath the body and is not directly associated with any organs, nerves, or systems. Since we have many points on our feet that correspond with specific areas in the body, this energy receives a boost from the deep grounding electrons that flow from Earth's core, mantle, and crust to mingle with the *nadis*, or energy channels, on the soles of the feet. Connecting to your Earth star chakra will provide the deepest level of anchoring available for your extended chakra system at this time on the planet.

Estimated Activation

It is our human birthright to be able to access all our chakras, whether they exist below, within, or above (outside) the body. Although higher dimensional chakras tend to open as we elevate and grow in consciousness over many years, the Earth star is one that you are born with as innately activated. Re-remembering is all that's needed to fully connect to this special gateway, which means you have access to all your past and parallel lives when you are born—even more so than when you age and begin to accept conditioned programming. You came from the earth, and you will return to the earth someday. As such, you are a part of the greater whole, and your oneness cannot be severed in this lifetime, except through willful rejection or reinforcement of separation. If you've ever felt a deep connection with gardening, playing with animals, hiking, observing nature in the wild, or feeling at home in the woods, your Earth star chakra has already tuned you in to the natural frequencies of the planet.

Body Parts

The Earth star chakra sits below your feet and therefore receives energy from Earth through the soles of your feet. Your foot pads create an energy bridge that connect the electromagnetic frequencies of Earth directly to your body. Your soles act as regulators that allow energy in and out as they plug Earth's energy directly into the nerve endings on the underside of your feet. Like an umbilical cord carrying nutrients to a fetus, this energy moves through your body's circuitry, carrying nutrient-rich Earth energy to all your limbs, organs, muscles, bones, joints, and systems.

Systems

If you follow the cord from this subpersonal chakra into the body, you'll find that it connects all the way up to the hara line and microcosmic orbit (see page 95). The Earth star, running down the sushumna into the ground, is a link between the hara, which is identified with identity, and grounding and umbilical functions.

Senses

Since the soles of the feet have nerve endings that connect to the entire body and all of its organs and systems, the grounding Earth star chakra plays a crucial role in linking Earth's energy to all the body's senses (sight, smell, hearing, taste, touch, and extrasensory perception).

Illnesses

Illness and disease aren't directly correlated with the Earth star chakra; however, since this vortex is under your feet, it's important to note that some of the elements that contribute to your health exist right beneath you. Soil contains dense micro- and macronutrients that are filtered into the human body through food or direct absorption. For the Earth star chakra, general awareness and mindfulness of what you consume and where it comes from (organic food instead of genetically modified food, for example, as well as processed foods) will benefit your immune system and have great long-term impacts on your health. About 60 percent of the human body is made up of microbes (bacteria, fungi, and single-celled organisms), which comprise your microbiome—a critical player in your health. These microbes affect your metabolism, immune system, and emotional well-being, so it's essential they get the nutrients they need.

Function

Distinct from the root chakra, the Earth star chakra goes beyond grounding and acts to stabilize the entire extended chakra system into Earth's crystalline iron core. While this subpersonal layer is considered more of a recent chakra to come online for humanity, its function seems to be as ancient as the stars. One thing is for sure: as you shift into new human templates that allow you to embody higher levels of consciousness, we usher in the Golden Age together. This Golden Age will be a time of harmony and elevated unity consciousness for the entire planet, and we've already begun the transition, which means we need to have strong foundations to grow in all quantum levels.

All your past and parallel lives, as well as the life of Earth itself, is recorded into the matrix of Gaia. This second-dimensional matrix is very dense and provides records of your personal incarnation stories as well as a general blueprint for your soul's journey, which was decided upon (by you) right before you chose to enter the Earth plane. It's helpful to be able to access these records so that you can gain insight into your life's purpose and path. You can do so by opening the Akashic records in a simple meditation to examine your queries (see page 71 for more about the Akashic records).

Your incarnation points are included in your Earth star chakra anywhere from 6 inches to 12 inches below the feet. These access points connect you to your ancestors, including the Earth family that came before you. Your heritage likely includes a tribe or clan or an ancient long-lost civilization that helped seed humanity. Connecting to your ancestry can be helpful, especially to receive additional support or wisdom that you may not otherwise have in your modern, day-to-day life.

Your Earth star chakra also contains entryways to archaic Earth energy, which can provide collective historical context for humanity as a whole. This would be a helpful tool for rediscovering your ancient roots throughout Earth's antiquity. Where did you come from? How does that impact your journey in today's timeline? These are important questions that play a role in your emotional and physical passages in this lifetime. Many of your questions can be answered simply by looking at the past through a new lens of interpretation.

And, finally, the Earth star connects you directly with Gaia goddess consciousness. All planets in the solar system, along with everything on them, possess their own consciousness. Earth is a playground for conscious manifestation, spiritual growth, and thriving natural resources, and she supports the rhythm of your life in all ways. Through her seasons and revolutions of change, she regulates your sleep patterns, supports your physical being, and sustains your life cycles. When you connect more deeply to Gaia, you reaffirm or establish a strong foundation for yourself to carry you through your days.

Archetypes

An archetype is a main model or prototype that represents a concept's first form. Originally brought to light through Jungian psychology, these patterns and primordial images are derived from the collective unconscious and are inherent in your existence. Though an unlimited number of archetypes may exist, Carl Jung identified four major archetypes: the Self, the Persona, the Shadow, and the Anima/Animus (True Self). Archetypes are meant to help you understand motives, and it is important to remember they are neither good nor bad (although each archetype can present a shadow archetype, which are uncomplementary characteristics when they become imbalanced). When you understand motives, you are in a position to make conscious choices.

One might argue that of all the archetypes, the Mother is the most important because she came first. Her womb is the space from which everything in creation derives. So, we begin our journey in the Earth star chakra with the Mother and her counterpart, the Destroyer. The Mother and the Destroyer are inextricably bound to each other.

We begin with the Mother archetype, who births all form with her life-giving energy. She offers resources, and regardless of your birth story, every single one of us has a mother and we each contain the Mother. The Mother within can hint to both dark and light aspects of the feminine. The archetype highlights that, on your journey, mothering yourself is just as important as the act of creating. It also hints at your own self-care. How do you nurture yourself and fill your own cup? Are you depleting yourself by giving away all your precious resources? How do you care for that which you have given birth to (projects, children, ideas)? In what ways are you restricting your own growth? A balanced mother is encouraging, benevolent, and graceful as she uses her power of control wisely.

We now turn to the Destroyer, as all life must be reclaimed by the earth. When we examine this archetypal energy closer, we see that which the Mother grips too tightly, she destroys in her grasp, prohibiting growth—sometimes clinging, sometimes crushing.

As humans have natural aversions to endings, the Destroyer is here to remind you that, though you may resist, change is inevitable and pain can be used to uncover your true purpose. Foundations are rocked, jobs and relationships dissolve, homes crumble, stagnancy becomes history, and we learn to let go of permanence. These destructive blows redirect the force of your life and teach you how to rebuild from the ground up. When the Destroyer is present in your life, you are embarking on a serious foundational restructuring. But don't worry; this path leads back home to the hopeful Mother, who is waiting to hold you as you begin again.

Personality

Once the Earth star chakra is rediscovered through active intention, it comes online. The personality of someone who has rediscovered their earthly heritage might be best described as one whose consciousness resonates with that of Earth. Advocates of peace and environmentalists alike could best be described as Earth keepers. They recognize themselves within the energy of the natural world and act in grounded awareness with consideration and respect for all life. They usually tend to be pragmatic, intuitive, and compassionate, and they possess a deep inner knowing about the planet and her inhabitants. They may recall past lives on Earth and other star systems that help aid in their life purpose in the here and now. Typically, these souls are highly integrated both in society and in nature, although they feel the most comfortable surrounding themselves in a natural environment like a forest, mountains, valleys, or the countryside. They have an attraction to helping others and usually take nurturing roles, like mothers and caregivers, in their personal and professional lives.

Underactivity/Overactivity

It's nearly impossible to have an underactive or overactive Earth star chakra, since this chakra exists in perpetuity and, as it is belowground, is not normally accessible. However, there are some cases when remembering our connection to the natural world might feel out of reach. City dwellers, for example, commonly feel disconnected from nature. If you live in the city, you'll want to make an extra effort to connect in a meaningful way to the natural environment. People who have not yet remembered their inherent connection to the natural world or have not gone through any levels of awakening will also feel disconnected. Then there are those who may seem not of this Earth. Such people may feel disconnected here because their soul is so new to Earth that the planet itself feels foreign. These beings need only remember their mission to ignite their true purpose and reason for being on Earth now.

Balanced Chakra

Since everything is energy, the molecules in your blood pulse to the beat of Earth, your home star. These molecules carry information and resonate with the center of Earth at her iron core. When your Earth star chakra is in balance, the frequency of the iron core of Earth syncs with the vibrating iron molecules of information in your blood, binding you to Earth and connecting you and every being directly to Gaia's heart center. The only time you might experience difficulty connecting to your Earth star chakra is if you have an iron-deficiency anemia or a medical condition that affects your personal electromagnetic frequencies. Otherwise, enjoy this natural connection—it's available to you every day!

Deities

Here we look toward the archetypal themes of the Mother and the Destroyer to point us to the deities associated with the Earth star chakra. These deities are Kali Ma, Durga, Osiris, and White Buffalo Woman.

We begin with Kali Ma, Hindu goddess of liberation and revolution. Her energy is present in the Earth star as both the giver of life and the one who takes it away. Kali Ma knows there is freedom waiting on the other side of shadow transformation, and she possesses fierce love that will most certainly be slightly, if not downright, uncomfortable. This revolutionary upheaval creates space for sublime change. Her message encourages you to find self-honesty and channel any rage or anger so that, through destruction, resurrection can begin.

Hindu goddess Durga is the protective goddess of the Universe and sits at the root of creation. In mythology, she is a goddess of war, preservation, and annihilation. Often called "the demon slayer," she combats anything that threatens peace and prosperity. She points with her eight arms to the dharmic path, and it is said that praying to her yields salvation. Call upon Durga for deep inner strength when you need to forge a new light path on your journey forward.

Osiris, the Egyptian god of the underworld, is the masculine deity representing fertility, death, and rebirth. He is the husband and counterpart of Isis (Mother of Egypt) and is a masterful energy manipulator. Osiris was a king, ruler, and protector of his people and served as a judge at the gates of the afterlife. Call on Osiris when a judgment is to be made, when you must make difficult decisions as a ruler would, and when you need Divine masculine assistance during times of extreme transition.

Finally, White Buffalo Woman's energy is present in the Earth star chakra due to her connection with ground spirits and the lineage of ancestors who came before you. A Lakota priestess, White Buffalo Woman is a shapeshifter who came from the stars and, in her human form, inhabits the body of a beautiful Native American woman. She created the *channupa,* or peace pipe, and her medicine brings peace and harmony to the Earth and all her inhabitants. Legend has it that when she returns to the land in the form of a white buffalo, a new era of ascension, unity, and peace will begin.

Planets

It's no surprise that we come home to Earth and her crystalline iron core as the governing energy for your Earth star chakra. Her solid inner core and molten outer core connect you to her inner being and original grounding essence. There's just no place like home! There is also a distinctly Plutonian aspect to the Earth star chakra, which I'd be remiss not to address. Pluto represents the underworld, filled with volcanic intensity, which brings intense change through transformation. This faraway outer planet of metamorphosis is aptly represented by the elemental and intense subpersonal Earth star chakra.

Earth Star Chakra Exercise: Despacho Ceremony

Despacho ceremonies are practiced in shamanic cultures as a way of showing profound gratitude to the Great Mother, Pachamama, and the mountain spirits, the Apus. As we reach deeper into Earth's core and take what we need to survive and thrive, it's important that an offering be made in return to complete the energy exchange between us and Earth. Humans have plundered Earth for her bounty for far too long, and traditional cultures recognized the value in making contributions back to the land so that Earth would be replenished and able to sustain its vegetation, wildlife, and human beings.

There are many ways to create a sacrificial offering to Earth in gratitude. We look to nature to help provide the tools so that we may create beauty and energy-rich rituals that honor her and give her thanks. Although most despacho ceremonies commemorate significant events (like a union, a birth, or a death), you can create a despacho ceremony as an act of gratitude to honor any moment that feels important for you.

Items needed for a traditional despacho ceremony should be meaningful to you, but they don't need to be a sacrifice of epic proportions. Gratitude is in and of itself a prayer of offering. For your energetic offering, you may collect a variety of dried herbs, essential oils, copal, wine, natural flour or tobacco, peppercorns, candles, crystals, shells, or, if you are female, even a small amount of menstrual blood from your moon cycle. You will use these items to create an altar, and they will form the basis of your offering. Each item you choose should be significant in its own right. For example, eggshells honor the unborn, red and white wine honor the moon and the Mother, flour or cornmeal signifies nourishment, and candles represent the transformational element of fire.

Pick a sacred place that feels special to you, like a private site off the beaten path and out in nature—near a river, in the woods, or on top of a giant rock, if possible. Arrange your items with care and say a prayer of intention along with a visualization of Earth receiving your prayers in reverence. One way to add to your ceremony is through song, mantra, or a powerful on-site meditation. Drumbeats help send the prayers down into the earth, so bring a sacred percussion instrument if you have one. As a general rule of thumb, the items work best if they are biodegradable so the offering can remain on the land, buried within it, or float away. Otherwise, leave no trace and take back with you any out-of-place debris or matter that you brought with you to preserve the integrity of your sacred site.

Akashic Records

Accessing the Akashic records is a way to gain insight and receive valuable information about any energetic imprints that could be affecting your well-being. The Akashic records are basically a database of all recorded energy that anyone can access, and it serves in your greater expansion. As all energy is a continuum between life and death, the Akashic records encode nonphysical information from other journeys for you to access here and now, including past, ancient timelines of Earth and every living thing on it. Earth has its own consciousness and therefore its own records. Think of Earth as a living library.

An experience of your Akashic records is much more than simply a psychic reading. It is an experience that reveals your soul perspective and soul-level truth. It serves as a restoration of your connection with your masters, teachers, and loved ones. The records are a glimpse into the highest, greatest expression and potential of you and an initiation into a world of accelerated expansion, transformation, and remembering. Connecting with your guides and experiencing their presence and love through their energetic transmissions, insights, and healing is tremendously empowering.

You can work with the transformative energy of the Akashic records through meditation to open yourself up to a greater and deeper remembrance and knowledge of your highest expression. If you'd like to start with a simple technique, begin with a question, get quiet, and say aloud, "Source, grant me access to my own Akashic records, so that I may work with my Ascended Masters and teachers in accordance with my greatest healing and benefit. Help me understand myself through your perspective."

Make this intention in a quiet place where you're likely to be undisturbed. As you start to receive information, do not second-guess yourself—just go with the answer you first receive, even if it comes in your own voice (it likely will). You can eliminate doubt and build trust by continuing to practice. Make sure to thank your guides before closing your session by saying, "Thank you, the records are now closed."

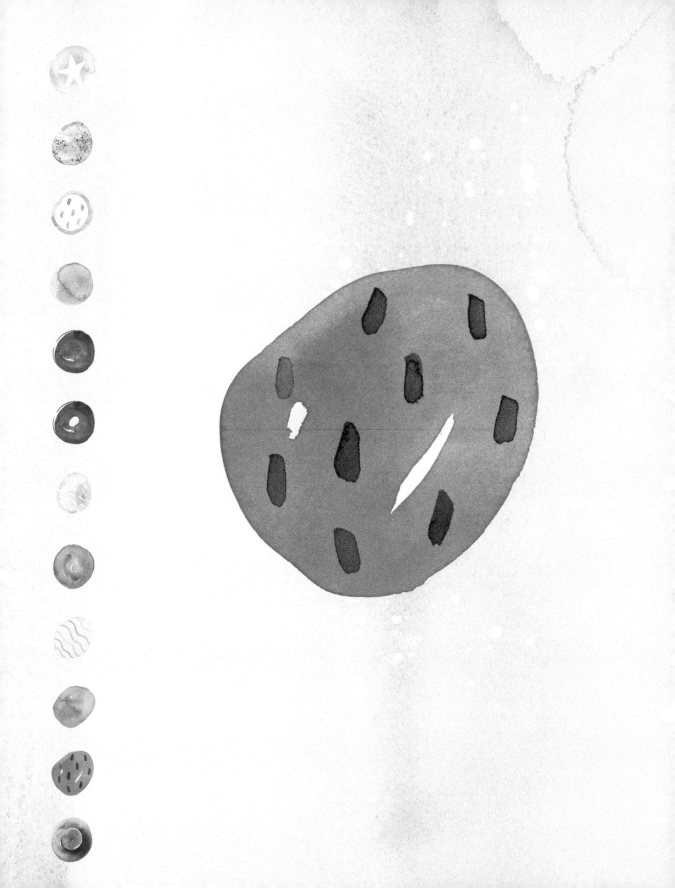

Chapter Six
The 1st Chakra: Root

The first chakra is called the root chakra because it is the center stabilizing point for the seven main physical chakras. Tied closely to Earth, this chakra rules the material realm along with basic survival blueprints and mechanisms. The mantra for this chakra is *I AM,* and it's no coincidence that this is the base statement on which the entire chakra ladder is built. Just as creating strong roots is important for plants, creating a sturdy grounding chakra is necessary for building the foundations you wish to cultivate for yourself in this life.

Self-preservation, security, stability, basic survival, and physical courage are hall-marks of the root space. The root forms the foundations on which your entire life will be built. These pillars must be solid and deeply anchored for your body to support all the life-giving functions for you not only to survive and thrive but also eventually move beyond human experience and merge into Divine consciousness. The root center carries a fire energy often associated with sex, yet it also carries a childlike innocence that imparts reliance on nurturing mothering and fathering energies (both biological and Divine). These energies assist you in overcoming challenges as you grow toward your highest expression.

The feet and legs are included in this base energy center, as they carry you from place to place and support your forward-moving actions and activities. There are two main energy channels, or *nadis*, that run down your legs called the ida and pingala. The ida corresponds to the left (or yin) side of the body and leg and is considered the introverted *lunar nadi*, which carries feminine aspects. The pingala runs down the right (or yang) side of the body and leg and is considered the extroverted *solar nadi*, which carries masculine aspects. The ida governs mental processes and is controlled by the right brain, while the pingala governs vital physical processes and is controlled by the left brain.

The sushumna is the final nadi, which can be considered the body's "great river." Located along the spinal column, it is the main channel for your chakras, or your ascension pillar. The sushumna flows from the crown to the root, where it is said to drop from the base of the spine into the ground below (and likely into your Earth star chakra). This energetic channel supports your kundalini (or shakti flow) as it rises from your root to your crown, sensitizing and activating you toward higher levels of consciousness.

Names & Meaning

The root chakra is also called the muladhara chakra; *mula* means "root," "support," or "base," and *adhara* means "lower." The name suggests its location on the physical body. Other familiar names belonging to the Tantric terminology include *bhūmi-cakra* (ground chakra), *brahma-padma* (Brahma's lotus), *catur-dala* (the four-petaled one), *mūla padma* (foundation lotus), or simply *adhara* (lower one). In the Vedas and Upanishads, *mūla-kanda* (root bulb) is also mentioned.

Color

The color most associated with the root chakra is a vibrant ruby red. This frequency on the color band oozes juicy passion, power, and energy. Red is the color of fire, blood, rage, desire, and love. It carries an intensity closely linked to kundalini (and shakti) energy. Known to raise metabolic and respiration rates, this color demands attention and turns on your primal instincts.

Location

The root chakra is specifically located at an area at the base of the spine, which is also home to sleeping kundalini, between the reproductive organs and the perineum. Its orientation is at the intersection of the three vital energy channels: ida (on the left side), pingala (on the right side), and sushumna (along the spinal column). This energy point is closest to the nerve bundle of the sacrum and coccyx (the sacrococcygeal nerve plexus) and can be located beneath the *kanda*, an energetic organ between the perineum and the genitals.

Estimated Activation

With motivations of security and survival, the root chakra theme is most apparent in your life between infancy and age seven. Really, it begins with *in utero* incarnation. Primal needs govern this time of rapid growth and development, with primary motivations being your base needs, including food, water, shelter, safety, sleeping, learning to become secure in the world, and working out your attachment style. Emotional needs of interconnection are fostered most during this time. A child of this age is mostly concerned with basic necessities, and any parent will attest that children will be self-centered (and rightfully so) as they are establishing their way in the world brick by brick.

Body Parts

Your feet, legs, parts of your genitals, and perineum are all managed by the root chakra. On males, the penis (*lingam*) is included as the main sex organ, and on females, this corresponds to the vagina (the womb space is included in the sacral region). In addition, the root chakra includes the skeletal system and various elimination organs (including the large and small intestines, the colon, the rectum, and the bladder), plus all the lower extremities (the hip joints and the coccygeal vertebrae, or tailbone). The root chakra shares responsibility with other chakras for the functioning of the prostate and with the sacral chakra for the functioning of the elimination organs.

Glands

The root chakra is associated with the adrenal glands, which are small, triangular-shaped glands that produce hormones, such as cortisol and sex hormones. These glands help regulate metabolism, inflammation in the body, blood pressure, the immune system, and the fight-or-flight response (the body's vital stress response).

Senses

In realizing your basic needs, it is a primitive function to gather sensory information about scent to identify nutrients. Therefore, the root chakra is associated with the sense of smell, and the key sense organ for this chakra is the nose. Working with essential oils through aromatherapy is an especially excellent resource for bringing the root space back into balance.

Illnesses

Diseases and illnesses associated with the root chakra can include eating disorders, obesity, anal and intestinal disorders (including hemorrhoids and constipation), sciatica, sexual dysfunction, chronic fatigue, and fibromyalgia. Foot and leg problems are included here, as are bone and teeth disorders, blood deficiencies, base-of-spine issues, arthritis, and varicose veins. Addictions like alcoholism, gambling, and drug abuse can crop up here, too.

Function

The root chakra represents your consciousness in its most concentrated form of incarnated matter. Because of this density, it is where your heaviest and most powerful emotions live (fear, anger, sadness, disgust), and it is the storehouse for your primal instincts. You store your feelings of self-worth here, and psychologically speaking, these thoughts and feelings are formed early in life.

Perhaps you were the child of birthing complications, divorced parents, or parents who endured financial hardship, or perhaps you suffered from abuse or were raised in a rough neighborhood. You may have been conditioned early on with emotional survival reactions that could include resentment, blame, despair, guilt, shame, rejection, or rage. On the flip side, maybe your childhood featured safe surroundings and caregivers, nurturing primary relationships, adequate food and financial resources, and healthy social connections. These factors all contribute to bolstering your beliefs in yourself and your view of the world. Your experiences become internalized, and it's not until you're a young adult that you start to finally unwind some of your past traumas. You suddenly become aware of your built-in attachment and abandonment issues, trust gaps, and boundary-making habits. The fact is that your beliefs about your circumstances helped support your identity as a physical and spiritual being in the world. When your physical being is threatened, your spiritual ability to create is diminished. It is not until you have opened up and cleared through some of these layers that the higher chakras will be able to fully open, creating gateways to higher realms of consciousness.

All the things you have gone through that make up your self-esteem and identity all point to one truth: although it may seem like you have little control over your circumstances, you *do* have a choice in how you show up to these challenges. It is perhaps the final frontier of self-discovery to integrate the understanding of how little control over anything you actually have. Once this universal truth is discovered, you begin to process and deconstruct years of programming, trauma, or loss, as well as any hardships or suffering you could face in the future. Once you realize this simple truth, things stop happening *to* you and begin happening *for* you. You will see your ability to rise from the ashes and nurture yourself, your role in manifesting your dreams into physical reality, and your past traumas softening through the new lens of healing you have created.

Archetypes

The archetypes of the root chakra are the Feminine and the Masculine. We begin with the sacred Feminine, as we are in a time of the Divine Feminine rising. The Feminine archetype in her essence is pure yin energy—grace, beauty, and shakti. She is nurturing and strong and a healer by nature. The Feminine balances the Masculine, and to feel inner balance, we must possess positive qualities of each archetype.

According to Carl Jung, the Feminine can include a multitude of archetypal energies within her and pass from phase to phase during the course of her lifetime (for example, with age or between seasons of life). The Feminine might pass through and embody any of the following during the course of her lifetime: the Maiden, the Lover, the Crone, the Huntress, the Queen, the Mother, and the Mystic. A mature Feminine is in tune with her emotions and fosters inspiration, connection, and love for those around her. This archetype magnetizes, attracts, and possesses natural intuitive and creative gifts. She recognizes there is much power in her ability to let go and surrender.

The Masculine contains five primary archetypal energies, which he can also embody during different stages of life. They are the Warrior, the Lover, the Father, the Magician, and the King. The Masculine archetype unifies, rules, loves deeply, activates and stabilizes the Feminine, and supports through action. A mature Masculine archetype will have confronted his own limitations and insecurities and learned how to temper and hold them with responsibility. He is interested in providing and caring for himself and others and has stopped letting defenses ruin his relationships.

Both archetypes belong to something greater than themselves and expand spiritually when they begin to embody one another in equal measure. Take a moment to observe your life as it currently is. Which phase or archetype do you identify with right now? Do you feel yourself leaning more into the Feminine or Masculine, or do you identify with both roles equally?

Personality

Dynamic and energized, a person with a balanced root chakra is likely living life to its fullest. Having worked through their own aggression, fears, and limiting beliefs, they can face any change that comes their way. Rooted in integrity, presence, and pragmatism, they will feel a deeper connection to others, which will help evolve their relationships as they continue to mature and stand in greater knowing of themselves. They naturally draw attention, magnetize energy within power dynamics, and hold stimulating conversations.

They are normally dependable and reliable and can bring things back down to earth when the situation calls for it. Success follows them, and they are most interested in creating a world full of resources, services, and foundations for others to build upon.

While the focus of these personality entries is on the qualities of a balanced chakra, it's important to note what this base chakra looks like out of balance. A person in this category may seem self-absorbed and completely focused on themselves. Their main objective is to meet their own primary needs (narcissists and abusers are included here). Other people's needs come after theirs have been met, and their general line of thinking follows this, too ("It's all about me!"). They have strong material desires and are preoccupied with physical orientation in the world. They often tend to act out of wounding and love to play the victim card. They may show signs of personality disorders (narcissistic, avoidant, paranoid), or they may have masochistic or possibly even suicidal tendencies that, at their root, are attention-seeking behaviors.

Underactive Chakra

An underactive root chakra is considered deficient in energy. Not enough energy in the root space may cause you to become unfocused, passive, and apathetic. You may feel spacey, as if you are disconnected from the rest of your body or even the rest of the world. It's possible this may manifest in the physical body through weight loss. If you have a weak root chakra, you will also have a difficult time setting proper boundaries because your sense of personal responsibility has been compromised or damaged. It may be easy for you to be taken advantage of, sucked into pointless arguing, or stuck in the middle of drama time and again. If this is true for you, it's important to try to rebuild your self-esteem so that you can begin to reestablish your sense of self-worth. Start with self-love exercises (such as mirror work) to foster a loving foundation of growth and support.

Overactive Chakra

An overactive or excessive root chakra has excess fire energy, and if this is the case for you, you may experience rage, anger, or jealousy or have a flare for the dramatic. You may suffer from a lack mentality (the feeling of not having or being enough), which can cause self-destructive and self-sabotaging behavior. Most of the time, this mindset can be attributed to a core fear or wound that has not been properly healed. Excessive spending, weight issues (overweight), greed, hoarding, extreme resistance to change, and rigid boundaries show up here as signs of surplus energy in the root space. Again, fear is at the root of most of these issues. Since fear is the absence of love, love is the antidote and medicine required to combat this imbalance. Pour it on in healthy doses as much as needed to see signs of improvement.

Balanced Chakra

When you have a strong root chakra, you will generally feel secure within yourself and have built up some solid levels of self-trust. Each time you listen to yourself and tune in to your own voice, you reinforce the fact that you are able to lean into this trust when you need it. Physical ease will be present, which means your basic needs are all met, contributing to a sense of security and eventually leading to abundance and prosperity. If your root chakra is balanced, you're in the driver's seat with your bodily and sexual desires, and you're sustaining a high level of practical awareness through nonjudgment. Presence, patience, calm, and renewal flow to you in this state of being, and you may feel a closer connection to others as well as the natural world that surrounds you.

Deities

The deities associated with the root chakra are Parvati, Shakti, Bhumi, and Brahma. These are all Hindu goddesses and gods who represent universal messages of foundational alignment on your path.

Parvati, the Great Mother, comes with a message that it is to your benefit to recommit to personal growth and inner devotion. It's not always easy to make your relationship with yourself a primary focus, but you owe it to yourself to be in service to this truth. When you are, you'll be your own best resource of love. Parvati knows how to root down to rise up, and this grounding leads to higher realms of spirituality through devotional channels.

Shakti, the feminine counterpart to Shiva, represents energy, movement, and sheer power. When she is present, great change is afoot. Shakti, whose essence rises as pure kundalini flowing up your spine, is an agent of transformation. When Shakti rises to meet Shiva (in the crown chakra), alchemically they combine to produce creation through sacred union. Her magical, Divine Feminine essence encourages a willingness to let go of the familiar things as she creates the metamorphosis needed for blessings to appear. Through embracing this spark, your inner fire is ignited to bring about radical new ways of being and seeing. A greater love for yourself is all Shakti asks of you in return.

Bhumi is the Hindu goddess of Mother Earth. She presides over the fertility of the land and the profusion of Earth's natural resources. In her guardianship, she offers her protection over the environment. When she is present, you can expect expansion and growth.

Brahma, one of the sacred gods in the Hindu holy trinity, represents the holy spirit and creator energy. Brahma created the four Vedas and is known as the self-born (*svayambhu*) as he was born from a golden egg, making him the first god. Like the ancient paradox asking which came first, the chicken or the egg, this deity is the beginning and end to all cycles, only to begin again anew. Creator of light and dark, he begs the question, can you find balance in neutrality within? What are you creating and what have your contributions been?

Planets

Earth's mantle, upper crust, and surface all belong to the root chakra. When you connect to Gaia's earthly layers, you connect to the lush essence of original sacred grounding energy. The root space also holds a Martian frequency. Mars, the red planet, is named after the Roman god of war. In its destructive expression, Mars can be quite primal and aggressive. In its constructive expression, Martian energy is instinctual and inspires action toward building a better world.

Root Chakra Exercise: Syncing with the Elements

As you move up in consciousness and continue to elevate through evolution, it will be increasingly important to continue growing a strong root system so that you will be able to navigate the higher dimensions and layers without losing yourself. As time is an element that exists primarily in the third dimension, higher dimensions are not controlled by this guiding principle. Instead, they operate from an ever-present now moment. The main way they travel is through shifts in vibrational perspective. As you begin to play with the thread of time in your ascension journey, being able to find your ground is especially valuable.

This exercise is a meditation that will always bring you back to your true self. Read the instructions first, and then select the perfect spot in nature to perform this meditation. If possible, you'll want to find a place with at least one tree (ideally one with leaves) and one body of water, like a babbling brook, stream, ocean, or water fountain, that's close enough for you to hear it running.

Position yourself between the tree and the body of water. Get into a comfortable seated position and settle into your meditation posture. Quiet yourself, and after a few deep breaths, listen to the beating of your own heart. Focus on your heartbeat, allowing all distractions to fade into the background.

After a few minutes, focus on the leaves of the tree. Observe the sounds of the rustling and focus your attention on the tree's sounds for a short time. Listen to the waves of wind as they pass through the leaves or the stillness with gentle stirring. Let everything else be in the background for now. Continue to deeply inhale and exhale.

Next, tune in to the sound of the water. Listen for the ebb and flow, the babbling, the bubbling, or the waves. Be with the water element for a few minutes, allowing the sound to wash over your ears. Notice how it makes you feel and where you feel it. Continue to breathe.

In the last 5 to 15 minutes of your meditation, draw your attention and breath back to your heart. Slowly begin to tune back into the tree sounds, focusing on your heart and the tree simultaneously. Finally, add in the sound of the water, syncing the sound of your heart to both the rustling of the tree leaves and the moving water. Listen for the beautiful harmony of total grounded coherence. Send gratitude to Earth for holding you in this space, enabling you to come home. Take an energetic snapshot of this moment—how you feel and the part you play in this harmonious swirl. You may come back to this essence at any time; your heart knows the way to get there now.

Schumann Resonance

The Schumann resonance, named in 1952 after physicist Winfried Schumann, may be among the greatest variables affecting the resonance of your consciousness. It is the measurement of Earth's base atmospheric electromagnetic frequency at any given time. In general, this measurement is normally around 7.83 hertz, although it has been on the rise.

This field of frequencies has a vibrational influence on your physical being as it oscillates. If you are out of sync with Earth's frequency, you may start to exhibit signs of dysregulation, including insomnia, sinus issues, allergies, illness, anxiety, suppressed immunity—the list of symptoms goes on. Dysregulation can happen during times of increased solar storm activity or when the sun is emitting dangerous solar radiation, like solar flares, that impact Earth's electromagnetic shields. But when you are in harmony with Earth's Schumann resonance, your ability to heal yourself increases exponentially; you feel aligned, balanced, and energy flows through you easily. This natural symbiosis with Earth allows for longer life as well as overall health and mindset improvement across the planet.

As the sun continues to emit more concentrated photonic plasma light that pummels Earth, Earth's frequency changes. Advanced scientific measurement systems all over the world publicly record these changes and show that, over the last decade and especially since 2012, these measurements have increased substantially, reaching frequencies far exceeding 7.83 hertz, depending on the day. Some recent measurements record anywhere from 60 to 100 hertz! What does that mean for us? Since we are connected to Earth, our vibrations are naturally rising as well. Sometimes you may experience ascension symptoms as your light body increases in size to accommodate the physical changes happening. The ionosphere of Earth resonates with all organisms, coupling us to Earth's electromagnetic field. When Earth changes, so do we!

Chapter Seven
The 2nd Chakra: Sacral

The second chakra up from the base of the spine, your sacral chakra, is thought to hold the sacred waters of life. Tied closely to the water element, this chakra is all about luscious sentience and receiving the nectar of the Universe, loving exchange through connection. This energetic center exemplifies polarity, as it brings together both feminine and masculine energies, which work to help you navigate your whole reality in all its dualistic opposing and complementary forces. You are both expanding into your own awareness as well as expanding outward as you touch others. Sentience, or your ability to perceive and feel, impacts how you connect to your inner world as well as your ability to empathize and associate with others—a primary theme of sacral energy.

The sacral chakra is associated with passion, intimacy, and abundance. Since the dawn of time, the Creator—an archetype of this chakra—has flourished. In the feminine essence, the Creatrix gives of her bountiful womb, nurtures, and receives. In the masculine essence, the Creator makes things happen. Understanding around this zone centers on the knowledge of creation. What you feel generates thoughts and behaviors, which then create your manifestations. Your sacral connection is all about stepping fully into your creatorship, full arriving in your feeling state of beingness, and recognizing that all experiences mirror back the inner landscape you have constructed.

This energy center's focal point is passion, and it's one of the things that almost all the Eastern chakra systems agree on. We'll be reviewing the passionate organs of the sacral chakra later in this chapter, and we'll note the connections here to the rest of your body's systems. Situated at your sacrum, or the small of your back, the lines to the brain and kidneys join up in your sacral and connect to the sushumna. Your sex organs, composing your endocrine system, make a direct link to your pituitary gland and hypothalamus in your brain. Signals here release hormones, mark the onset of puberty, menopause and andropause, and regulate body temperature. Some of the sex gland functions of the sacral chakra also support the adrenal glands, and all these (adrenals, sex organs, pituitary, and hypothalamus) link to your kidney meridian line in traditional Chinese medicine.

Names & Meaning

The main Sanskrit term for the sacral chakra is *svadhisthana* (*sva* means "self," and *adhishthana* means "established"). There's also a variety of Tantric names: *adhisthana, bhima, shatpatra, skaddala padma,* and *wari chakra.* In the Vedas, this chakra is referred to as *medhra.* In Sanskrit, *swad* also means "to take pleasure in," which is fitting for this sensual abode.

Color

Orange is the primary color of the sacral zone, and it evokes a bright and creative state of being. Combining the intensity of red and the joy of yellow, orange is vibrant, stimulating, fascinating, and encouraging. This color frequency elicits creativity in all forms and gives birth to sensuality, playfulness, and innovation. The warmth of orange is a symbol of strength and endurance, as well as abundance and happiness.

Location

The sacral chakra is found about one to two inches below your navel, between the coccyx (tailbone) and the sacrum (the flat, tiny triangle at the small of your back). Its nerve plexus lies in the pelvis. This area of your spinal column is wedged between your hip bones, or about halfway between your navel and sex organs. Its location in general is the womb space (for women), the lower abdomen, the genitalia, the sacrum, and just below the navel. Appropriately, the energy centers are fluid, just like the element that presides over your sacral region, so don't get too hung up on exact placements.

Estimated Activation

This chakra becomes activated in the body between age 7 and 14, according to the Hindu system. This is the time when children begin to transform and move away from what was considered their purity or innocence and begin blossoming into adulthood as they enter puberty and become explorative teens. As their hormones kick in, they start to express and create new versions of themselves. It is also around this time that kids begin to turn their self-absorption into bonding with friends and forging connections beyond the family unit.

Body Parts

Your hips, pelvis, internal sex organs, kidneys, bladder, intestines, and lower back are thought to be managed by your sacral chakra. Your kidneys and bladder are the part of your elimination system, which become engorged with the water element, which makes sense for this chakra. Since they are so intricately involved with water, these organs fit best in the sacral region as water is its governing element. For women, the uterus and cervix are included in this region, and for men, the testicles are included here (lingam is included in the root chakra); the pelvis in general is included for both. Your appendix falls under here, too, as do your lower vertebrae.

Glands

Since the sacral chakra is considered your sexual chakra, this chakra manages your gonads, or internal sex organs. For women, this will be the ovaries, and for men, this includes the testes. In some systems, you'll see the prostate gland included in this grouping, but technically, it is shared between the root and sacral spaces. These are both part of the endocrine system.

Senses

The sacral chakra is all about sensuality, feeling, and inspiration. The sense associated here is taste, and the sense organ is the tongue. Eating bright, colorful foods such as oranges or other citrus fruits will tantalize and help satiate the sacral chakra's seemingly unquenchable desire for more, more, more!

Illnesses

Health issues associated with the sacral chakra include reproductive concerns such as menstruation, infertility, egg reserves, and sperm count and problems with the urinary system such as infections of the urinary tract, bladder, and kidneys. Sexual dysfunctions, like loss of sex-drive, arousal, and orgasm, and pain disorders will come up in this region. Appendicitis, chronic lower back pain, some sciatica (also linked with the root chakra), and some joint problems may also be present here.

Function

The portal to creating new life exists within the sacral chakra, and it's no mistake that this is one of the most sacred of the chakras participating in the creation of the world of form. Both a Tantric magnet for miracles and a hospitable cocoon for baby's first home, the womb is often thought of as one of the greatest shamanic mysteries of the ancient feminine. It is a great source of power, a well of ecstasy. It can carry great love stories or shame. Betrayal and hurt live here, and once healed, the ability to clear through your worst fears and wounding arises.

The womb naturally speaks to the cycles of the moon and flows with its gravitational waves, stirring a beautiful dance of raw shakti and mystique. Females are the custodians of life, and our expression here illuminates an unspeakable power: magic exists in the world, and it is wom(b)an. The womb is both the crucible of creation and the original voice. Of course, males have an obvious role to play in genesis, too; their sperm must be healthy and strong to reach an egg for fertilization to occur. A man's testosterone levels and sperm count are factors, yet for conception, only one sperm needs to make it all the way to begin cocreation. A man's mood, health, and behavior all affect the quality of the sperm produced and therefore what gets passed on in his DNA.

The remaining physical aspects of your sacral chakra include the bladder, small intestines, and kidneys, all of which are elimination organs that help remove toxins from your body. Detoxification is beneficial, as your body is constantly renewing itself in each new moment, cleansing and purifying your internal systems to assist in optimal energy flow. Some of these responsibilities are shared with the root chakra, so they will have some crossover.

Now let's take a look at the emotional aspects of your sacred sacral chakra. Your deepest feelings of pleasure and well-being live here. Think about the greatest heights of bliss and sexual gratification that come through the ecstatic orgasmic state. That force of energy doesn't really exist anywhere else in the cosmos to the degree that it does on the physical Earth plane. It's this energy that lights up galaxies and creates universes—we are all a reflection of the macrocosmic on a microcosmic scale in this fractal Universe. Remember: as above, so below. You hold the same power that forms whole worlds deep inside of you. The sacral region is a major creation zone for women and men alike.

In addition, your sacral chakra taps into your sense of intimacy and belonging. Intimacy here doesn't necessarily equate to sexual intimacy, although that is included in this junction. The sense of closeness you feel and the sensitive frequencies you exchange with another are precious and subtle, and that is the type of intimacy I refer to here. This intimacy can be cultivated through conscious connection and through hard work and dedication to moving through your shadows. The process is not for the weak, and the payoff is second to none. As human beings, we came here for connection, and that is exactly what this chakra helps us achieve.

Archetypes

The archetypes that most closely correspond to the sacral chakra are the Creator and the Womb.

The Creator, an artist and alchemist, uses its powers of innovation to generate something from nothing. The spirit of this archetypal energy is collaborative, constructive, open, and boundless. The Creator is present when we choose to step into a relationship with our own abilities, offerings, and gifts and share them with one another and the world. The Creator also knows that destruction is a necessary part of creation. Old walls must fall for a new castle to be built. From a void comes new life. Where there was emptiness, the Creator manifests abundance and abolishes lack. This archetype ceaselessly combats apathy and burden with the notion of creating new and infinite possibility.

The Womb speaks of an origin story, beyond gender. It is a nest of sorts that holds you in its warmth and comforting abode of love. Holding a feminine light to soften all injuries and suffering, the Womb is the place inside where we all feel held and supported. This place is where healing and growth are happening. We can also seek refuge in wombs of the world, places where we feel nourished and comforted. Whether these are inner or outer temples, the Womb allows for our rebirth and renewal should we choose to explore her solace.

Personality

A person with a highly developed and gifted second chakra shows signs of high emotional intelligence. They are empathic and are aware of and in control of their emotions; it's easy for them to tune in to the sensitivities of others. They will be more likely to handle relationships judiciously and, instead of being reactive, will be even-keeled in their responses to even the most intense situations. This person displays balanced feminine and masculine energies in resonance with their internal harmony. Nurturing, instinctual, devoted, and loving, these people are influencers in the world. They are charming, resilient, and self-reliant, and their adaptability adds to their captivating characteristics. Enthusiastic by nature, success follows them. They tend to effortlessly attract others toward them for groups, teams, and projects and are usually the determined ones of the bunch. You will usually find these people in roles such as creative director, designer, musician, architect, account manager, or editor. They also typically possess creative interests such as film, photography, music, and art.

As empathy is a gift of this chakra, empaths must be careful here. They can often be tempted to focus their attention on the needs of others rather than on their own. By training the mind through simple, mindful awareness, this can be easily corrected over time and with practice.

Underactive Chakra

When the sacral chakra is underactive, your emotions or expression may be dangerously withheld or avoided altogether. Men tend to run this risk more naturally than women because of their childhood social conditioning. When this toxic programming is in place, rigidity is held in both the physical body and belief systems. For example, programming like "crying is for girls" or "feelings make you weak" will need to be worked through in adolescence and adulthood for males to step more fully into balance within the yin, or feminine, domain of the sacral. Females may also combat toxic social programming of their own as they learn to balance their dual nature.

Another sign of an underactive sacral chakra is that you may be prone to feelings of denial or lack intimate bonds with others. Your sex drive may be low or even non-existent. You may feel creatively stifled, like you are at a dead end. All these feelings of inadequacy can create insecurities, so if you have an underactive sacral chakra, your self-confidence may be lacking.

Overactive Chakra

Emotional instability is a hallmark of an overactive sacral chakra. If you are overactive in this area, you may feel out of control, perhaps feeling overwhelmed or feeling things much more deeply than normal. Severe mood swings might be an issue, causing you to act irresponsibly toward the feelings of others. You may be indecisive, inconsistent, or domineering. Some may view you as insincere and superficial. Know that it can feel unsafe to be in the presence of someone with an overactive sacral chakra. Symptoms of excess energy here can show up in sex addictions, overt self-indulgence (hello, carbs and wine), exhibitionism, aggression, arrogance, or mania. Excess energy in this chakra can also be expressed through any obsessive attachments (codependency, seductive manipulation, and invasiveness).

Balanced Chakra

With a balanced sacral center, you feel present in your body, and when all your primary needs have been met, your sacral chakra feels supported enough to reach out and establish deeper relationships in the world. Engaged and connected, this energy bonds with others in a way that shapes true intimacy. You understand your own needs and have learned to check in with yourself often to gauge your own emotions—this is considered emotional stability.

Creativity is a hallmark of this chakra. When you are tapped into your inner inspiration, you have the desire and capacity to create your vision or execute your artistic expression. When creativity is stimulated, you notice that everything manifesting around you (your career, a new relationship, parenthood, success, abundance, and so on) is your creation. In fact, you control everything as your ideas birth new forms around you.

Deities

The goddesses and gods that correlate to the sacral energies are Lakshmi, Mary Magdalene, Yemanja and Oshun (orishas), Mama Qocha, Poseidon, Neptune, and Varuna.

Lakshmi, the Hindu goddess of prosperity, purpose, and good fortune, shows generosity by sharing her luck with others. She will show you how to multiply and amplify your manifestations as you consciously cocreate inner and outer riches in the world. This goddess is a magnet for miracles and believes in your unlimited power to attract the possibilities most in line with your highest good.

Mary Magdalene is an Ascended Master who comes to heavily anchor the new energies of Divine Feminine. A disciple of goddess Isis, Magdalene has an entire order of angelic beings with her called the Magdalenas, who are here to support you as you step into your sovereignty. This collective consciousness is awakening and activating the shakti energy on Earth now. Ask Mary Magdalene to help mentor you in your journey of kundalini activation and feminine strength.

Yemanja and Oshun, goddesses (*orishas*) of Yoruba descent, are deities of the ocean and river, respectively. They represent eternal nourishment, prosperity, fertility, and healing. They encourage you to ride the eternal waves of creation without worry and to give freely of yourself without expecting anything in return. They temper your expectations and invite you to trust in the flow of life.

Mama Qocha, the Incan goddess of water, has a shamanic influence and mystical, spiritual ties to all water bodies. She rules cycles and offers you the chance to reveal your life's evolutionary path by recognizing the cycles in your life. She is here to assist you when tidal waves of emotion threaten to engulf your shores.

Poseidon (Greek), Neptune (Roman), and Varuna (Vedic) are the analogous water deities who hold the masculine presence in the sacral chakra. All gods of the sea, they rule the waves, revealing conditions in life for which you will need to gain the courage to overcome by swimming against or with the current.

Planets

The moon in all its feminine essence is the primary luminary body governing the sacral chakra. Just as the tides reflect formless possibility and watery depths, this lunar energy stirs creative forces deep inside of us. The moon presents a simple statement, "I need," and is the most essential piece to understanding your own psyche and internal world. She conveys your nurturing aspects as well as your maternal relationship; she advocates emotional authenticity.

Sacral Chakra Exercise: Yin/Yang, Light/Shadow—A Balancing Ritual

This ritual activates polarity equilibrium, helping neutralize any energies within yourself that you wish to bring back into balance. It is considered a yin/yang balancing practice because it also stabilizes the feminine/masculine energies you exude. It is meant to be a practice in honest self-observance, acknowledgment, and release—not a time for judgment or self-loathing.

You will need two stones or crystals for this exercise, a pen and paper, and some herbal cleansing materials like sage or palo santo for smudging. Select one light and one dark stone or crystal. Here are a few suggested pairings: tourmaline and white moonstone, onyx or obsidian and selenite, smoky quartz and clear quartz, or hematite and howlite.

Ensure that you will have some quiet time for yourself where you'll be uninterrupted for about 30 minutes. Begin by smudging your space to clear any existing energies. Have your pen and paper nearby so you can reach them when needed. Lie on your back and begin to relax, breathing deeply in and out and following your breath for a few minutes to drop into your body.

Say aloud, "I ask to connect to my highest self now to gain clarity and insight of myself. I ask to know myself in my light and in my shadow and to bring into balance any energies that have not been beneficial to my highest good. And so it is."

Place the dark stone on your left hip first. Spend 5 to 10 minutes recalling anything that has been surfacing for you that has felt negative, which is bringing out your shadow. This could be a pattern or toxic behavior you want to change or perhaps a part of yourself that hasn't felt supported in a long time. Let yourself feel and acknowledge anything that comes up with the statement, "You are felt and seen." When you feel complete, remove the dark stone.

Next, place the light stone on your right hip. Spend 5 to 10 minutes contemplating the ways in which you have recently shown up for yourself, your behaviors and moments that made you most proud of yourself, and your positive qualities and attributes that need recognition now. These will be accomplishments or achievements that you want to praise or actions that made you feel good about yourself. Again, let yourself feel and acknowledge anything that comes up with, "You are felt and seen." When you feel complete, keep the light stone in place, and place the dark stone on your left hip again.

Notice how the energies feel when they are both present on your body. Next, say, "Bring me into balance." You may feel the need to swap the left and right stones to feel more of the balancing energy. Keep the stones on your body for 10 to 15 minutes or until you feel a shift and the balancing is complete. Remove the stones when you are done and put them away after cleansing.

To close your ritual, say aloud, "Thank you, Spirit and higher self, for assisting my healing today. With a heart filled with gratitude, I feel and I see that I am balanced, perfect, whole, and complete in my light and in my shadow. And so it is."

You may choose to then write down some of the uglier shadow aspects that came to mind under a heading "Things to Love." Keep the list and revisit it every few weeks as you work through those shadow elements. When they have all been loved or brought into the light, you may ceremonially and safely burn the sheet.

The Hara Line and the Microcosmic Orbit

The hara line is a small chakra point in some complex chakra systems. It is located about two and a half inches below the navel in a center also called the *dantian* ("the field of elixir" or "sea of chi"). In certain Eastern systems, this point is off the body and located in the astral field, but here, we'll look at this line in respect to its presence on the physical body. The amber hara point enables the generation of your soul's purpose and helps connect your personal will to that of Earth's. In fact, the hara line splits in three meridian-like rivers that run from it, one going down the left leg (grounding functions), one going down the right leg (creation functions), and one dropping down through the root to the Earth star chakra (freewill connection).

Energy practices like Reiki and qigong use this power point to anchor qi, or chi, to the physical body. The dantian forms the base of an ascension column that runs vertically up your sushumna. This spiritual center is where your higher mind, or monad, is seated. It is said that this is the original supply of chi with which you were first born.

The microcosmic orbit (MO), originally a Taoist energy technique, is a way to circulate energy inside the body with the breath. It is used to cultivate, raise, and refine more chi reserve in the physical body. The MO runs from the Governing Vessel (from the perineum up the spine to the head) to the Conception Vessel (from the head down the sternum to the perineum), passing through the hara line as it summons chi for cultivation. To practice, take a few deep breaths, and on the last breath, hold. Now, circulate your breath in a loop down the front of your body and up your spine in a circuit. You'll want to immediately close off all your typical chi exits, so ball your fists, press your tongue to the roof of your mouth, squeeze your perineum, and practice holding and circulating the breath for 30 to 45 seconds. You'll feel the energized effects instantly upon total release. The spinal fluid released here travels up to your third eye to stimulate the release of small amounts of DMT (scientifically known as *N,N*-Dimethyltryptamine, a naturally occurring hallucinogenic tryptamine), so practice this one often!

Chapter Eight
The 3rd Chakra: Solar Plexus

The solar plexus chakra is your central chakra, and like the sun in our solar system, its fiery energy is the center of your personal power. It maintains your vital energy and connects you to your purpose and sense of self. A major player in forming your identity, this chakra also helps you develop integrity, leadership, sovereignty, strength, and confidence. Many people think of the solar plexus as a manifestation gateway in the body, and it certainly can be thought of as such. This chakra illuminates the role of cause and effect in our lives. For example, when we take action or create a cause (a central theme to the solar plexus), it produces a specific effect whose ripple creates the world as we know it. In this way, this chakra teaches us the laws of creation: we get back what we put in. As you begin to empower yourself, you'll open new doors in your life and find that you become a magnet for attracting all you desire.

This energy center critically supports your digestive functions and regulates your body's stress levels. Your digestion here supports your physical processes, which contribute to your overall health. As for your stress levels, anytime you go through a life crisis (moving, changing jobs, gaining or losing a loved one, divorcing or breaking up with a partner, etc.), you may internalize the stress, especially if these are layered on top of one another in the same space of time. Over time (usually within two years), this internalization manifests as a major illness. It's important to take steps to manage your stress so that you are better able to deal with life changes and take yourself out of the fight-or-flight response. No system exists in isolation in your body, so stress and anxiety can affect your whole system.

I encourage you to remember that you are a being of light living and operating in a physical body. As a light being, you are constantly assimilating new information in the form of energy into your body. This mind-body connection to your subconscious mind happens in your solar plexus chakra. When you integrate these energies, you expand and connect more deeply into your greater purpose as a spiritual being, and more spiritual energy becomes available to you. Through this spiritual empowerment, you're better able to heal your physical body and align to right relationship in the outer world.

Names & Meaning

Manipura is the Sanskrit name for the solar plexus. *Mani* means "jewel" or "gem," and *pura* means "dwelling place." In Tantra, several other names exist: *dashachchada, dashadala padma, dashapatra, dashapatrambuja, manipuraka, nabhipadma,* and *nabhipankaja.* In the Vedas, the solar plexus is also referred to as *manipuraka* or the *nabhi* (navel) chakra.

Color

Yellow is the invigorating frequency of the solar plexus, and it's no surprise as this is the color of happiness, joy, optimism, and inspirational action. Sometimes the color can be a bright yellow-gold, fiery like the sun's rays. This vibration awakens inner vitality and exudes confidence, strength, and power. It is a color of remembrance, enabling you to tap into past timelines. Its tone feels fresh and clear.

Location

The solar plexus can be found at the base of the sternum (or the curve of the upper rib cage) and above the navel. This location correlates most closely with your belly area and midback. Think about the center of your body as your core. Just as the core of Earth contains the most dense and vital energies on the planet, so does your solar core. The belly is the area most associated with this chakra.

Estimated Activation

The Hindu system has this chakra activating between the age of 15 and 21. During this time, you are developing a sense of who you are in the world. This understanding can be considered ego development, which grows alongside your worldly identity. A sense of personal power blossoms during this time and begins to weave a wonderful interplay between your self-worth and maturing confidence.

Body Parts

The solar plexus chakra manages your upper digestive system and organs like your stomach, gallbladder, liver, spleen, and small intestines. Your lower esophagus is included here since it provides an entryway to your digestive organs. Although the adrenals are mostly managed by your root chakra, parts like the adrenal cortex are comanaged by your solar plexus, as are parts of your kidneys. Your skin and breath, as well as your diaphragm and upper abdomen, are also associated with this chakra. Also managed here are the muscles in your midback, your spine, and your pancreas.

Glands

The pancreas is this chakra's hormonal gland. It is an oblong organ that sits underneath your stomach beneath the left rib cage, nestled in the curve of the small intestine. As an endocrine and exocrine gland, the pancreas releases hormones, such as insulin, and enzymes directly into the bloodstream and ducts.

Senses

The dominant sense associated with the solar plexus chakra is vision, and the sense organ is the eyes. Someone experiencing impaired eyesight may also feel tension at the level of their solar plexus chakra, which may correlate to central issues around power, control, and freedom. This chakra is also referred to as your "lower third eye" because we tend to feel things as a gut reaction in the pit of the stomach as our first instinctual vision into what's happening in or around us.

Illnesses

Most commonly, issues in the solar plexus chakra are related to vital energy and digestion. Disease and illness associated with this chakra include total energy burnout, irritating digestive disorders (stomach ulcers), eating disorders (anorexia, bulimia), certain colon diseases, diabetes, pancreatitis, low blood pressure, hepatitis, heartburn, hypoglycemia, and leaky-gut syndrome. The latter is caused by leakage of bodily toxins into the bloodstream, which can also create chronic fatigue. Muscular disorders also show up here, too, especially mid- to lower-back issues.

Function

The digestive system is central to your solar plexus and plays an important role in the assimilation and absorption of food in your body. The organs in this system, starting with the stomach, help chemically break down foods via hormones and digestive enzymes. The pancreas is the main organ that performs the important task of the endocrine and exocrine functions, carrying hormones to the bloodstream and enzymes to the ducts. Digestive juices are released directly into the small intestine to break down food that has left the stomach. New nutrients travel from the digestive tract to adjacent blood and lymphatic vessels to be absorbed so that your entire body can carry out all the things it needs to do.

Psychologically, the solar plexus chakra's role in the body is to maintain your personal power and create a sense of self through internal beliefs and external behavior patterns. This includes building self-esteem and self-discipline. On your journey to becoming your best self, you will go through periods of needing to be in control of everything and periods of letting go. You will be motivated and disenchanted with projects. You may be the manipulated or the manipulator at different times. You will be the observer and then the judge. You will feel self-criticism and pride. Just as your solar plexus metabolizes food, it also digests ideas and beliefs we have about ourselves, others, and our place in the world. All these feelings help you fulfill your spiritual contracts through character building and growth.

Just like you choose what food to put in your body, it is up to you to continue to make choices that feed your soul expansion. I invite you to make small choices in each moment that enable you to walk in integrity, drop limiting beliefs that hold you back, and empower you through inspired action. After you have gained enough self-mastery through solar plexus energy patterns, you will be ready to journey into the deeper loving space of the heart chakra, which is next in line.

Archetypes

The archetypes associated with the solar plexus chakra are the Queen/the King, the Sustainer, and the Martyr.

Aspects of the Divine Feminine and Divine Masculine are exemplified here in terms of their leadership roles in the Queen and the King archetypal energy. The Queen and King are counterparts and rulers of the kingdom. Originally thought to be a title designated directly from God, in modern times, royalty can be a self-appointed energy. Both the Queen and the King lead through deep resolve, trusting themselves, and knowing the difference of when to be still and when to strike. These archetypes recognize their dual nature and are in balance when they are guiding themselves and others toward peace. If these archetypes are out of balance, beware of their wrathful, oppressive, highly critical, and demanding ways.

The Sustainer is a peacemaker who works best behind the scenes, tending to the meticulous and sometimes mundane details of life (paying the bills, picking up groceries, cleaning the house, etc.). Naturally inclined to preserve and support, the Sustainer can easily become overworked and undervalued, which can lead to resentment and burnout. Reliability is a hallmark of this archetype, but the Sustainer must be careful to listen to themselves when they need to hold their own boundaries instead of catering to the will of others.

The Martyr knows strength through sacrifice and steps into that role with humility and integrity. At its core, this archetype represents doing the right thing, even if social programming and "rules" say otherwise. They may ask, "What is the right thing for me to do, independent of anyone else?" They take time to acknowledge themselves, and this creates personal empowerment. Reliability, strength, and selflessness are their hallmark traits. The Martyr must be careful because when they are off balance, they can slip into manipulation and control, self-sabotage, or worse yet, attach their sacrifices to their self-worth. A balanced Martyr knows they do not need to suffer to feel as though they are making a difference.

Personality

Someone who has a balanced solar plexus chakra has the full range of emotions in check and is able to experience and exude healthy assertiveness as well as cooperation with others. They can tap into their internal well of energy and enjoy sustained energy levels, especially when dealing with other people at work, in school, in a partnership, or out in the world. They can see the bigger picture because balance in this space leads to highly imaginative and idealistic states. Because their emotional connection needs are met, they can further refine their behavior with others, specifically in the areas of communication and productivity.

Mental focus is one of the traits of balance in this area. This ability can be particularly useful when it comes to getting work done. As employees, these people are factually grounded, tactically minded, thorough, practical, and organized. They also tend to be charmers, as they radiate warmth and exude confidence. They tend to be generally happy, cheerful, and optimistic, treating people the way they would want to be treated. They are also more likely to have a sunny disposition toward controversies.

Because they are dependable, faithful, and stable, these individuals make loyal partners. Often seen as flirts and extroverts, they broadcast their friendliness far and wide, leaving a spirited energetic imprint on everyone they meet. Occupations of people with balanced energy here may succeed in entrepreneurial leadership roles, public speaking, and life coaching. They may do well as attorneys, judges, scientists, and researchers due to their strong analytical abilities.

Underactive Chakra

If you have an underactive solar plexus chakra, you may suffer from anxiety and the many forms it takes. This is the primary reason many people feel a knot in the pit of their stomach; anxiety is very much a *felt sense* that pops up through an inability to stay present and detach from certain limiting beliefs. For example, you may have an expectation on a timeline or outcome, and the thoughts you have around them when they are not met can create an anxiety response in the body, which is sensed both physically and emotionally until you choose to let go of it. Jealousy, unhappiness, emotional fragility, and cowardice live in this place when they are not well managed. These types of feelings can pull you out of the present moment and cause a downward spiral into low self-confidence, self-doubt, and victim mentality.

If you are suffering from energy deficiencies in this chakra, you may be more likely to feel completely tapped out, like your battery has been totally drained. An underactive solar plexus chakra can lead to poor digestion and a lack of self-discipline, which negatively impacts your ability to create and manifest.

Overactive Chakra

An overactive solar plexus chakra can be a sign that your sense of self is out of alignment. Oftentimes, we think of this as the ego taking complete control. Pride, egotism, and demanding and dominating behaviors can show up with too much of the solar element present. An overactive solar plexus chakra may present in a number of ways, including displays of perfectionism or being overly critical, arrogant, controlling, hyperactive, excessively stubborn, aggressive, and angry. Because this chakra is connected to your sense of sight (remember the lower third eye), blurred vision may be a sign of excessive energy in this center. You may also suffer from back problems or weight issues.

Balanced Chakra

A balanced solar plexus chakra allows you to draw on the powers of the sun to fuel you—in this case, the sun that exists within. Self-reliance is a big theme for this vital energy center, and an open solar plexus will give you the feeling that you have claimed (and, in some instances, reclaimed) your essential power. Although this is a center to grow personal power, it is also a space to cultivate partnership and leadership energy.

A healthy mental focus along with a flourishing digestive system directly correlates to great overall physical health and mental well-being. Don't forget, an entire world of microorganisms assists in regulating your mood, and a good portion of the microorganisms live and thrive in your gut, which is central to both the solar plexus (upper digestive tracts) and sacral (lower digestive tracts) chakras.

Deities

There is a whole entourage of goddesses and gods that are perfectly aligned with your solar energy and solar plexus. They are Sekhmet, Ra, Surya, Agni, Hanuman, and Indra.

In Egyptian mythology, Sekhmet is the fierce but loving warrior goddess with the head of a lion and body of a woman who carries a sun disk on her head. This lioness means business: she is a protector who holds the energy of powerful and intense motherly love. Call on her when you need to command inner strength and courage.

Ra or Re, also a sun god, ruled over Egypt as one of the central gods in the ancient pantheon. Ra united Upper and Lower Egypt, and in mythology, it was said he was born in the East each day only to die in the West each night. He has the body of a man with the head of a hawk and is also adorned with a sun disk on his head. In typical creatorship fashion, he was responsible for making the world and everything in it. Calling on Ra means serious manifestations, empowerment, and action headed your way.

Surya, the Hindu god of the sun, is the source of all life who brings light and warmth to the planet. He is glorified as a supreme being with at least 12 names (the 12 splendid suns). He stands for vitality, respect, and power. In traditional belief, he is responsible for healing the sick.

Agni, the Hindu god of fire, brings this element to heal digestion issues. He rises in inner power through yoga, and his extreme focus burns away unwanted desires and habits.

Hanuman, a Hindu monkey god, is the symbol for strength and energy. He has the ability to acquire things at any time (think: control). When he is present, ask him to help you carry your burdens and lift you up against difficult odds.

Indra is our last Hindu god presented here, and he is the king of the gods. He harnesses the power of physical virility, wealth, success, heroism, and leadership. He presents security in difficult times. Call on him to help move you through a challenge to personal victory.

Planets

The sun is the luminary body that ignites your solar plexus, and so the title "solar" is ascribed to the chakra itself. The sun is a glorious transmission of outward-facing expression and exuberance. And just as the sun is the only star in our solar system, you can think of your solar plexus as the fundamental sun of your central self. This energy represents sense of self as well as how you present your "I AM" presence to the world.

Solar Plexus Chakra Exercise: Abundance Generator Ritual

Abundance can mean a number of things to different people—financial solvency, a circle of friends who love you, prolific health, or opportunities flowing your way. To generate inner and outer prosperity, we need to start with what we know: wealth is a mindset. According to the Law of Attraction, beliefs are more powerful when said aloud, written down, and put out vibrationally into the Universe. Lack mindset causes more lack, while gratitude for what is here causes more of what is available to you to keep showing up. To make new forms of abundance visible, you must act as though the vibration of these things is already here now. In this ritual, you will make a prosperity grid to magnetize money, opportunities, and abundance to you and check in on it from time to time for one month.

The things you will need for this prosperity ritual are green/white candle(s), green and gold crystals (for example, green calcite, malachite, amazonite, moldavite, jade, pyrite, tiger's-eye, or citrine—several of each), four blank checks, and a pen and paper.

The ritual should be started within three days (before or after) of a new moon, the lunar symbol of new beginnings. Find a space in your home where the crystals can remain for the next month until the next new moon (altar spaces, dressers, and tabletops work best). Wash all your crystals in cold water to clear the energy from them before you begin.

To start, tear off a small sheet of paper or use a sticky note—one for each crystal you have. Next, take some time to arrange your crystals in a circular grid. For each crystal, write something on the piece of paper that you are manifesting now. Write it as though your blessing has already arrived: "I'm so grateful that I have _____ (fill in the blank)." Put each manifestation under a crystal as part of your grid. Finally, to call in prosperity, write yourself a check with all the details filled in. You may choose to write your check for a specific amount. Put this in the middle of your crystal grid, with the blank checks underneath.

Light your candles whenever you are standing at your grid or charging it with your positive thoughts about the blessings coming in. This is a beautiful daily or weekly practice, and you can do it as often as needed. Say aloud, "I ask these crystals and positive energy here to assist me in building the life of my dreams, with all of these elements already in place to bring me abundance and prosperity. And so it is!"

Each week, check in with your intentions, and if you want to, write yourself a new check for a higher amount. If one of your manifestations has been fulfilled or you no longer wish to have it in the grid, take it out. Leave the grid for up to one month (from new moon to new moon) and watch the blessings pour in around you, taking time to express gratitude and loving appreciation for all the good fortune that is here and now.

The Photon Belt

The solar plexus chakra is all about tapping into solar energy, so let's take a look at this special solar light ascension energy that has recently become available to the planet. The Photon Belt is a band of energy that can be seen as a toroidal field made of condensed light particles that circles the great central sun of the Pleiades, Alcyone. Both Alcyone and Earth circle the Galactic Center (the central region of the Milky Way), and this rotation happens in cycles, which we measure in time. If you were to measure the time it takes to cross it, the Photon Belt is approximately 2,000 years wide. Every 26,000 years, our solar system orbits Alcyone, and every 11,000 years or so, we cross the path of this band of light. This cycle of orbiting means that we have galactic periods of darkness and of light, and we just so happen to be in a light cycle, which we entered on December 21, 2012. Since the Photon Belt is 2,000 years wide, this means we'll be in this light cycle for the foreseeable future.

Since light is energy and energy carries information, when Earth is exposed to these particles, it is bathed in highly charged photonic light. This light creates acceleration and excitement in our subtle energy fields, much like solar flares from our sun can cause disruptions in our biomagnetic field, except in this case, our light bodies are expanding from the gentle photonic light. This change in our energy fields is creating a rise in consciousness for all of humanity and everything in the Photon Belt's path. This supraconscious energy that has been flooding the planet has been intensifying for decades, and as we move through it, it will not be an option to remain asleep for long—the Great Awakening is here, and it's just getting started. It is up to us to rediscover what the ancients of our planet knew so long ago through these solar upgrades, to learn how to restore ourselves to consciousness and elevate humanity for the benefit of all living beings. Ask yourself every day, "How good can it get?" What could be more sovereign and solar than that?

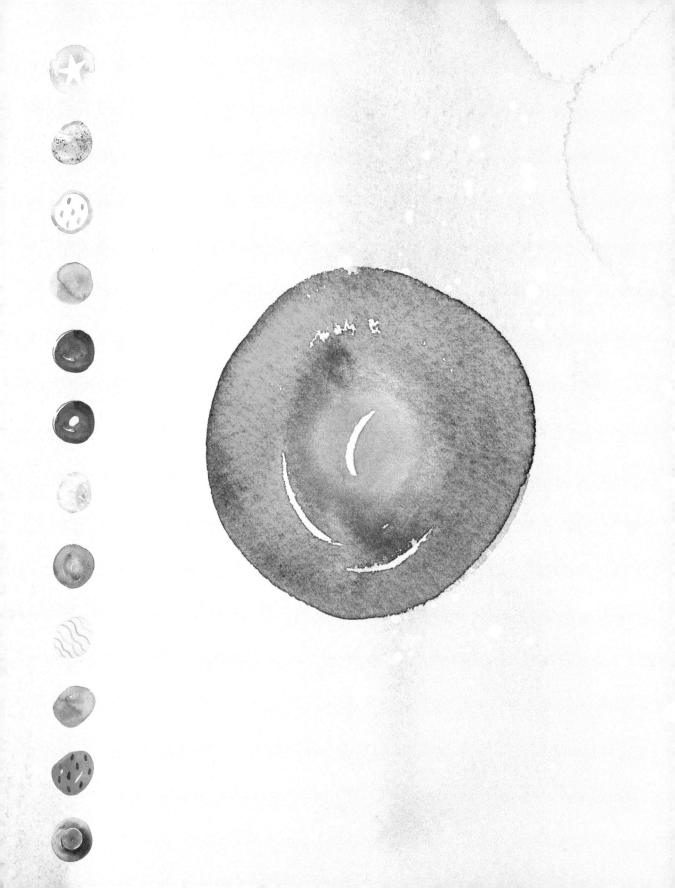

Chapter Nine
The 4th Chakra: Heart

The doorway to the sacred is found within the heart. This gateway houses your anatomical heart and thus is named the heart chakra. It is a path to the alchemical and miraculous and a means by which negative patterns are reversed and cleared. This chakra is about dropping all judgments and embracing the beauty that is your innate spiritual perfection. By surrendering in the heart chakra, you will be able to tap into deep wells of compassion, restoration, purity, grace, and acceptance for all that is. Strengthening the heart space creates a beautiful unified field around you, allowing you access to wisdom beyond intellect and words. This is the wisdom of the Divine. We call it heart-centered consciousness. Practicing staying inside heart wisdom and allowing it to guide you will better connect you to the cosmic heart, which belongs to the highest chakra, the Divine gateway chakra (which we'll discuss in chapter 16).

The heart chakra is responsible for the physical systems governing circulation and respiration as well as for the subtle emotional and spiritual connections we experience. The heart functions like a brain. This emotional brain (your heart) secretes hormones like oxytocin, the "love-bonding hormone," which contributes to your romantic bonds. The heart is also connected to your sushumna and the vagus nerve (part of your parasympathetic nervous system), which runs along the spinal column in the back of the heart space. These central avenues for the nervous system form an intricate network with the web of blood vessels streaming into this fist-size muscle in your chest.

In modern times, the focus is on the higher function of the heart, and the ability to access the intelligence of the heart relies on heart coherence. Recently re-emerging into the collective consciousness, heart coherence is nothing new; however, the way in which we have been able to think about it has been reimagined so that it's becoming accessible in this new time of awakening. Coherence is a state in which your heart, mind, and emotions communicate in alignment.

Your heart actually sends more information to your nervous system than your brain does, and the quality of these signals profoundly affects brain function. The brain interprets the signals of the heart to tell you how you feel. To change how you feel, you need a doorway to the heart to alter the ascending information moving from it to the brain. By using meditation and other heart-centering techniques, you can use the rhythms of the heart to send different neural messages to your brain, like when you feel stressed, for example. You need to send different messages to the brain if you want to establish a new baseline and sustain positive changes. When your heart and brain are aligned, your inner guidance system turns on, and your heart coherence goes up!

Names & Meaning

Anahata is the Sanskrit name for the heart chakra, which translates to "unstruck, unhurt, unbeaten." This name refers to the seed syllable *yam*, which is generated without friction through pure vibration at this chakra level. Tantric names include *anahata-puri, dwadasha, dwadashadala, hridabja, hrit padma, hritpankaja, hritpatra, padma sundara, hridaya kamala,* and *hriday ambuja.* In the Upanishads, you will also see this chakra referred to as *hridaya* and *dwadashara.*

Color

The primary color of the heart space is emerald green, which is the frequency of harmony, renewal, nature, and growth. The secondary color of this chakra is pink. Pink represents universal love, affection, intimacy, and compassion. Sometimes, the heart chakra is viewed with a white and pink inner core and a green outer shell. Other times, green is viewed as the primary heart color with the high heart (see page 118) having a pink frequency.

Location

As opposed to your anatomical heart, which is located in the left side of the chest, the ethereal heart chakra is located directly in the center of the chest, between the breastbone in the rib cage and between the lungs. The sushumna is aligned with your heart chakra, which corresponds with the cardiac plexus, a nerve bundle at the base of your heart. This vortex holds the space of neutrality as it divides your body into hemispheres, with the lower half of your chakras performing primal functions and the upper half sustaining interaction with higher forms of spirituality and consciousness.

Estimated Activation

The heart chakra is activated from ages 22 to 28. During this tender time, the passionate and fiery-red root chakra is tamed and tempered by the pink caress of the sweet and gentle energy we call romantic love. Romantic relationships open up a time for bonding, affection, and intimacy. This period is a time when your nurturing abilities are cultivated and turned on. It is also a time for heart-sacral connection. With this connection established, it's more likely for you to form a deeper relationship with your own self-care, sensuality, and creativity.

Body Parts

The heart chakra manages your heart, thymus, lungs, rib cage, circulatory system, blood, breasts, milk ducts, shoulders, arms, and hands. It shares functionality of the diaphragm and esophagus with the solar plexus chakra. The cardiac plexus links to the epicardium, the pericardium, and a number of branches directly intercepting the vagus nerve. It connects your sympathetic nerve trunks and a number of other ganglia (nerve masses) to cardiac nerves running from the heart to the nervous system (and eventually to the brain). This information superhighway connects to the vagus nerve, your "second brain."

Glands

You may be surprised to learn that your heart is considered both an organ and a gland. Because the heart has a unique function of secreting oxytocin, this circulatory pump serves multiple vital functions in the body. We'll chat about the thymus (the high heart, a minor chakra) later in this chapter, but for now, know that your thymus sits under your collarbone in front of your backbone. Your thymus regulates production of white blood cells and T cells, which help your immune system battle infections and outside invaders.

Senses

The dominant sense associated with the heart chakra is touch, and the sense organ is the skin. Your epidermis, your largest organ, helps you sense everything in your environment, including temperature, air pressure, and humidity. Perhaps most importantly, your sense of touch connects to pain receptors that warn your body of injury and danger.

Illnesses

Illnesses associated with the heart chakra include diseases of the heart, lungs, lymph, and immune system. Autoimmune diseases mistakenly attack your immune system instead of protecting it. Disorders here include lupus, Crohn's disease, Addison's disease, Hashimoto's disease, Lyme disease, multiple sclerosis, psoriasis, type 1 diabetes, rheumatoid arthritis, irritable bowel syndrome, and more. Chest pains (angina), allergies, blood pressure, circulation, breast and lung cancer, asthma, pneumonia, and thoracic spinal issues, as well as issues in the upper back and shoulders, all fall under this category as well.

Function

Physically, your heart chakra is responsible for your respiratory system—from the origins of your beating heart to the blood circulating in your arteries and veins. The breath of life (*prana*) animates your lungs and keeps oxygen moving to every single cell through a network of blood vessels. Your blood transports nutrients and removes cellular waste such as carbon dioxide and nitrogen from your system. Neurotransmitters regulate body temperature, acid-alkaline balance, and the water content of your cells. The circulatory system protects your body by managing proteins, white blood cells, and antibodies to defend you against foreign invaders. Clotting mechanisms in the bloodstream prevent blood loss after injury. The blood has so many jobs; it's hard to name them all! And we aren't finished here yet.

Your heart and thymus produce an array of hormones and neurotransmitters, including oxytocin and thymosin, which play a role in immunity, social bonding, childbirth, and reproduction. Since there is an inextricable link between emotions and physical health, restricting your emotions in your heart space can shorten your overall lifespan and lead to autoimmune disorders.

When you can come to a place of balance and harmony inside your heart walls and feel completely safe, you experience bliss. When you are in extended periods of this bliss, you are immersed in love. The more you learn to love in the face of oppression and obstacles—the unlovable—the more you recognize love as a state of being rather than something you simply give and receive. Love is the natural frequency of All That Is. It is the unconditional wavelength of the Divine, and your portal is the multidimensional heart space.

We learn through heart coherence how to combat lower-vibrating emotions like disappointment, pain, or disgust. Through an attitude of gratitude, we learn how to surrender and gain the courage to know ourselves and to forgive and accept or release those things that aren't in our highest alignment. We generate sensitivity to others and master the use of our gifts. Sensitivity is the degree at which we respond, shift, or change according to outside inputs, including how our environment or someone else treats us in the moment. Sensory processing, which starts in the heart, involves deeper cognitive processing of physical, emotional, and social stimuli, affording us the opportunity to react with empathy and kindness. Heart-based sensitivity is a superpower that we have started to reclaim in the era of the Divine Feminine, and its resurgence signals a greater movement of consciousness into the heart center.

Archetypes

The archetypes associated with the heart chakra are the Lover and the Healer.

The Lover, or Beloved, is a devoted muse. Inspired by art, music, and sensuality and driven by dreams, the Lover is an ever-evolving matrix of consciousness and beauty. This energy is stirred into awakening by the nectar of life, a profound experience of connection, supreme devotion, or the kiss of a beloved. This archetype savors the slow merging of two becoming one. To fully feel its depths, we must be completely present and drop all expectations about how love will or should arrive, or what it will look like when it does. The Lover is grateful and holds the world and all its musings in total awe.

The Healer is the natural progression of an open heart. Once you have gone through your own shadows and transformation through self-love, it is natural to wish to deepen those lessons by sharing your path with others so that they may experience healing. You don't need to label yourself a lightworker to claim this title for yourself. Anyone who has navigated through trauma or pain and come out on the other side has experienced their own healing abilities (often as a multilayered and circuitous process). Anyone who has been broken knows that healing comes in waves and precisely when we need it most.

Personality

Love, happiness, cooperation, and compassion are core values of someone with an open heart chakra. They naturally exude these values within all inner and outer dynamics. They can deeply empathize with someone without playing into any victimization roles. They are self-aware enough to check in with themselves so that they don't unnecessarily project any unwanted beliefs or opinions onto their relationships with others. When two people operate from an open heart chakra, a healthy relationship ensues. They are whole and complete individuals who bring themselves to the table fully while maintaining their individual characteristics and qualities that make them valuable people and partners, whether romantically involved or not. Each person takes turns being the one to step up in times of turbulence, and both are capable of listening to each other and holding space for processing triggers and wounds.

A gentle and nurturing nature, friendly warmth, and calming radiance are traits of heart-centered individuals. Emotionally, these people tend to be pretty even-keeled and are naturally intuitive as they empathize easily with their environment and everyone around them. They tend to do well in occupational roles such as nurses, doctors, therapists, teachers, healers, volunteers, and social/charity workers.

Underactive Chakra

We think of an underactive heart chakra as being shut down and closed off emotionally. There are many ways a heart can break—grief, loss, betrayal, abandonment, and rejection. You may feel pain, emptiness, or loneliness inside. If the flow of energy from the higher chakras to your lower chakras becomes interrupted, it can cause isolation or depression. An underactive heart chakra can present in the inability to forgive others, poor coping and sharing skills, apathy, aimlessness, loss of self-love, and withdrawal in general. Hardening of the heart can look and feel different to everyone and is sometimes marked with victimhood, defensiveness, and bitterness.

Overactive Chakra

Since your heart chakra connects you to your loving energy, dysfunctions of excessive energy in the heart chakra center can lead to dysregulation of the ego (egotism) and emotions. When you become ruled by these things, you basically fall away from your loving center. An overactive heart chakra could manifest as stubbornness, narcissism, obsession, unchecked comparison, codependency, jealousy, self-aggrandizement, and self-centeredness.

   If your heart chakra is in overdrive, you may notice that you lack appropriate boundaries within friendships and romantic relationships and may be misusing the power of love. You may throw yourself headfirst into love and choose romantic partners indiscriminately. You may have lost touch with your sense of identity and the power of your own discernment. An overactive heart chakra can result in people-pleasing and saying yes to anyone and everything, even if it might not be in your best interest.

Balanced Chakra

The heart chakra is generally seen as a point of integration (zero-point calibration) of personal and altruistic aspirations. Within a context of love and relation, a host of abilities start to come together when heart coherence is reached, including good judgment, empathy, compassion, motivation, and acceptance.

   Since the heart is the bridge between physical reality and the metaphysical realm, balancing the heart chakra will mean harmonizing all layers of Divine energies with the more dense layers of your lower chakra system. Your personal needs and desires will be purified, allowing you to calibrate to your zero-point center, which at its heart is pure unconditional love. In turn, this will open you up to greater expansion, connection, and possibilities in every area of your life as your heart rhythms exude waves of gratitude and joy.

Remember that the key to the heart space is to hold a high-vibrational attitude, infusing laughter into more moments and refreshing your stagnant energy by getting out of your routine and exploring to gain a fresh perspective. There are many levels of consciousness that you can gain access to, and if you align with the heart truth inside you, it will always guide you on the right path!

Deities

The deities associated with the heart chakra are Jesus Christ, Mother Mary, Quan Yin, Krishna, and Inanna.

The heart space is considered to house the high heart, which is home to Christ Consciousness. We start by taking a look at Ascended Master Jesus Christ (Yeshua), the Son of God in Christianity, who once lived on Earth as a human. He is known universally by his galactic name, Sanat Kumara, as head of Shamballa (the Ascended Master retreat). He stands for compassion and served as a guide to seed the darkness with light so that others might follow in his footsteps in their personal ascension journey. He makes a wonderful Ascended Master guide, as he has lived through the challenges of life on the Earth plane and has much experience dealing with humanity.

Mother Mary, Yeshua's mother, is also an Ascended Master who emanates pure and compassionate motherly love. She serves as a mother for all those in need and as a pillar of inner strength. She challenges oppression and invites you to see how you can serve others with your own heart wisdom and medicine. Whenever you encounter a rose, it is a sign that Mother Mary is with you.

Quan Yin is an Ascended Master and collective consciousness that is available to Earth at this time to teach us compassion and Divine lessons of self-love. She is considered the bodhisattva of mercy and a warrior goddess who can help you forgive and battle your inner demons. Call on Quan Yin to help you see your own inner beauty, grace, and ability to let go.

Krishna, an incarnation of Lord Vishnu, is one of the most widely revered Hindu gods. He is the god of love and represents ideal Divine love embodiment. He is a warrior, philosopher, and teacher. Krishna was celebrated here on Earth and left his incarnation to ascend and help others in their search for destiny and to aid them in remembering pure love.

Inanna, an ancient Sumerian goddess (and perhaps the most popular of all Mesopotamian deities), is a goddess of love, sensuality, fertility, and martial aspects. Associated with Venusian heart-based energy, she is worshipped for her sense of benevolent justice and feminine/masculine balance. She has traversed the underworld and has an incredible story of strength and perseverance.

Planets

The planet ruling the heart chakra is Venus. Ruler of love and beauty, this planetary energy invokes pleasure, acceptance, attraction, and love in all forms. It has a distinct feminine characteristic that influences your desires and seeks harmony in all areas of your life. With this intoxicating amorous energy present, seek some playtime with a creative muse or become a muse yourself!

Heart Chakra Exercise: Opening the Back of Your Heart Space

This special Venusian-inspired meditation from the guide and teacher Paul of Venus, which will take anywhere from 10 to 15 minutes, helps open the back of the heart chakra to take in loving Source energy. Begin in a seated position where you'll be undisturbed and able to focus your energy.

Start by taking a few long, deep inhalations into the belly for three counts, and exhale for a count of five. By breathing into the diaphragm and releasing a longer exhale, you help slow your nervous system, which signals to your body that you are safe. Begin to focus your breathing on a point between your shoulder blades behind your heart, in the middle of your upper back. Breathe into this space a few times to release any tension.

Imagine a white shimmering diamond light above and behind you. This liquid crystalline light is pure Source frequency, glimmering with golden reflections. Feel it streaming into the back of your heart space through your back and shoulder blades, like a beam of light penetrating the center point on your back. As the back of your heart chakra opens, shift your attention briefly to visualize the front of your heart chakra shrinking down and closing to the size of a quarter. Shrinking the front of the heart chakra helps you keep the love within you that you are sourcing from your back heart space.

With your attention on your back once again, feel this loving light pouring in, filling up your heart from behind. Feel the warmth and love as you allow it to fill up your entire

The Heart Torus and the High Heart Chakra

Toroidal (doughnut-shaped) magnetic energy fields exist around everything in nature. They spiral upward, around, and then downward, forming an infinite loop of energy that propels itself energetically in an unending emanation, circulating feminine and masculine energies. The toroidal field around the heart can be up to three feet in diameter, if not bigger. The heart torus (or toroidal energy field) is nested within your body's larger layered torus (your aura). The heart's electromagnetic field arcs out from the heart and then returns to the heart's zero-point center. It is from this center that neutrality is reached. This center also aligns with the center of the toroidal fields of your physical body and light body. This field helps us visualize the geometry of pure aligned consciousness, and it helps us understand and connect with our soul's higher intention of unconditional love.

The zero point is a very tiny space that maintains stillness—accessing it can open up doorways to infinite impossibilities and multidimensional realities. It's important to grasp this concept to understand that the heart space is wildly important for gaining access to higher consciousness. It will take the full connection of your heart, body, mind, and spirit to reach the zero point.

When your heart chakra is activated and you begin to work with the heart torus, you create a pathway to your high heart chakra, an energy point (and minor chakra) located at your thymus between your throat chakra and heart chakra. Your high heart chakra can become fully activated after all your other chakras have fully developed and opened. The high heart chakra is sometimes referred to as your etheric heart and is said to be where intention originates from. It helps you connect language with emotions like compassion, which creates a profound heart coherence and therefore a profound healing effect on your body. This sacred space bridges your emotion and intellect to connect you more fully to Divine love.

You can locate this point on yourself by finding the divots a few inches beneath and at the center of your collarbone. Using Emotional Freedom Technique (EFT), or tapping, you can tap on this point to begin reprogramming your subconscious mind and rewriting old patterns. You can also gently press your fingers on this point, moving in a clockwise position around your high heart and notice how you feel after about 30 seconds.

heart space until it is overflowing. You may even feel the energy beginning to radiate and ripple out around your heart chakra as well.

When you feel complete, invite the diamond light beam to slowly dissipate. Take as much time as you want to feel the renewal in your loving energy center before opening the front back up and closing out your session with the statement, "I am grateful for this love that I am. And so it is."

This technique allows you to receive Source energy whenever you need it. No matter where you are during the day, you can draw on this white diamond light energy to sustain and hold you during moments of struggle.

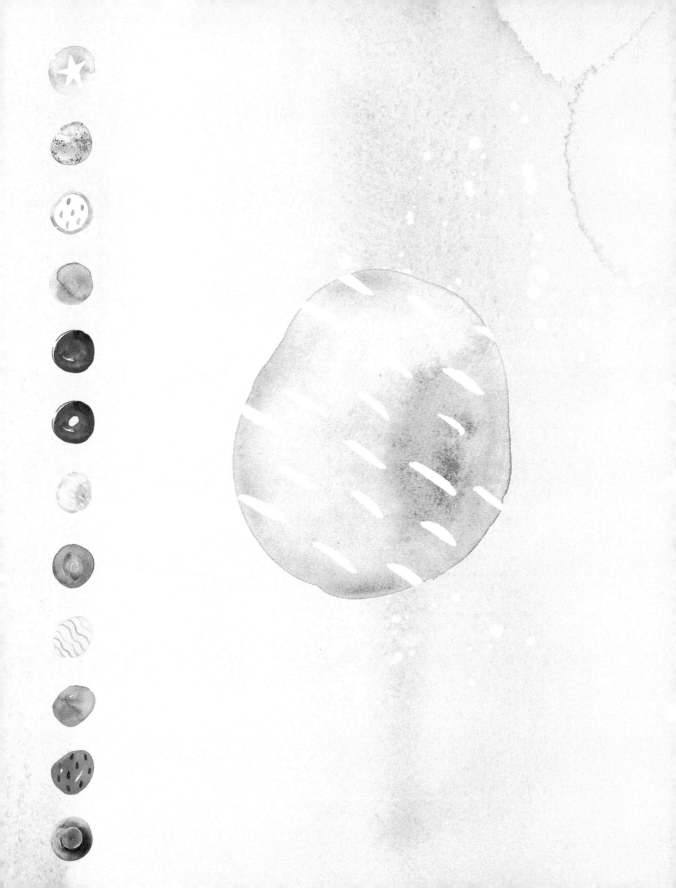

Chapter Ten
The 5th Chakra: Throat

The throat chakra is about expression in all forms: verbal, nonverbal, internal, and external. This chakra's element is ether, as it begins to connect you to realms of higher consciousness and more subtle spiritual levels. It is this center that projects your creations into the world, giving structure to and maintaining your reality through expressive vibration. Vibration is an oscillation of energy waves—in this case, verbally spoken sound—that create correspondence with your environment. Let's take a look at exactly how you create your reality through your throat chakra.

Your word is your wand—that is how much magic your throat chakra holds. This chakra is so special because it has the power to speak your entire world into existence. Since everything is energy, it is vitally important to be aware of what you speak aloud in order to consciously cocreate your life. Life isn't happening *to* you; it's happening *for* you. For example, imagine your voice echoing off a canyon wall. If you create a low tone with your voice, that sound is mirrored directly back to you. This is what happens when you utter words: what you say is mirrored back to you in the form of your reality. In essence, you are casting spells with your words in each moment (that's why it's called spelling!).

The key to welcoming in everything you desire is knowing what you want and being able to verbalize it. The throat chakra is your center of expression and allows your truth and desires to be told. To feel connection with others, we all need to feel heard and understood. We need to take responsibility over what we are communicating and how we are communicating it. To place your order with the Universe, you need to get clear and focus your message. The Universe is always listening, and it is your job to be flexible and trust that what you are creating will come to you with no expectation about how or when it will do so.

Besides manifesting your reality, the throat chakra is home to your thyroid and parathyroid, which are important endocrine glands in your body that are responsible for metabolic function and hormone production, which we'll review in this chapter. This chakra is also responsible for the entire area around your shoulders, neck, upper back, and clavicle. When you think of yourself as being burdened or weighed down, focus healing efforts on relieving tension in this area. When you take the weight of your own stories off your shoulders, you can move mountains. It all starts with finding your inner truth, which happens here, in your throat chakra.

Names & Meaning

The most familiar Sanskrit name for the throat chakra is *vishuddha*, which means "especially pure." In Sanskrit, *shuddhi* means "pure," and *vi* is a root word that intensifies the word to which it is adjoined. This chakra is a place to purify your truth through verbal expression. Some Tantric names for the throat chakra are *dwyashtapatrambuja, kantha, kanthambuja, kanthapadma, kanthapankaja, kanthadesha, shodasha, nirmala-padma, shodasha-dala, shodashara, shodasha-patra,* and *shodashollasa-dala.* In the Upanishads and Puranas, it is simply called the *kantha* chakra.

Color

The color for the throat chakra is blue. You can imagine this as a sky blue or royal blue, depending on your mood—all shades of blue are welcome. Blue is often associated with depth, stability, balance, healing, loyalty, sincerity, and intelligence. This frequency is calm and tranquil and invokes security, integrity, and trust.

Location

The throat chakra is aligned at the base of the throat, along the sushumna. It is associated with the carotid plexus (nerves that run parallel to the carotid artery) and the laryngeal nerves. Your carotid arteries are major arteries that supply blood to the brain, face, and neck. Your laryngeal artery lies beneath your thyroid and is responsible for the muscles, mucous membranes, and glands of your neck. The focal point of this chakra is at the center of your throat, which is located a few inches below the Adam's apple.

Estimated Activation

Your throat chakra likely goes through multiple stages of development in life, with different development theories to support this claim. Some argue the ages for this development begin anywhere from 6 to 12 years old, to be further developed later in life. In the Hindu system, ages 28 to 35 is the range in which the throat chakra is thought to be fully activated. This developmental period is when you are learning to hold your truth against the opinions of the world. You are motivated more and more by the expression that wisdom and love take in your life, and you are becoming more willing to share. This period is a time for opening up to a higher alignment of integrity and more fully knowing and sharing yourself.

Body Parts

The body parts managed by the throat chakra include your ears, neck, jaw, teeth, mouth, trachea, vocal cords, thyroid and parathyroid glands, upper esophagus, cervical vertebrae, and the bones, joints, and muscles of your shoulders. The pharyngeal plexus and brachial plexus connect to your mouth, tongue, pharynx, palate, and jaw. This is considered the passageway between the lower parts of the body and the head, brain, and upper spinal cord, which control your body's higher functions.

Glands

Your thyroid and parathyroid are the glands associated with your throat chakra. Your thyroid, a butterfly-shaped gland at the front of your neck, makes two primary hormones (triiodothyronine and thyroxine) that regulate how your body uses energy for metabolism, growth, and development. Your body produces these important hormones naturally by converting iodine from food. Meanwhile, your parathyroid produces parathyroid hormone (PTH), which causes the release of calcium, increasing your body's ability to absorb it from the foods you eat.

Senses

The dominant senses your throat chakra is associated with are hearing, listening, and speaking. The sense organs are the ears and the mouth (vocal cords), which makes sense because the throat chakra is mostly concerned with the honest vocalization of your thoughts and feelings.

Illnesses

Health issues related to the throat chakra can include throat-related illnesses such as sore throat, tonsillitis, asthma, bronchitis, mouth ulcers, and laryngitis. Problems can arise in the mouth, jaw (such as lockjaw or grinding), larynx, upper lungs, respiratory system (the heart chakra shares responsibility for this system), upper esophagus, teeth and gums, ears (such as earache or tinnitus), and cervical vertebrae. Upper arm pain, hay fever, and allergies fall into this category as well.

Function

Within the energy of the throat chakra, we deal with psychological and emotional issues of decision-making, faith, personal expression, dreaming, and creativity (which is itself a high form of spiritual inspiration). We each have the ability to carefully select the words we use. Depending on social conditioning, and some might argue manners, we choose what to share in a conversation and what to keep as internal dialogue. The key here is discernment, not judgment. It's just as important to select what you will ultimately share in an honest and clear manner as it is to select which opinions you'll choose to internally acknowledge instead. As we grow, we learn to communicate our beliefs with tact and grace, connecting our spiritual lens with our vocal filters as we grow beyond cultural hypnosis and programming.

Through practice, we learn to let go of patterns of unconscious decision-making and expression such as gossiping about others, slander, or stretching the truth. This deconditioning allows you to align authentically with your truth instead of having to work for it. Practice releasing guilt and showing yourself forgiveness when facing key challenges so that you can move forward in a better way. You can practice this consciously or in your dream states. (Dreaming helps us process things on a subconscious level and make sense of all the thoughts we didn't get to process during the day.)

Physically, the health of your thyroid gland plays a crucial role in your overall immunity. Hormones and amino acids are generated in your thyroid gland and directly impact your metabolic rate. Your rate of metabolism determines how fast you use the energy that you consume through food. If you have a fast metabolism, you generally need to eat more often to keep your energy levels up and maintain your weight. With a slow metabolism, your body processes slow down, and the body can tend to gain weight as it prepares for holding on to fat supplies for energy maintenance. Here, the parathyroid controls regulation of calcium in the body. Without enough calcium, your bones run the risk of losing density and hardness (osteoporosis), which can negatively impact your skeletal system and teeth.

Your throat (pharynx) is connected to your auditory (eustachian) tubes in your inner ears. It helps drain fluid from the middle ear into the throat behind your nasal passages. This function clears your auditory passages so that your eardrums can vibrate, allowing you to hear. Since hearing is such an important part of listening, keeping your throat chakra clear can also help you take in and hear the world around you more closely. They say you have twice as many ears as mouths so that you have the opportunity to listen more than you speak. Listening is definitely a skill set of the higher-mind functions, and it takes practice to become a successful listener, so be patient with yourself and others in your communications together.

Archetypes

The Communicator and the Silent Child are the archetypes associated with the throat chakra.

The Communicator has a natural knack for putting words to feelings and opens up easily to others. This archetypal energy thrives on integrity and alignment by focusing on the truth of the matter and making sure that one's truth is conveyed appropriately. The Communicator's word can be trusted, and they can be depended upon to stand up for themselves—even if it comes with a cost! Self-honesty, which is required to get to the core of an issue, is a quality of the Communicator. This archetype reminds us that listening is an active part of communicating, so when this energy is present, you will listen often. The Communicator may push you outside your comfort zone to get your message across, but rest assured, when this energy is present, you will have the courage to do so.

The Communicator must be diligently attended to, or its shadow, the Silent Child archetype, may come around. Silent Child archetypal energy is reflected in withholding one's voice or opinion due to fear or shame. When the Silent Child energy is present, we see suffering without expressing pain or hurt. The Silent Child tends to hide their true feelings and bottles up their emotions. Often, those with this archetypal energy aren't really connected to their higher truth. They may not know how to access radical self-honesty to look at their blind spots objectively, which results in a lack of inner knowing. This energy is often seen in adults, in job settings, or romantic partnerships, where a person might keep silent to avoid potential repercussions or rejection.

Personality

Someone with a balanced throat chakra is an open and authentic communicator. Even though they have hard conversations just like everybody else, these people find a way for their words to come across as tactful and understanding. Exuding confidence when they speak, they naturally tend to attract others through their open invitations to join in or participate in the conversation. Even through disagreements, they try to keep the argument respectful while they express their perspective. A "go with the flow" attitude often accompanies a balanced throat space, and it's no surprise that these people often adjust well to a change of plans.

The throat space is the center for creativity and expression. Life is about the journey, not the destination, and the same applies to the process of creation. People who have a well-balanced throat chakra will understand that sometimes this process looks messy and that they must flow with both the challenges and the opportunities for magic to appear. They understand each new moment has the potential for magical manifestation. Musicians, singers, writers, producers, actors, attorneys, talent agents, podcasters, artists, food critics, and speech therapists tend to put their throat chakra front and center, so these are often great careers for people who have lots of energy surrounding their fifth energy center.

Underactive Chakra

When you aren't receiving enough energy to the throat chakra, a variety of communication issues may manifest. Nervousness, timidity, introversion, or insecurities preventing you from speaking up for yourself are common with an underactive throat chakra. Having a small voice here can cause delayed personal development and adversely affect relationships and business (for example, public speaking). Being shy isn't always a bad thing, but suppressing your truth usually ends up causing inner turmoil.

Additionally, symptoms may present in illnesses in the throat, earaches, voice loss, strained vocal cords, stuttering, and nasal problems. Thyroid problems manifest here without proper energy balancing and, in the case of energy deficiency, hypothyroidism. Hypothyroidism is defined by the body's inability to make enough thyroid hormone, which can slow all your body processes down, causing weight gain and mood disorders.

Overactive Chakra

Coincidentally, an overactive throat chakra also tends to show up as communication breakdowns or lack of control over speech. Habitual lying to cover up intentions or gossiping can be important indicators that your integrity needs to be checked and brought back into alignment. When the throat space is overwhelmed with energy, you may become highly self-critical and impede the flow of ideas and thoughts you share with the world. You may feel as though you are very picky with yourself or others, particularly in regard to how you talk. A critical attitude could also manifest as being condescending to others, arrogant, or rude with your speech.

Another disorder known as hyperthyroidism can be caused when the thyroid produces too much of the hormone thyroxine and can cause rapid heartbeat and excessive weight loss. People with excess energy in the throat could also suffer from compulsive behaviors like overeating, jaw clenching, or teeth grinding. Over time, these issues can cause major problems if left unchecked.

Balanced Chakra

When you have a balanced throat chakra, you are an open and authentic communicator. The throat space is the center for creativity and expression, so your ability to take what you intend to say and translate it into spoken or written word is a sign that your throat chakra is open and unblocked. You'll be able to speak confidently and listen well, and you won't have any issues speaking up for yourself, even though this practice can feel uncomfortable at times.

The ability to project your creations into reality is another sign that your throat space is functioning optimally, since creativity is a hallmark of this energy center. Expression flows freely, too, helping you access your creative flow more deeply by tapping into your highest potential. You're able to get ideas out on paper and start and finish projects almost effortlessly. This optimal state can be achieved with some dedication to your own truth.

Deities

The god and goddess presented at the throat chakra are two of the most powerful Egyptian deities who ever walked the earth: Hathor and Thoth. Both of these souls have Earth roots originating in Atlantean times, so they've been around for thousands of years.

Goddess Hathor is one of the most revered ancient Egyptian deities. She is also an ascended collective consciousness known as the Hathors and is comprised of an entire civilization that was said to have gone through the earthly ascension process together. Hathor is the goddess of the sky and a master of music and sound. Her essence is a multidimensional shapeshifting woman who moves through quantum reality and has the ability to embody a multitude of emanations as well as her total expression of being at will. She can exist in multiple places at once (bilocation) and call those facets into one expression when she needs to. Her medicine is unconditional loving energy through sound transmissions. Call on her when you are learning to share your medicine through your voice's expression.

Thoth, another ancient Egyptian deity, is often depicted as a man with the head of an ibis. As the supreme god, he brought the written word (hieroglyphics) to Egypt and created his legacy through scriptures called the Emerald Tablets of Thoth. These tablets sought to disclose and illuminate the nature and structure of reality so that the information would live on for those looking to awaken humanity to its highest destiny and purpose. Associated with magic, lunar energy, science, wisdom, and the moon, Thoth's energy is powerful for relaying your expression through the written word. Invoke him when you need to get clear on your ideas and organize them into form or when starting a writing project.

Planets

The ruling planet of the throat chakra is Mercury. Mercurial energies represent your mind, your thoughts, and how your ideas move and are expressed, making communication a vital pillar of this center. Planetary aspects ruled by Mercury denote how you wish to be communicated with and how you are seen and heard.

Throat Chakra Exercise: Toning

Your voice is so powerful. In fact, when it moves through your sternum, it creates a vibration that helps clear obstructions in your chakras and meridians, signaling safety. This thoracic vibration moves through your chest, decreasing ventilation by 20 percent—in other words, your breath signals your body to relax and slow down. Your voice also stimulates your immune system, because it oscillates the thymus gland in the high heart area of your chest (see page 118 for more on the high heart chakra).

It's scientifically proven that music has a healing effect on the body. Sound waves create resonance in your body that vitalize your cells; it's like each of your cells receives a micro-massage. Optimal resonance also stimulates the parasympathetic nervous system, which has a multitude of beneficial impacts, including lowering blood pressure and heart rate. Using the sound produced by your own vocal cords, sound creation is effortless to practice, and it doesn't pose a risk to your well-being. Although each chakra in the Hindu Tantric chakra system has a seed syllable that ties it to the element ascribed to each energy portal, you can practice installing these seeds into other chakras or making up your own vibrations to see what resonates with your specific energy. For example, water is traditionally associated with the sacral chakra, but this element (and corresponding seed syllable *vam*) can be installed into the solar plexus to dampen the fire energy naturally present there.

Pure sound is vibration with no words and brings the right brain online, which allows for massive transformations. The nature of the work with sound transcends the human thinking brain. In this exercise, you'll learn different ways to experiment with and improve upon your vocal tone by chanting, humming, singing, or toning.

The important thing is to sit with each sound, breathing out the stagnation so you're able to make some space for new energy to come into your system. You don't need to clear all the space at once; just know that each time you sit down and dedicate your time to healing, every little bit helps you move toward your greater goal. Each time you sit down to practice (ideally uninterrupted), you can do one or more of the following:

FIND GROUNDING: STABILITY COMES FROM A PHYSICAL CONNECTION. Squeeze your muscles and release a few times. If you are having trouble, try sitting on your hands to really feel your body.

PRACTICE DIAPHRAGMATIC BREATHING: AS YOU BREATHE, DESCEND YOUR BREATH INTO YOUR BELLY. Breathing only into your upper chest is called shallow breathing; it's a less than ideal way to breathe. So, breathe deeply and fully.

MAKE BUBBLES: PRACTICE BLOWING IMAGINARY BUBBLES WITH YOUR MOUTH. This will help you sustain your breath and help you get used to projecting your voice.

EXPLORE YOUR RANGE: AS YOU READ OR SING, ALTERNATE BETWEEN HIGH AND LOW TONES. This is called "going up and down the stairs." This exercise improves your range, especially if your voice is fairly monotone. You can also try alternating between speaking fast and slow.

REPEAT *A* AND *O*: THESE SOUNDS CAUSE VIBRATIONS IN THE CHEST AND STERNUM. You can practice saying them quickly and drawing them out.

HUM THROUGH YOUR NOSE: THIS IS CALLED NASAL HUMMING. When you hum through your nose, the air from your nose and sinuses mix together. The nose and sinuses produce nitrogen oxide, which is beneficial for your body and has antibacterial and anti-inflammatory effects. Try humming the notes of a popular song!

TRY "SEED SWAPPING": EACH CHAKRA IS ASSOCIATED WITH A SEED SYLLABLE. For example, *yam* is the seed syllable for the heart chakra. When you swap seeds, you can chant a seed syllable into a different chakra. For example, you could chant *yam* into the throat chakra instead of the heart chakra.

MAKE ANY SOUND: GENERATE ANY SOUND THAT FEELS GOOD TO YOU FOR ANY LENGTH OF TIME. It doesn't have to sound musically perfect—it only needs to feel good. (Sometimes these results won't go hand in hand!)

Do these techniques as many times as you'd like. When you're in the process of healing your throat chakra, practice a few times each day. Happy toning!

The Zeal Point Chakra

The zeal point chakra is located on an upward-facing angle at the back of your head, where your spinal column meets the base of your skull. This chakra is over the occipital lobe in your brain, the center for visual processing both in your waking and dream states. Also referred to as the Well of Dreams, the Jade Pillow (*Yu Chen* in Chinese), or the Mouth of God, this focal point is an emerging minor chakra that some systems use as part of a main chakra ensemble.

Although it's not mentioned in the Tantra chakra system, the zeal point chakra is a significant point in most modern ascension models because it is now opening up for more people. This important energy point is used to balance the mind, body, and emotions, and its gift is to allow you to express your spirit's powers consciously and fully through your true voice. Since this chakra responds to higher-vibrational energies, such as sound, its musical note is a G♯ (G-sharp), and it opens up to this frequency.

With this chakra point open, you will have greater access to spiritual abilities, including advanced dream recall, astral travel, lucid dreaming, and clairaudience. It is said that having this chakra open also helps connect you more to your spirit guides because of its proximity to the crown and third eye chakras. As the gateway to your consciousness, this chakra allows you to harmonize insights from the lower chakras as you assimilate the information into your higher purpose in life.

Chapter Eleven
The 6th Chakra: Third Eye

Known as a mystical center, your third eye chakra transmits important visual information from both your sensory sight and psychic sight. Psychic sight, also known as subtle information or your sixth-sense knowledge, goes beyond normal sensory inputs to the paranormal or metaphysical. Essentially, the gift of sight belongs to this chakra—both inner and outer vision. This chakra allows you to experience self-reflection as well as spiritual thought. You can only receive messages from your higher self and the Divine after you have opened yourself up to receiving and cleared through your higher physical gateways. Your third eye offers higher perspective and allows you to receive alternate answers and solutions so that you can translate higher consciousness information. This gateway allows you to internalize the outside world and externalize your inner multidimensional self.

Your ida (lunar nadi) and pingala (solar nadi), or energy lines, come together in your third eye zone, behind your pineal gland. There, these lines represent your feminine and masculine energies coming together and meeting your sushumna, initiating an opening of your third eye. In ancient Egyptian alchemy, this point was used in sex magic to enhance the *ka* body and build up energy through subtle channels to help reach immortality. Historically, this spot is important in Hinduism as well. The three elements of consciousness join together here: higher mind (*buddha*), ego (*ahamkara*), and the thinking mind (*manas*). The latter helps us move beyond right and wrong into a unified field of oneness, transcending duality as we know it.

Located in the center of your forehead, the sixth chakra contains a small gland the size of a grain of rice in the shape of a pine cone called the pineal gland, which we'll discuss shortly. The pineal gland can accumulate calcium over time, which can block important subtle streams of information coming in. This small gland is responsible for your psychic sight and holds the power to cut through any illusions in your way. This area of the mind is where you get to observe the perceptions that form your reality.

Seeing and understanding go hand in hand, and the energy from your higher chakras, as well as your lower chakras, plays a part in this chakra's opening and functioning at high capacity. This space is considered the seat of your consciousness, and it has a delightfully mystical quality to it. While most of your lower chakras have elements tied to them in their metaphysical organization, your third eye combines all the elements (matter) into its next evolutionary phase of light. This light element is the least dense of the other elements associated with the lower chakras. As you travel up the consciousness ladder, the vibrational states of your chakras buzz higher and higher with excitement, whirling and spinning as fast as the speed of light.

Names & Meaning

The Sanskrit name for the third eye chakra is *ajña*, meaning "summoning," "command," "authority," and "unlimited power." This name conjures the notion that this chakra directs your other chakras, especially in the realms of the unseen. Tantric names include *ajña-puri, ajña-patra, ajñamhuja, ajñapankaja, bhru-mandala, bhru-mula, bhru-saroruba, bhru-madhya-chakra, bhru-madhya-padma, dwidala, dwidalambuja, dwidala-Kamala, dwipatra, jnana-padma, netra-padma, shiva-padma,* and *triweni-kamala*. The Upanishads refer to the third eye in texts as the *bhru* chakra. This energy center is also called *trikuti* (third eye), *divya chakshu* (divine eye), and *gyana netra/gyana chakshu* (the eye of knowledge).

Color

The colors associated with the third eye chakra are indigo and violet. These colors invoke spirituality, self-awareness, and reflection. Violet is a secondary shade, as it has also been associated with the crown chakra in many systems. Indigo, a midnight blue, is both the frequency of deep blue and violet and holds the attributes of these two colors. Indigo conveys devotion, integrity, and justice. Violet carries a frequency of dignity, sensitivity, and intuition.

Location

Your third eye chakra is located in your brain, an inch above the center point between your eyebrows. It rests at the top of your spinal column, specifically at your medulla oblongata; this area forms the lower part of your brain stem and contains your pineal gland. This location isn't exact, but the chakra is behind and above your sinuses. The focal point of this chakra is in the mid-brow region of your face.

Estimated Activation

The third eye chakra has multiple activation timelines; some systems mark ages 8 to 14 as initial development stages for your third eye chakra. The Hindu system vaguely conveys that this activation takes place much later, between the ages of 35 and 42; however, most systems do not correlate a time period for the third eye development. In this 12-chakra ascension system, activation is likely very early on in childhood, as the wave of children being born after 2012 (when the ascension timeline began for us on Earth) are naturally spiritually open, awake, and aware.

Body Parts

The third eye chakra includes your eyes, parts of your brain and ears, your pineal gland, hypothalamus, and nose. In some systems, the pituitary gland, which we will dive into in the next chapter, is associated with this chakra. Your optic nerve, the main nerve responsible for vision, links with your pituitary gland and pineal gland to fully activate functions associated with awakening your third eye. The pineal and pituitary glands are partners in perception and work together for its full opening. Additionally, the nerves of the pineal gland cover the lower part of the brain, linking to your limbic system, which is responsible for memory, automatic emotions, and the stress response.

Glands

Your pineal gland, the size of a pea, is located in the central part of your brain, close to the pituitary gland. The pineal gland's primary function is to create melatonin and serotonin, which help your body regulate your sleep/wake cycles. This gland also contains magnetite (a magnetic form of iron oxide), which sensitizes you to the magnetics of your environment. Emitting hormones that regulate body-wide endocrine functions, the pineal gland is a master gland of sorts. On top of all of this, your pineal gland secretes psychedelic-producing substances (specifically, 5-MeO-DMT and DMT), which are present at birth, death, and times of intense bliss. These emissions can produce visionary and spiritual states, are thought of as doorways to other dimensions, and are often sought after by psychonauts and researchers alike. Luckily, we don't have to go far to experience other planes as they are already inside of each of us.

Senses

The sense associated with your third eye is inner sight, or insight. Your third eye is your sixth chakra, and this space produces your sixth sense. Your extrasensory perception (ESP) is managed by your lower left eye and the lower part of your brain. This sense goes beyond the commonly recognized five senses (sight, smell, taste, touch, and hearing), and we know it as our intuition. It includes expanded clairvoyance and psychic abilities of various degrees.

Illnesses

Health conditions that develop in the third eye chakra include vision problems (cataracts, glaucoma, blurred vision, poor eyesight, dyslexia, and blindness), headaches and migraines, and hearing problems such as deafness. Other illnesses include brain tumors, strokes, blood pressure issues, depression, nervous breakdowns, insomnia, dizziness, sinusitis, and learning disabilities or impairment. Illnesses of the third eye chakra affect a number of systems, like the endocrine and hormonal systems, which are responsible for growth and development, and the autonomic nervous system, which regulates automatic body processes.

Function

Your third eye chakra is all about transcending duality through correspondence of opposites. Correspondence in the third eye means that everything you have within you, you create outside of you. One way you can see who you truly are is through another. You hold both polarities inside you (feminine/masculine, positive/negative charges, light/dark). You are even built symmetrically (two eyes, two ears, two nostrils) to highlight your need for balance. When you begin to examine this, you see that there is no need to look outside yourself to find anything. What you need to transcend duality is already here; you only need to pull it into the light to truly see what is there.

The third eye chakra only perceives light, which combines and raises the frequency of all other elements. Therefore, working with light will help you increase your third eye's spiritual and intuitive awareness. Physically, the pineal gland has receptors that capture light and let your body know when it is night and day to help regulate your sleep/wake cycles. This inner vision is responsible for assimilating light in such a way that your body can process images and even pick up on extrasensory information. Your pineal gland works in congruence with your hypothalamus gland, which monitors your body's hunger, thirst, sex drive, and aging processes. Proper functioning of the pineal gland is synonymous with good health, while calcification (the buildup of calcium crystals) in this area can potentially lead to health hazards.

Another function of the pineal gland is its magnetic sensitivity. In animals, magnetite crystals are found inside the brain at the third eye, which primarily function as a navigation system that works in tandem with circadian synchronization. This electromagnetic sensor is present in humans as well and serves as a compass. Because of its sensitivity to artificial electromagnetic frequencies (EMFs), the pineal gland is easily disturbed by outside magnetic forces such as cellular frequencies (5G and above), Wi-Fi, radiation, microwaves, and most modern electronics. A good way to keep your intuition intact is to minimize, disable, or neutralize these devices wherever you spend the most time. You can purchase EMF shields and shungite (crystal) plates for your electronics to dampen their EMF emissions.

Since your thoughts create the same mental instructions as your actions, what you think, feel, and believe is especially important. Mental visualizations impact many cognitive processes in your brain, such as attention, perception, motor control, memory, and planning. Practices such as meditation and visualization have been found to increase self-efficacy and motivation, improve performance, and prime your brain for success. (Your brain is in training each time you actively feed it a program.) These practices actually improve your mental health as well as your physical health—*mind over matter*. Once you discover the true power of your mind, you can step into creatorship with every thought and emotion you have.

Archetypes

The archetypes depicted through the third eye chakra are the Mystic and the Judge.

Bringing the mysterious realms of the feminine into the light, the Mystic is a seeker and dreamer who aims to share lunar energies through illumination and integration. The Mystic's critical role is transmuting darkness into light and offering that medicine to society. Mystics cultivate this power within before they share it with the world. They must come to know their own power and harness their own latent potential before beaming it back into the world as medicine. This process takes patience and the desire for growth. Above all, the Mystic can get stuck when too much energy is stalled in expectation or the need for attention gets in the way. This archetype represents the visionary and creative changemaker that embodies heart-centered, connected consciousness. The Mystic trusts in order to transcend.

The Judge is a diplomatic advocate of neutrality. Sitting in a place of discernment, the Judge is concerned most with seeing all sides of a matter and making a decision of right action based on omnipotent information. This archetypal energy helps you discern what is right and just, and ideally those opinions should be formed from a heart-conscious mindset and clear vision. When this archetype is in its shadow, it can become attached to separateness, and this polarity ironically builds walls instead of removing them. Through healing, this archetype has the ability to see things as they are, in all the love they represent. Forgiveness and presence are key.

Personality

People with an open and balanced third eye are imaginative, strongly intuitive, and intellectual. They can easily tap into their inner mystic and have learned to trust their intuition, or inner knowing. They are both self-actualized and self-empowered. Since they have a healthy relationship with their own consciousness, they are immensely powerful manifesters and typically have a positive relationship with their reality. They refrain from overanalyzing and sway toward more contemplative and meditative thought processes, which enhance their life experiences. We think of the awakened person here in more subtle conscious, visionary roles such as therapist, healer, holistic health practitioner, detective or crime scene investigator, or veterinarian.

Underactive Chakra

Energy deficiencies in your third eye chakra are tricky to self-diagnose. In my experience, when we are battling our own mind, it can be difficult to see outside of our own frame of reference. When clues show up—negativity, self-doubt, chaos, difficulty visualizing or planning the future, memory loss, and perception issues—it's important to pay attention to them.

If you have less energy or a blockage in your third eye, you may be unable to see the obvious, and you may tend to regard your issues with denial. You might want things to change but aren't able to see what is required for the change to happen. With an underactive third eye chakra, it's easy to be deceived, and so you may end up being taken advantage of if you aren't careful. If you find yourself in a codependent or abusive relationship and this is a pattern for you, take a look at your boundaries, needs, and wants, and seek assistance from an outside source to get the clarity and direction you need until you are able to guide yourself to safety.

Overactive Chakra

Excessive energy in your third eye chakra can lead to fantasizing, daydreaming, and overthinking. In general, your ability to focus is hindered so you may have trouble manifesting your deepest desires if you keep finding yourself pulled down a rabbit hole out of the present moment. Difficulty concentrating, obsessiveness, and delusions are signs that you have too much energy going into this chakra. In these circumstances, remember that you create your reality, and if you continue to fuel the fire of your negative thought cycles, you'll continue to perpetuate them. Stopping the cycle with meditation and seeking clarity outside yourself should help you rebalance. Refocusing on the things most in alignment with you will allow you to achieve successful results.

Balanced Chakra

An open third eye chakra allows you to see things as they truly are in full understanding. When you recall feelings that you now know you should have listened to, that was your intuition signaling to you that you can lean in to your inner voice of reason and trust it. Sometimes it seems like this is just your imagination, and it will require an openness in your heart and causal chakra (see page 145) for you to access the truth of the matter. When the third eye chakra is in balance and you are completely open, there is nothing to distrust.

So much of your life depends on this level of openness, since the way you interpret your thoughts is how you visualize and perceive your reality. You, as a creator, have the ability to change your mind and, therefore, your reality, oftentimes through thought alone, which is one reason why visualization meditations are so successful. We create everything twice: once internally and once externally out in the world. With a balanced third eye chakra, you should be able to focus at will, leading to a keen intellect. Strong intuition along with the ability to see the bigger picture is another sign this psychic center is balanced. You are innately aware, often receive hits or hunches, and use the power of your mind to help others in their own vision quest. After all, what is the point of waking up if we allow others to stay asleep?

Deities

The deities represented in your sixth chakra are Vishnu, Ganesha, Ardhanarishvara, and St. Germain. These masters are stationed in the seat of consciousness.

Vishnu is revered as the most important part of the Hindu holy trinity (Vishnu, Shiva, Brahma). As a supreme god, he has many emanations and avatars, which means he can arrive in various forms (although he is usually depicted blue in color). He is seen as the preserver and protector of cosmic harmony. His name means "one who pervades, one who has entered into everything." His presence represents transcendence of duality and illuminates the true reality of any situation.

Ganesha, the elephant Hindu god, lord of all creatures, sometimes resides in the root or solar plexus chakra because he has success in initiating new ventures and many physical and mental powers. However, Ganesha resides in the third eye in the 12-chakra ascension system because he is the remover of obstacles and the destroyer of sorrow. Clearing the path to enlightenment, Ganesha helps dismantle anything obstructing your path forward. Call on him for Divine assistance to create new visionary pathways.

Androgynous Ardhanarishvara is the perfect blend of Shakti and Shiva (feminine and masculine). Reminding us of the power of neutrality and balance, this gender-neutral Hindu deity is white (right side) and golden (left side) to represent both genders. Call on Ardhanarishvara for healing and equalizing your feminine and masculine energies.

St. Germain is an Ascended Master who is guardian of the seventh ray and violet flame. These energies are healing frequencies that support the alchemy of transmutation (change), freedom, heart healing, grace, and ascension. St. Germain has had many earthly embodiments and is well qualified for his primary role as an ascension guide and master teacher in the Aquarian Age. His energy can be felt and accessed through Earth portals such as mountains (primarily Mount Shasta) and other sacred sites.

Planets

The planet associated with the third eye chakra is Neptune. Neptune's energy merges the dreamy, mystical psychic senses with spiritual intuition. It is a watery planet, which means it has depth. It also has a distinct artistic and creative feel, as it rides the waves of imagination and intuition.

Third Eye Chakra Exercise: Violet Flame Meditation

The violet flame is an advanced light technology brought to us from St. Germain. It's a type of energy that can heal those separated by location (space), time, beliefs, family rifts, core wounds, and relationship issues. It is known to bring harmony and elevated unity consciousness to those who use it. Just as Ganesha removes obstacles to clear your way ahead, the violet flame allows you to see behind the masks people wear and get out of your own way.

This meditation is meant to provide healing between you and another person you are connected to by bringing your souls into alignment. Set aside about 15 minutes for your meditation in a private space.

Start by selecting the person you'll be doing this meditation for—a current or former lover, a parent, a sibling, a friend, or a coworker. Ideally, select someone you are unable to physically give your message to, such as the departed or people who are separated by distance or rifts. Know that, especially in this meditation, your soul is quite capable of delivering your memo!

Close your eyes. Imagine yourself encased in a white or rainbow diamond light bubble, which floats around your aura and contains you. You are in an alternate astral plane, where there is no one else. Next, imagine the person you've selected appearing inside this setting with you. Invite the person inside your bubble, and sit there with them for a few moments, noticing their energy and their openness to receiving your message today. When they are quiet and you feel comfortable, give them your message directly. Notice the reaction you receive.

Now it is time to heal whatever is between you. Bring your attention to your third eye and call forth the power of the violet flame. Say aloud, "I call forth the violet flame and ask for healing between myself and _____ *(fill in the blank)*, for the benefit of our highest good. And so it is."

While your violet flame is glowing inside your third eye, imagine extending it out in front of you in a lemniscate (the infinity symbol). Imagine the loops encompassing both you and the person you're struggling with right now.

Allow the lines to flow fluidly, representing harmony between you. The center point provides a common ground and point of unity. See what comes to you from this place of higher perspective and understanding. Thank their soul for arriving on the etheric plane with you to do this sacred work, and then close your meditation in gratitude to your higher self.

At different times, the subject across from you could simply be a name or an object. It can even be an obstacle you're facing. It doesn't matter what or who it is, as long as it is something you wish to connect with and heal.

The Causal Chakra

Located about three to four inches behind the upper back portion of your head, the moon-white causal chakra is another emerging chakra center that is coming back online for humanity at this special time. Legend has it that this was a main chakra with a physical place on the body back in Atlantean times, when the shape of the human head was elongated. In modern times, this energy portal sits outside the body, and as it is being energized, it is pulled into vertical alignment with the rest of your chakras and encapsulated within the head. This alignment is part of your ascension pillar of light that aligns with your sushumna. The frequency that matches this chakra is the musical note A#, or A-sharp (also used for the pineal gland).

This special energy center closely adjoins your crown and third eye chakras and has a similar function of illumination. The causal chakra brings in lunar energies for Divine Feminine consciousness and amplifies and ignites the feminine energies you already have within you. This chakra draws on wisdom and compassion as its primary vibratory resonance. These energies are needed to balance the planet right now as we are dissolving outdated patriarchal systems put in place to suppress the Divine Feminine. These energies bring peace and balance to humanity and allow us to see the bigger picture through our own powerful intuitive ability. When your causal chakra is activated, the light of your soul is superimposed into the conscious and subconscious mind. To activate this chakra, you must have a level of self-mastery that comes with the dedicated practice of stilling the mind and consistent conscious awareness.

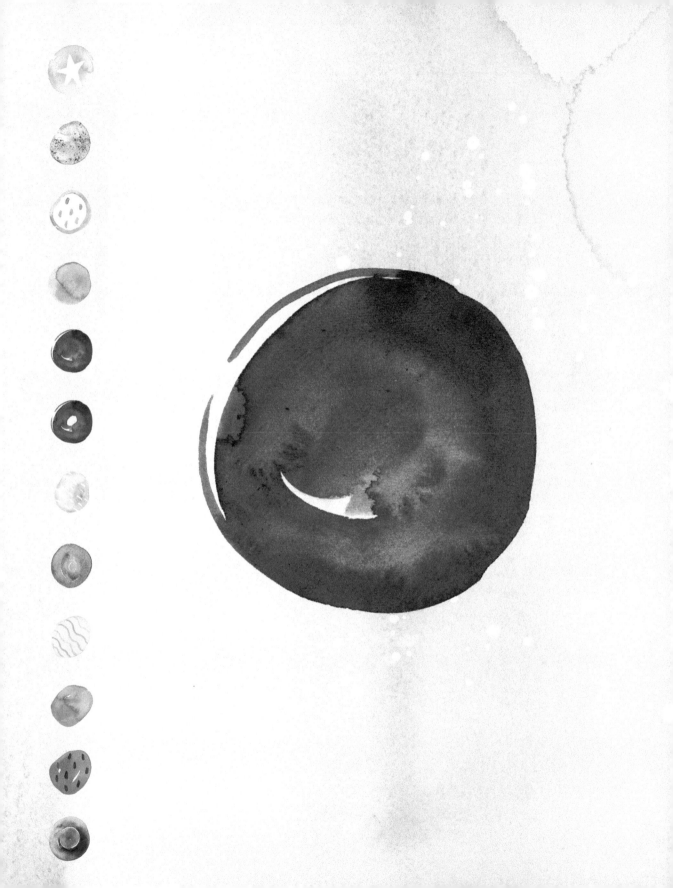

Chapter Twelve
The 7th Chakra: Crown

We have reached the crown chakra, the pinnacle point of the physical chakra system and the seventh energetic gateway of transcendence. The crown chakra sits at the top of your head and is the perfect celebration (through coronation) of you stepping into your inner Queen or King. A true ruler is knowledgeable, wise, and judicious, and cocreates with Divine inspiration. As you open up energetically, the crown chakra sits atop all your other corporeal chakras, opening a pathway of light. This elevated chakra is known as the abode of truth, or *satya loka*, and here it is possible to achieve attainment of nirvana and samadhi. In these final meditative stages of a true eight-limbed yogic practice, enlightenment is gained through the higher channels downloading their ultimate knowledge into your consciousness. Hinduism, Buddhism, Jainism, and yogic schools all regard the crown chakra as a place to break through the *anandamaya kosha* (the "bliss-illusion sheath"), or causal body.

The crown chakra is an energy vortex that acts as a bridge between the Universe and you. Breakthroughs here will happen when it opens up to the transpersonal chakras, linking you to different supraconscious states. Take note that while you may have an open crown chakra, there are still more layers for you to go through to fully open up and use your crown as it was intended.

The seventh chakra is where your nervous system begins to stretch down the brain and spinal cord. This area of your body not only produces hormones and neurotransmitters responsible for most of your voluntary and involuntary actions and thoughts, it also enables a host of your behavioral and psychological characteristics as well. Your consciousness rests in your upper sixth and seventh chakras, as do your master glands. Energetically, your crown and root chakra are linked in that they bookend your physical chakras and represent poles of your body's gateways.

When we explore the crown chakra, we take a look at the law of creation called mentalism. If you are operating from this consciousness, you understand that everything you are living is your creation. You operate in a world of vibrations that are constantly adjusting to show you different perspectives, and this creates your reality. With this inherent knowledge, you are able to tune in to new realities at will. You hold the power and courage to break free from all limiting beliefs and abusive or manipulative relationships. Disillusionment vanishes as you remap your internal wirings to make room for the right kind of knowledge. Think of stripping away reality to its core truth of unconditional love—that is what your crown chakra is for.

Names & Meaning

Sahasrara is the Sanskrit name for the crown chakra, meaning "thousand." This is based on the Hindu lotus chakra system, where the crown is represented by a thousand-petaled white lotus. There are a variety of other names for the crown chakra in the Tantra system: *sahasradala, sahasradala adhomukha padma, sahasradala padma, sahasrapatra, sahasrara padma, sahasrara mahapadma, sahasrara ambuja, shuddha padma, shiras padma,* and *wyoma.* The Upanishads and Vedas have a few additional names, including *akasha, sahasrara kamala (pankaja or padma),* and *sthana.* In the Puranas, this chakra is described as *parama, sahasrapatra, sahasraparna padma, shantyatita,* and *shantyatita pada.* Lastly, in Agni yoga, it's called *brahmarandhra,* or "the hole of the Brahman." Whew!

Color

The crown chakra is said to contain all the colors of the rainbow and, because of this, will appear white. It is also occasionally represented by a secondary color, violet. White represents purity, light, neutrality, and hope. Violet is a more dynamic color, associated with spiritualism, creativity, and mystery.

Location

The location of the crown chakra is at the very top of your head. Many sacred texts describe this exact location as inside your cerebral cavity, near your choroid plexus, a group of nerves that produce spinal fluid in your brain. In Hinduism, it is the site of the supreme *bindu* or *bindu visarga*, or "where the soul enters the body." Some ancient texts have this chakra an inch to two inches above the very top of your head. Since the location isn't exact, use your judgment to feel where it is located on your body. Remember, every body is different.

Estimated Activation

Since your crown chakra develops over a lifetime, it makes sense that this energy space is open at a young age, when we don't have many preconceived notions about the world around us. Over time, opinions and programming begin to shape how we perceive reality, and we must unlearn all the rules and containers that keep us controlled. For example, if you grew up following a certain religion, chances are it wasn't something you chose; you just didn't have a chance to form your own opinion about that until much later in life. As we age, we get to choose the spiritual paths we follow, the level of conditioning we will accept, and the truth that feels right to us. According to the Hindu system, the crown fully develops around ages 43 to 49. As we are ever evolving and advancing, new generations are helping open the door to earlier advancement of this spiritual gateway.

Body Parts

Your crown chakra manages your skull along with most everything located in the top half of your cranium, including parts of your brain, cerebral cortex, brain stem, pituitary gland, and nervous system. Your cranial nerves, plexus, and bones also fall under this classification. That's a great deal of responsibility for the crown chakra. Think of this area as the command center for your physical, spiritual, and emotional self.

Glands

A partner in perception to the third eye's pineal gland, the pituitary gland is the crown chakra's endocrine gland. This master gland is located in the middle of the brain in front of the pineal gland. It is responsible for the production of growth and sex hormones, the aging process, and the inflammation response. It works with your other endocrine glands as a director of sorts.

Senses

The crown chakra transcends your physical senses and thus does not associate with a primary sense in the way we know it. You can consider this space a bridge between your physical and metaphysical senses. As you begin to open up to higher gateways of light on and above your seventh chakra, you will tap into new layers of consciousness that reveal themselves subtly through light, frequency, and vibration.

Illnesses

Illnesses related to your crown chakra include muscular and skeletal disorders, as well as neurological disorders, including depression, dementia, Parkinson's disease, Alzheimer's disease, epilepsy, schizophrenia, psychosis, neurosis, and insomnia. The crown space is where you absorb knowledge and process information, so learning disabilities could also show up here. Because your brain governs your nervous system, coordination challenges, as well as sensitivity to light, sound, or your environment, present through the crown space. Head-related illnesses such as migraines, dizziness, and brain tumors are also ascribed to the seventh chakra.

Function

The crown chakra controls parts of the brain and your entire nervous system, so it's a critical juncture of your body that's responsible for your physical, emotional, and spiritual self. Your nervous system is composed of nerve tissues and branches that transmit chemical and electrical messages that run your entire body. Your peripheral and somatic nervous systems receive stimuli, your central nervous system interprets them, and your motor nerves initiate a response. Your sympathetic nervous system prepares your body for activity and response, while your parasympathetic system lowers your physical activity to conserve energy.

Your brain is divided into two hemispheres: the left, your verbal and analytical brain, and the right, your visual, artistic, and intuitive brain. It is here above the pineal gland (sometimes shared with the third eye) where the *amrita* (immortal nectar) of life begins to flow, an energetic liquid which symbolizes enlightened immortality. The crown chakra is the place where your kundalini sits in the top of your head once it has made its long journey up from your root space. This is the crown of enlightenment.

Your pituitary gland is a great conductor that links your thyroid, adrenals, and sex organs as well as your optic nerve (in conjunction with the pineal gland). It has so many functions that, like the pineal gland, it is considered a master gland. Some systems have the crown space governing both glands because they share so many vital functions. Your pituitary gland produces vasopressin and oxytocin, two hormones linked to amrita, kundalini energy, and states of ecstatic bliss.

This chakra is your center for ultimate realization. Spiritually, this means forming connections with the formless as you lift higher into limitlessness and communion with elevated states of consciousness. You'll be able to access a state of neutrality and begin the work of opening up to the nonphysical in order to bring more of the universal energies into your physical body and mind, including information from your multidimensional higher chakras. These states are not governed by space or time, and the quality of awareness you feel here is transcendent clarity.

Your dominant connection to Source is held by your body through the matrix of your emotions (frequencies). In the past, this connection has been blocked by the human consciousness through fear and control. This ability to gain control over our own emotions in the recent past few decades has meant that we can begin to take control of our own frequencies. Every energetic manifestation holds an imprint, so pay close attention to the frequency you hold. You carry a signature imprint, and everything you see is a mirror of that imprint; your energy is always working to manifest its match out in your physical reality. Carefully managing your emotions as they arise from your crown space will allow you to fully step into your creatorship as you begin to be more present with the frequencies you give your attention to. Remember: where the mind goes, energy flows!

Archetypes

The archetypal energies ruling the crown chakra are the Queen and the King. Both of these counterparts have a dualistic nature and deep shadow work to overcome. They either preside over their kingdoms with grace and kindness, or they fall into patterns of fear and allow their insecurities to cast shadows and cause demise. These are transcendent energies that are outside and above the inhabitants of the kingdom. In this case, they are divinely appointed godheads who rule not through royal bloodlines but by Divine assignment.

The Queen (or Empress) energy represents the sovereign feminine. In a world of rulers, she is an equal with her King and confidently rules with or without him. She is the embodiment of grace, forgiveness, intelligence, resolve, dignity, and courage. She is a fair judge and has the powers to see the full scope of the realm (and other realms) she rules. When she is in her light element, she is a balanced and fearless leader. When she is in her shadow, she can be demanding, self-righteous, and caught up in vanity and overwhelm.

The King (or Emperor) is the ruling commander over the entire spectrum of his kingdom. This Divine Masculine works alone but even better in tandem with a Queen who can provide the yin to his yang. He tends to all the high-level details and sits in his strength as a protector and noble leader. His duty is to create a safe kingdom for all to live peacefully. This archetype must beware of the shadow expression of ego, oppression, corruption, and control. To best maintain benevolence, the King needs to surrender to the Divine with humility and allow it to use him as a channel for good. This form of ego death is necessary for true transcendence to occur.

Personality

If you've ever met someone who comes across as patient and wise as they rise above the messiness of life (especially when the going gets tough), they likely have an open crown space. People with balanced and activated crown chakras tend to be highly connected to their own sense of objective awareness. They have no problem placing themselves as the observer in the game of reality. They are aligned with their beliefs and can see, express, and feel into the heart of a matter almost instantly. They have likely spent time meditating, working on themselves (in no small way), and have learned a great deal in life.

These individuals can distinguish life-force energy in other things (people, ideas, food, etc.), and because they are able to connect with heart-based wisdom through mental capacities, they intuitively feel their way through many situations, using both the heart and mind. They have achieved greater self-awareness and have healed many old patterns and attachments. Such people have a lot to teach and share with humanity, and they are natural teachers, eager to share and educate others on a higher path.

Underactive Chakra

Energy deficiencies here tend to be really noticeable, as they cause issues that are based on separation consciousness rather than unity/oneness. Loneliness and separation from others, feeling like you just don't belong, spiritual cynicism, and abandonment of religion or spirituality show up here a lot. An underactive crown chakra can also cause disassociation from your higher self and from spiritualism in general. This disconnect might look like forsaking your spiritual beliefs for a fatalistic view, reinforcing separation. Usually, you'll know right away if you fall into these categories. Many of us know someone who seems closed off to "woo-woo" ideas, and they typically fall into the left-brain category. They may also suffer from apathy, disconnection from joy, poor discernment, and even learning difficulties. With an underactive crown chakra, various neurological conditions, nerve problems, muscular atrophy (degeneration), or dullness of the senses may also be experienced.

Overactive Chakra

Energy excesses in the crown chakra can show up as many things, including overthinking, feelings of superiority, manic-depressive thinking or behavior, or obsession. Deeply analytical thoughts can be helpful, especially in certain instances; however, if you get stuck in your thinking, it can be paralyzing. The inability to decide on the smallest of things can really halt your life. Obsessing over an ex-partner, a toxic situation, or other minute details are all awareness issues. If you can shift your attention when these things come up, you'll create more balance in your crown chakra.

Balanced Chakra

A balanced crown chakra allows you to feel connected with your spirituality and a higher sense of your soul or spirit. This feeling of connection permits you to lean in and cultivate more trust in yourself, allowing your soul to guide you more fully. Openness here will feel like a refined sense of empathy and a decreased sense of egoism. Feeling separate from everything else falls away, revealing a sense of connectedness and oneness with All That Is. Self-trust and selflessness become central traits as do right action through increased awareness and perceptive abilities.

As you open up the higher chakras, each chakra below it will be enhanced, feeding into the next and amplifying their synergistic energies and relationships. A crown chakra that is open and balanced channels higher energies into the body to create not only your physical reality but also inspiration and higher levels of creativity in your life. Examining your beliefs will help you identify any distortions and patterns you are holding on to so that you can clear your path to healing the crown space and keep it open. Opening the crown chakra ultimately opens you up to greater self-leadership, spiritual self-improvement, and more embodied higher-self attributes, which expand with each higher chakra that opens.

Deities

The deities associated with the crown chakra are aligned with purity and transcendent consciousness. They are Shiva, Saraswati, and Buddha.

Shiva, in his Divine Masculine presence, represents pure consciousness. His beloved, Shakti, sits at the root space while he sits at the crown of creation, and they are different sides of the same coin. Shiva is included in the Hindu trinity (Shiva, Vishnu, Brahma) and holds this space at the crown chakra as a vigilant observer. He is known to be both creator and destroyer, endlessly sustaining the cosmos with his dance of creation and destruction. When Shiva is finished with his dance, this Universe will end and a new one will begin. Resurrection is his superpower, and you can call on him when approaching new beginnings and cocreation.

Saraswati, the Hindu goddess of learning and wisdom, is adored by the gods Brahma, Vishnu, and Shiva. She protects your intellectual abilities and guides you to successfully integrate the knowledge you acquire through education. Call on her to help you improve and perfect your memory, especially if you are studying.

Buddha, lord of compassion, is well known in almost every country across Southeast Asia. Born Siddhartha Gautama Buddha, he was an ancient philosopher, spiritual teacher, meditator, and religious leader who inspired nonviolence and enlightenment. He proposed the Eightfold Path to free humans from the incarnation cycle, which became the primary teachings for his followers. Buddha was said to have attained nirvana, and through his gifts, he was able to pass his knowledge on to others, as well as continue to live on as an Ascended Master. Call on him when you are calling in peace and enlightenment.

Planets

Jupiter rules the crown chakra. With its big, expansive nature and theme of optimism and growth, this planetary energy is the luckiest of all. It signifies higher learning, elevated consciousness, and capacity for growth. Jupiter governs philosophical and moral principles, making it the wisdom center of the solar system.

Crown Chakra Activity: Mandala Ritual

In this exercise, you'll be designing your own mandala so that you can begin to connect your inner world with your outer reality. *Mandala* is Sanskrit for "circle." It is a sacred geometric design typically used in Hinduism and Buddhist Tantra for meditation purposes. The shape of a circle represents oneness and unity; it is endless and timeless. It is the most common shape found in nature and is the container for all other forms. An atom, a seed, and the planet are all spheres and contain an enormous amount of innate intelligence. From inside a sphere, you can see all angles, all possibilities, and every timeline.

To build your circle, you can use objects you have around your house, or if you are feeling creative, you can pick up a blank piece of paper and some colored pencils and get to work. When foraging for materials, crystals and stones hold energy well, but be sure to select items that have meaning to you, hold beauty, or are inspiring. For example, you can use the following: crystals, seeds, shells or coral pieces, dried floral or herbal leaves (such as sage leaves and rose petals), little statues of beloved deities, or mala beads.

Arrange your items on a blank but dedicated altar space in the shape of a circle. Take your time organizing and placing each item carefully with nothing in the center.

If you are drawing your mandala, start with one center point and create an array of lines, shapes, and forms emanating from that point. You'll want this to be colorful, so take

Sacred Geometry: Flower of Life

You may have seen or heard of sacred geometry, but what is it exactly? These are geometric shapes that have unique mathematical properties along with ancient history and symbolism. Many believe that sacred geometry was brought to Earth from beings in alternate dimensions that needed a way to anchor important information about the nature and structure of reality for the inhabitants of Earth to access on this physical plane. Thus, the Flower of Life is depicted in many ancient temple sites and sacred texts across a wide variety of religions and writings.

The Flower of Life is more than just a simple grid of interlocking circles that build outward in a flowerlike shape. This sacred geometric pattern symbolizes creation and unity, metamorphosis and transformation. Think of this pattern as a blueprint for all life. Within it, you can glimpse the start of one cell (the seed of life) as it divides into two, four, eight, and so on. This shape is seen as more of an underlying building block that works in unseen harmonics to bring matter into form. It is thought to be the template for everything in existence for many cultures around the world, as the geometric forms found within it include foundational shapes such as the platonic solids, Metatron's Cube, the Kabbalistic Tree of Life, and the merkaba.

When the Flower of Life comes across your path, it is a reminder of your innate power as a creator being. It is a gentle pull back into the awareness that you are becoming what you think, feel, speak, and believe. The Flower of Life asks you to align your foundations with the field of oneness that is love. Each pattern you create from a strong foundation of love will replicate and grow so that you can be a more whole expression of yourself in your true nature.

some time to color it in afterward. Let your creativity guide you. This in itself is a whole meditational process that should be honored.

Set aside the next 10 to 15 minutes to sit with your mandala once it feels whole. You can add to it later—all art is a work in progress! As you are present with your mandala, a question you are contemplating may arise, or you may simply start receiving incoming downloads about a situation in your life. Be open to all angles, even the unexpected ones! Simply be present to what comes up, as this is your time to reflect on how the value of new perspective shows up in your life. Thank your higher self for assisting in its creation and allowing you to access infinite knowledge. You may come back to the mandala for more insight when you feel called.

When you are done with your ritual, allow the mandala to stay where it is for a moon cycle or until the next new moon or full moon before removing it.

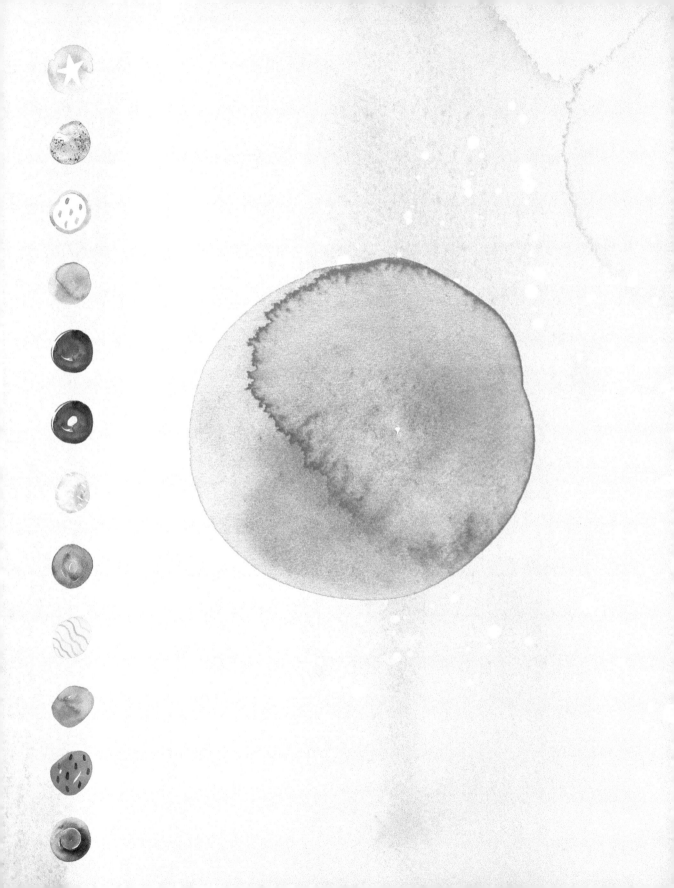

Chapter Thirteen
The 8th Chakra: Soul Star

The soul star, the first of your transpersonal chakras, connects you to your soul's journey, serving as a bridge to higher energies in the Universe. This is where your ascension journey officially begins. Your eighth chakra contains information about your soul's eternal blueprint. It is the template from which you pull your physical incarnation, depending on the soul's contracts, needs, wants, and lessons you wish to accomplish in your lifetime. Most of the major milestones of our lives are believed to be set up in a life-planning stage before we arrive Earth-side, and of course, free will plays a major part in the direction your life will go and how exactly your choices will play out. Once this transcendental chakra is activated, you begin to define yourself through your soul's gnosis (inner knowing) rather than through external influences. Your soul star chakra is also a center from which you access Divine love, the unconditional love that flows to you from Source energy—this is the highest frequency of the Universe.

Your soul star chakra has a silver cord running through all of your higher chakras directly connecting to your high heart chakra (see page 118). Once this connection has been established, you can download your soul's true purpose, which is passed down from your oversoul (see page 170 for more on this). Your soul access gives you the ability to be conscious in this life, moving you into your core self so that you can reclaim more of your wholeness. Think of this connection as a gateway between the spiritual and physical realms.

Upon opening this chakra, you acquire the acceptance of reality beyond the space-time continuum. This space holds all your potential for your soul's journey as well as your soul's purpose. If you are wondering just how big your soul and its potential are, know that your soul is much greater and more expansive than can be put into words. It would take a cosmic level of understanding to truly know the vastness of it. In fact, you are working with just a small portion of your soul in your current incarnation.

Just as your crown and root chakras create polarity with similar functions running in different directions, so do your soul star and Earth star chakras. These two chakras provide access to your Akashic records—one cosmic and one ancestral. Your soul star chakra feeds information in the form of light from your oversoul into your corporeal template from the present and future quantum potentials you are experiencing across all your incarnation journeys. Your Earth star chakra feeds information from your past experiences directly from the heart of Gaia as well as from your earthly ancestors.

You may have heard of karmic records, but this is an old template as we move into New Earth. Karma has typically been thought to be stored in the Earth star and soul star chakras and in the sushumna of the physical body. However, after the first wave of the Great Awakening in 2012, there has been a flow of light energy supporting the complete removal and dissipation of old karmic records that are no longer serving humanity. Since we are moving into more ever-present now moments and time is illusory, karma no longer exists as we have known it. That means we are no longer carrying debts from other lifetimes (they are being erased), and the only debts you have during this lifetime are the ones you continue to create and harbor yourself. This lifetime is the lifetime when we must learn to truly let go of the past and master all the lessons we are here to integrate.

Names & Meaning

The Sanskrit name for the eighth chakra is *vyapini*. In Hindu, this translates to "the all-pervading, reaching through, all-covering, diffusive," which makes sense for this chakra because the nature of your soul is all-encompassing and expansive. Your soul star chakra is also known as the "seat of the soul." Your connection to this chakra allows your soul to connect to your conscious mind. Your soul waits here to be downloaded and translated into your everyday awareness.

Color

The color of your soul star chakra is an iridescent rainbow with various hues of pink. To the naked eye, it would appear a shimmery pink, which changes as light is reflected and refracted. This chakra is pink because of its relationship to your high heart chakra. Sometimes another heart shade, sea-foam green, is associated with this chakra, making that its secondary color. The rainbow essence here allows your soul star to shine in many aspects and frequencies at once, representing your multidimensionality.

Location

Your soul star chakra is located about six inches above your head. The higher up we go, the more liquid these chakras of light become. One can seem to flow into the next, and, as a reminder, their estimated placement is not exact. This chakra resembles a halo around your crown and is often represented as such in ancient texts and depictions. Many people who have out-of-body or near-death experiences have also described a silver cord running from their body to their light body or soul star chakra. This cord is said to connect your body to your soul.

Estimated Activation

Your soul star is a transpersonal chakra, which, as a reminder, is any chakra outside your traditional seven corporeal chakras. This chakra will open after all your physical chakras have been activated. Your soul star chakra is intimately connected to your high heart chakra (see page 118), and there is a line of energy linking the two energy centers. Your eighth chakra usually comes online at the same time or shortly after your high heart begins to open. This opening allows you to fully access your spiritual codes, which have been waiting for you to re-remember them during this incarnation. Once you have advanced far enough to move most of your awareness into a heart-centered space, activation can happen anytime.

Senses

The higher your vibrational levels resonate, the more your advanced senses open up. Gamma brain waves (40 hertz or higher) put you into a flow state, a state of higher mental perception. Flow states are considered a type of heightened consciousness where attention and focus create a bubble around you in which time seems to melt away altogether. In this bubble, it's easy and effortless to accomplish everything you need to do and to access unlimited creative potential. Advanced meditators and those who are consciously aware are naturally optimized toward this state.

Function

Your transpersonal chakras, including your soul star, do not associate with body parts, glands, or systems like your physical chakras do. Instead, these "sleeping" chakras are accessible to you on your path of self-actualization and enlightenment. They open once you consciously awaken to your multidimensionality. And, once open, they generally stay open. They are considered ascension chakras that reveal themselves after significant work and clearing has been done on the inner planes and heart coherence has been reached. We might be conscious of a few of these chakras, but for the most part, they remain untouched by our everyday awareness. These higher chakras have the function of blending transformational energies coming in from everywhere in the Universe with our physical being. Our brains and bodies adapt to frequency changes to enable us to process new levels of perception. In this way, we can extrapolate many more layers of our existence and apply it to the scope of the reality we are creating.

Your soul star chakra extends up toward the higher planes as it pours energy and information into your physical body, and it takes information from your crown space back up through the soul star portal to be transmitted to your higher self. Think of an ethernet cable versus an old dial-up modem. We have to upgrade our software to be able to move more information very quickly, so we need to make sure our upper chakras are extremely open. To aid in this function, your soul star chakra activates your smaller secondary chakras in your hands, feet, and ears to open more fully. This opening helps accommodate you in channeling higher levels of information to and from your environment. More than ever, your mission as a human being is to bring in direction and alignment from your soul and anchor that within your physical body (embodiment) and ground it with Earth energy.

Your soul star chakra is a place where specific Akashic soul-level information resides, and many of those who are able to reach this information do so through this portal. If you are searching for a greater truth regarding your soul's mission, you can ask to access this information, and you will be shown all relevant information from a higher perspective. Author of *How to Read the Akashic Records*, Linda Howe, states that information from this realm is compassionately delivered and guided to you by your masters, teachers, and loved ones, but you can also think of this information as coming from different versions of yourself—past, present, and future.

This space is also a connection point to your high heart, which physically holds the capacity to strengthen your immune system as it generates thymus-stimulating heart rhythms. As your vulnerability, openness, and heart-centered awareness grow, this connection strengthens and opens wider. With both of these advanced chakras open, a channel forms that allows spiritual inspiration to flow in and take root as personal expression. The author of *The Crystalline Transmission*, Katrina Raphaell, refers to this as *octavation*—activating a higher octave of frequency to benefit all humans and the New Earth. With these higher frequencies recoding your DNA, you are becoming more and more of your true self every day!

Archetypes

The archetypes associated with your soul star chakra are the Self and the Seeker.

The soul is a watcher, a witness, an observer. In its full radiance, it is an uninhibited, nonjudgmental, rainbow of prismatic light. The Self is a unified consciousness, which experiences the full spectrum of life's offerings. This archetype represents all potentials of you, in any manner of individuation. In its light representation, the Self is autonomous, accepting, and integrated. In its shadow, it is disjointed and scattered. You can also choose to see the shadow aspect as the Other, or anything that is outside the Self. The Self is whole and therefore comprised of both light and shadow and requires this knowledge to be fully actualized. This can be a challenge for the ego, which is always seeking to assert itself. Once enough of the ego mind can be reconciled (not dissolved!), a more whole you can blossom through your true self.

The Seeker arises when the Self decides to go on a journey. Also referred to as the Traveler or the Apprentice, the Seeker understands that the journey is just as much inner as it is outer. The deepest meanings are just beyond casual conditioning, and the Self can take you to the edges of that. To go a step farther, the Seeker rallies you to new adventures waiting on the other side of your current reality. Seekers follow a path to truth, increasing the soul's expansion and growth. If you find yourself stuck in the slumber of day-to-day life, you need only awaken the Seeker to attune you to the great unknown.

Personality

Someone whose soul star chakra has been activated will be attuned and open to the guidance, wisdom, and intuition from their higher self. These beings will practice internal alchemy because they are curious about their own nature and that of reality. They will explore and master work within the subtle energy realms and are likely experienced meditators able to highly focus their attention for extended periods. A person with an activated soul star chakra will possess a high degree of self-awareness and is usually capable of seeing the many different angles of a situation and the larger picture. They will be extremely balanced, having done work to consciously raise their kundalini energy and balance the yin and yang energies inside the physical body to work toward wholeness and integration. Since they are connected to their heart wisdom, they are compassionate and understanding.

You don't have to be a monk in a monastery to live a life like this. In fact, many spiritual people in the world are simply awakened people who are trying their best to uphold heart-based values as core principles in their everyday lives through basic means. Because they have done extensive inner work, they are more likely to choose to align themselves through their work as either spiritual teachers or healers. However, people with an advanced spiritual interest and knowledge may also be found in nonspiritual careers.

Chakra Awakening

There is no overactivity or underactivity in your transpersonal chakras. They are simply asleep or awake. When you have activated your soul star chakra, you will experience accelerated spiritual awakening. This awakening can come in many layers and levels, and as you progress through evolutionary shifts, you will continue to unlock different states of consciousness, expanding your perception and opening you up to galactic, universal, and Divine energies. With the high heart and soul star chakras activated, the soul begins to sense itself as a part of a larger community of beings, as well as a part of the collective energies of the Universe. Here, the soul is connected to the mind so that you are able to sense energetic blockages on the physical and spiritual levels.

Deities

The goddesses and gods associated with the soul star chakra are Sophia, Isis, and Horus.

Goddess Sophia, the great ineffable mystery of Divine Feminine essence, helps usher you into ascension through her embodiment of higher-power alignment. Traditionally, she is well known in Gnosticism for being a creatrix of All That Is and in Hellenistic mythology as the goddess of wisdom. She is perhaps one of the most important deities, as she arrives to show us how fate and destiny operate in relationship to free will and synchronicity. She is a reminder that the spiritual unseen aspects of us are the most vital pieces to call into alignment and that we are always pulling that spiritual aspect into form through our conscious choice, creating magic. If we want to create heaven on Earth, the most meaningful expression is your own inherent expression of unconditional love.

Isis (Auset) is an Ascended Master and ancient Egyptian deity known as the goddess of 10,000 names (this represents her number of forms and associations across cultures). She is a multidimensional and multifaceted being, capable of playing roles beyond form. Isis is devoted—she put her husband Osiris back together when he was in pieces—and motherly, though those roles don't limit or define her essence. Through her strength, Isis asks you to let go of any old identities and embrace your true spiritual self, because you are much more than meets the eye. Call upon her for assistance reaching your uncontainable, eternal, infinite, and endless true nature.

Horus, the Egyptian sky god, is known as "the one far above." He is depicted as a man with a falcon head wearing a red and white crown, a symbol of the serpentine kundalini energy uniting with the enlightenment of the spiritual sushumna and creating *amrita,* or "nectar of the gods." Horus was the name for any godly incarnated king, and thus there were many (and all of them ruled Egypt at some point). Though he took on a multitude of different incarnations, his spirit was always the god Horus. Summon him to remember who you truly are: a sovereign being of light in this world here to accomplish your earthly mission.

Planets

The soul star chakra has two luminary bodies that rule it: Saturn (the planet) and Chiron (the comet). Saturn shows up to represent the lessons you are here to harmonize and work through. Saturn will show you the harsh aspects of you that indeed need healing in this lifetime. In its positive connotation, this energy presents an initiation into self-mastery as a gateway to healing.

Chiron is also known as "the wounded healer," and although this orbiting comet is small, he is mighty. The wounded healer refers to the notion that one who has gone through the shadow is best equipped to teach others how to heal. Chiron energy is a reminder that we must be prepared to look at our own wounding to be able to hold the space of grace for others to step into themselves. This is the energy of wayshowing.

Soul Star Chakra Exercise: Syncing to Your Oversoul Meditation

When we think of ascension, we often associate it with an upward flow of energy. In reality, it's likened to energy that radiates everywhere in all directions simultaneously. Ascension energy is the gradual ability of your body, mind, and spirit to incorporate more light, vibrate higher, and realize its higher multidimensionality. To get there, you need to start by realizing the potential of your own soul in its fullness. Your soul star chakra is all about self-actualization, and in this meditation, you'll tap into your true self by syncing to your oversoul (see page 170).

First, find a quiet space to yourself, and allow 20 to 30 minutes for this meditation. Breathe in and out deeply, slowing your breath and focusing on your high heart (in the center of your chest between your throat and heart chakras). Start with stating your intention aloud: "Spirit help me to connect to my oversoul today. Help me reach self-realization to my highest capacity beyond the understanding of my mind. Allow me to surrender into the truest essence of myself, now."

Next, proceed down the following list of small requests for your oversoul. Your job is to simply witness and listen for the responses you receive without judgment and without trying to force an answer. If you get stuck, move on to the next query. Try to get through at least two each time you do this meditation.

SHOW ME A DIFFERENT LIFETIME IN WHICH I HAVE LIVED (IN THE PAST OR THE FUTURE) THAT PLAYS A ROLE IN MY LIFE TODAY.

WHAT WAS THE BIGGEST CHALLENGE I FACED IN THIS LIFETIME? WHO WAS INVOLVED?

WAS THERE A RESOLUTION?

WHAT WAS THE GREATEST LESSON I HAVE LEARNED ACROSS ALL LIFETIMES? WHAT LESSON DO I HAVE YET TO LEARN?

SHOW ME THE HIGHLIGHTS OF THE MOST JOYFUL MEMORIES ACROSS ALL MY (PAST OR CURRENT) LIFETIMES.

SHOW ME THE TIMELINE, EITHER IN THIS LIFETIME OR ANOTHER, IN WHICH I AM STRUGGLING MOST.

SHOW ME A TIMELINE, EITHER IN THIS LIFETIME OR ANOTHER, WHERE I AM EXPERIENCING SUCCESS, LOVE, OR FULFILLMENT.

SHOW ME THE MOST IMPORTANT CONTRIBUTION I AM MAKING ACROSS ALL TIMELINES.

ALLOW ME TO WITNESS OPTIONS FOR RESOLUTION OF A RELEVANT SITUATION I AM CURRENTLY EXPERIENCING.

You may come up with other questions to ask once you have practiced listening for the answers. People who have the most success receiving responses are those who practice patience above all else. In time, these answers will start to flow to you consciously as you reinforce this connection through practice.

Afterward, thank your oversoul for joining you and for making time to connect with you in meditation. Take a few moments at the end of your practice to journal any observations or insights you have that you'd like to expand upon.

The Oversoul

Your oversoul, the main umbrella of your soul, is a composite consciousness that manages all your incarnations at once—some on Earth and some in other places of the galaxy. Think of this as a wider version of you that is present in many realities simultaneously and offering you guidance, support, and direction in each. All are working with different pieces of you across multiple timelines, integrating lessons along the way. In fact, each time you acquire new levels of consciousness, the information is uploaded to your oversoul and transmitted to all your incarnations, allowing you to access your multidimensionality during any of your lifetimes in any reality or dimension.

Your soul's purpose includes all the soul contracts you are currently connected to or have agreed upon. Once you begin to access this information from across your lifetimes, you can begin the work of rewriting it to your current needs, bringing healing to all timelines.

Your oversoul manages all your lifetimes beyond your current awareness, even those taking place on other planets. As it does so, it filters your conscious access to them. This can feel limiting to the ego, but remember that you chose to be in this incarnation and you are permitted access to any information that will help you serve your higher purpose. Much of this information comes through in subtle ways through the nonphysical realm for direct integration. You can rest assured you have everything you will ever need in this life to complete what you came here to do.

Chapter Fourteen
The 9th Chakra: Stellar Gateway

A scending up our chakra's pillar of light, we reach the stellar gateway chakra, the next layer of consciousness and spiritual achievement that opens us to worlds beyond our own. Your stellar gateway is a cosmic portal to the rest of the galaxy. Directly above your soul star, this chakra is a stargate to your galactic heritage and lineage of light. With both of these centers open, very high-frequency golden light (from the Divine Mind) can be channeled into the soul and all its incarnations. Your oversoul extends to include energies from this plane (including your galactic incarnations!). Your stellar gateway chakra bridges your humanity to your star family.

This gateway represents a more formal link to your celestial connections, such as the Pleiadians, Arcturians, Sirians, Lyrans, Lemurians, Cassiopeians, Mantis, Andromedans, or Zetas. There are so many more civilizations that exist across all the planets that it would be impossible to name them, but these races are just a few representing our neighboring systems, constellations, planets, and galaxies. The stars are home to many different races and beings. It is rumored that beings from these systems helped create the great Earth experiment and seeded the DNA of Earthlings here to create humans. Most of the celestial connections exist within higher dimensions and are not considered embodied beings; rather, they are forms of light consciousness. There are a few of each of these beings on the Galactic Federation of Light that serve together as a collective to aid humanity through its current process of ascension. It's through the stellar gateway chakra that they may be reached.

While it's not necessary to identify with one origin story or another, many of us have stepped down from various star systems and lineages. Humans are a composite of our stellar ancestry. We were made from the stuff of stars, and back to stars we shall go when our time here is over. While you're here, though, take your time enjoying all the lessons you came to learn about mastering the physical, emotional, mental, and spiritual parts of your true self. Remembering your cosmic link in all of this is part of the adventure.

Understanding your unique gifts and how you came to be is part of decoding your multidimensionality. It is the next step to deepening your understanding of your true purpose and receiving guidance from outside yourself as you work toward your highest good. As you focus on the smaller details of living, remember your true expansive nature, which is Divine love and light. You are beyond your body and beyond form. As you overcome challenges and transmute energy here, you send that freedom back across the cosmos. And anytime you need a cosmic perspective, all you need to do is ask.

Names & Meaning

Stellar means "of the stars," and gateway means an "opening" or "doorway." The Sanskrit word for the ninth chakra is vyomanga, meaning "cosmic" or "space body." It's no surprise that the energy connecting you to the stars flows through this channel. This chakra is celestial in nature and gives you access to energies beyond this Earth. You may also hear this chakra referred to as the galactic gateway or cosmic gateway. These terms allude to your connectivity to worlds beyond the Earth plane.

Color

Gold best represents your stellar gateway chakra because it is known to be the highest healing frequency in the galaxy. Golden light energy contains wisdom, accelerated healing, optimism, and enlightenment. As we increase our vibrations, the pillar of white light streaming down from the Divine gateway all the way through the body and into the Earth star chakra slowly takes on golden hues. One day, this entire pillar will be gold, as will our merkaba light body. We will be known to our star sisters and brothers throughout the Universe as the Golden Ones.

Location

The stellar gateway chakra, the second of your transpersonal chakras, is located approximately 12 to 18 inches above the top of your head, directly situated over your soul star chakra. One arm's length above the head is a good approximation. This etheric spiritual chakra relates to star systems, or Logos, from outside our own.

Estimated Activation

Your stellar gateway is a sleeping chakra that activates once your soul star chakra has been activated. This activation can happen any time after significant work has been done to clear through blockages of current and past lifetimes. Most people who have worked with connecting to their soul-level energy will see this activation occur during this lifetime on Earth.

Senses

There is a burgeoning brainwave state that researchers have just barely started to identify and explore called lambda (100 to 200 hertz). This is the fastest brainwave and can be found in Tibetan monks who have spent decades meditating. According to eyewitnesses and personal accounts, some of these individuals have started to open the doors to their multidimensionality, including awakening abilities of levitation, telepathy, telekinesis, and teleportation (known as bilocation, or being in two places at once).

What's even more interesting is that this brainwave rides on the slowest wave, an epsilon wave (0.5 hertz or less). This means that to tap into our highest potential, we must begin to integrate these energies (that is, slow down) in order to wake up.

Function

This energetic chakra raises your awareness to more than who you are as a physical being on Earth. The stellar gateway chakra is all about the realization of your cosmic blueprint. Your cosmic blueprint is a map of your multidimensional self and a template for accessing your embodiments beyond the Earth grid and related timelines. These timelines include the past, present, and future ones that you are incarnated within on different planets and star systems.

You are always operating and integrating all your lifetimes into your current now moment. This brings awareness and connection to your personal space-time continuum and helps you realize where you are along your ultimate path. If you need help or direction on your mission or your life's work, you can call on help from your star sisters and brothers. Your stellar gateway chakra enhances communication with enlightened beings, even the ones in the higher dimensions like the Arcturians or Andromedans. Remember, the higher the dimension, the faster the vibrational frequency (and the more challenging it is to receive messages from them). Frequencies in the easy communication bandwidth for us tend to be fourth to seventh dimensional beings like the Sirians, Pleiadians and Lemurians.

Another function of the ninth chakra is its ability to pull in information to your monadic core. Think of a monad as the aspects of your consciousness belonging to your higher self. Your monadic core is comprised of your seventh (crown), eighth (soul star), and ninth (stellar gateway) chakras, which work in a triad to pass information down to your physical form and integrate this information into your body on an atomic level. In other words, this triad is in charge of the synthesis of cosmic energies into physical matter. It widens its scope when your stellar gateway chakra opens, and the monad is able to download more complete galactic information from your holographic architecture. It can do this because the flow of stellar information in this triad actually helps shape the surrounding aura from an ovoid (like an oval) to a toroid (like a doughnut). This flow of energy is beneficial for your aura and helps increase the strength of your energy field.

Perhaps my favorite function of the stellar gateway chakra is that it opens a prominent channel for astral travel. Astral travel is a way to move through space and time to be able to witness yourself in different places and timelines, anywhere in the Universe. With this gateway open, it becomes easier to access these inherent abilities. Some people have no problem astral traveling effortlessly, but for many, it comes easiest through a lucid dream state. Astral travel becomes another way to visit versions of reality you haven't experienced before or want more information about. For example, you could visit the moon, other nearby planets, the rings of Saturn, or even take a quick visit to the Galactic Federation of Light mothership—a ship believed by some to be docked close to Earth for the current awakening. How exciting!

Archetypes

The archetypes associated with the ninth chakra are the Shapeshifter and the Seed.

The Shapeshifter is truly a multidimensional being, able to morph into another form at will. This archetype is complex and asks you to consciously choose which direction you are headed at any given time. If you aren't satisfied with the results of your choice, you have the opportunity to change paths rapidly. Changing paths may require your complicit willingness to shift into another version of you to get your goals accomplished. This archetype points to the part of you that can always choose to switch to an alternate perspective to receive a wider view of your circumstance. The Shapeshifter is in all of us. With each click of the kaleidoscopic lens, you have unlimited opportunities to access various versions of realities at your fingertips.

The Seed archetype alludes to your cosmic origins and speaks to the greater part of you that may feel small but holds much power. A pumpkin grows from a pumpkin seed—the entire lifecycle process resides in a compact container. Yet it is whole. It is the beginning and the end. Similarly, we were born from the stars, and we'll each return there someday. Our genes express a celestial ancestry in which ancient stories are embedded. When we look to the Seed, we can see where we came from. This archetype has generative qualities and appears when you are going through growth phases. The Seed knows that to become a fruit, there must be many different transformations and elements that pull together to manifest your creation, just like you are tasked to pull in all the extra-dimensional layers of you.

Personality

On top of having a loving, considerate, and conscious presence, someone with an open stellar gateway chakra is likely an unconventional thinker and extremely connected. A person who has tapped into their cosmic potential has conscious knowledge and connections to their galactic star family and community. They know that we are not alone, and they are open to connecting with cosmic energies. These other energies may seem alien to some, yet for star seeds, they feel right at home. Those who are cosmically connected can likely tap into their multidimensionality in a more conscious way than others.

Want to know where you came from? Just take a look at the life you're living now. For example, you may be living another interdimensional reality in the sixth or ninth dimension within the Pleiades star system. In this alternate lifetime, let's say you are contributing toward creating advancements in technology. It's likely that your Earth work reflects aspects that are being carried out in your other lifetimes on these planes. With an open stellar gateway chakra, you would have conscious access to information that you are working on from this separate dimension as it applies to your current lifetime. In your current reality, you might take an interest in science, math, or quantum physics. Maybe in a lifetime on Arcturus, you are practicing healing (most Arcturians are natural healers). In this lifetime, you would likely find yourself drawn to crystals, Reiki, sound healing, and various spiritual practices. Perhaps you are a life coach or in a healing profession yourself. Your other lifetimes have a very direct (although mostly unconscious) influence on your current lifetime, whether you know it or not. Consciously accessing these lifetimes will allow you to directly integrate your various experiences into your higher self and oversoul.

Deities

The deities represented in the stellar gateway chakra are Green Tara and the Galactic Federation of Light. These beings carve an ascension pathway for us through the stars and beyond.

The goddess Green Tara is one of the 21 emanations of Tara, a Tibetan Buddhist deity. In her galactic Green Tara form, she descends from the Sirius Star Nation and is known as "she of a thousand stars." She is a renowned cosmic diplomat and experienced shapeshifter. She has helped many civilizations through their own ascension process by helping them understand the nature of reality and the quantum universe, the Law of Attraction, regeneration, and spiritual advancement. She helped the people of Sirius begin to track the progress of the soul through incarnation cycles, just as the Buddhists do in their ancient culture. Call on Green Tara when you are looking to increase your involvement with the multidimensional aspects of yourself and working on expanding your natural abilities (like telepathy) for your ascension journey.

The Galactic Federation of Light, also known as the Sphere Being Alliance or simply the Alliance, is composed of beings from neighboring dimensions who support the light forces within the Universe. They are benevolent in nature and cluster together in collectives representing their various star systems like the Pleiades, Sirius, Arcturus, and Andromeda. It is said that there are several hundred groups working together on different councils and a high council. These advanced civilizations have the best interest of Earth at heart, and they are providing much unseen direction and protection for humanity at this time. They have varied characteristics as they are mostly different species, but they all share a unified purpose: to bring a heart-centered focus to Earth at this time and preserve the peace within the cosmos at large. Ask for their direction and protection while you go about your Earth mission, as they have much wisdom to share.

Planets

The dual luminary bodies that represent the stellar gateway chakra are truly galactic in nature. The points Alcyone and Ophiuchus are on the same axis as the Galactic Center, which form a pair of polar-opposite stargates. Alcyone, known as the Great Central Sun, is the main sun of the Pleiades. It is known as the Silver Gateway to Heaven and sits at 0 degrees Gemini. Directly across from Alcyone and through the Galactic Center sits Ophiuchus. This constellation is sometimes referred to as the thirteenth sign of the zodiac, a more recent astrological hypothesis. It's also known as the Golden Gateway to Heaven, sitting at 0 degrees Sagittarius. These two stargates form a galactic portal and bring you to the Gate of God, a place of transitional energy. When you are at this point, you cross over or ascend into another realm.

Stellar Gateway Exercise: Merkaba Galactivation Meditation

As you've read, your merkaba is a light body ascension technology that surrounds your physical body, but what exactly does it look like and how can you make sure yours is activated? The shape of a merkaba is formed by two intersecting tetrahedrons that interlock to form a three-dimensional star. The moving shapes are spinning in opposite directions as they rotate, forming a three-dimensional field. Your merkaba is a technology that has come back during this time of Great Awakening on the planet, so if you haven't specifically done work to activate your merkaba, you'll want to now!

In this meditation, we'll astral travel through your merkaba to explore the galaxy. To start out, you'll want to know where you wish to travel, and set aside some time free of distractions so you can focus. Take several deep breaths to clear your headspace, and as you exhale, imagine your breath cleansing your immediate energy field.

Start by building your light body. First, visualize two luminous golden-tinged translucent tetrahedrons that intersect—one pointing up and one pointing down with you in the middle. (A tetrahedron is a four-faced three-dimensional triangle.) Next, program your merkaba for where in the galaxy you'd like to visit. You could travel to another part of the solar system, a different planet, a constellation, the Galactic Federation of Light, an undiscovered area of the Universe, another timeline, or even another dimension—the possibilities are unlimited! After you select a choice, you'll need to *galactivate* your merkaba to make the journey.

Focus on your breathing and the merkaba field surrounding you now. Visualize the interlocking sides beginning to spin. This may appear as a fuzzy unified field or bubble around you as it spins faster and faster. Then clear your mind and allow the blackness of space to surround you. Follow your mind where it wants to go; don't block yourself from overthinking during this process. Simply allow yourself to travel to your destination, observing with an open mind.

Pay attention to any feedback the mind may be communicating to you. What do you see? Do you want to get out of your merkaba and walk around? Do you feel energized, open, positive? Try to absorb as much information as you can about the experience, even if the first few tries aren't visually stimulating for you. Maybe you just sense color, warmth, or shifting energies. Remember to only observe. You aren't here on your journey to fix anything. If you encounter any other beings or versions of yourself, you may converse with them.

If you are having trouble traveling, you may prefer to sit quietly inside your merkaba and just ask where it is you should go, if anywhere. Notice if your consciousness is able to connect outside of your physical body with your higher self. And remember, you are not your thoughts or actions—you transcend that—you are just the observer in this vehicle.

When you are ready to come back from your alternate reality, parallel dimension, or place in the stars, simply return to your light body. Ask to return to the Earth plane and then open your eyes. Imagination is a vehicle you can use to explore yourself and the stars as you shift into your highest potential, so give it a try. You may discover the mysteries of the unknown are closer than you expected!

The Sixth, Seventh, and Eighth Dimensions

The six, seventh, and eighth dimensions, or the higher dimensions, represent a fuller picture of reality at this time. As we open the higher, transpersonal chakras, they correspond more with the dimensional levels of vibration than anything on the Earth plane. It is important to understand that they are mere frequencies apart and are nestled inside one another. Each dimension presents a new viewpoint and a broader and higher perspective, along with carrying higher vibrations with less matter or density. Many of our galactic ancestors reside in these dimensional belts.

The sixth dimension (6D) is a plane that is relatively easy for us as humans to access. This plane creates much of the blueprints for our reality through sacred geometric templates. This level of consciousness exists beyond time, and beings here fully realize the illusory game of physical reality. This dimension is considered host to Christ Consciousness and spiritual realization. Beings operating at a sixth-dimensional level know inherently that they create their entire reality and do not need to use choice to manifest; instead, they use thoughts.

The seventh dimension (7D) is a conscious container that is slightly larger with a higher perspective that there are many creators and infinite realities. The beings here no longer need to use thought to manifest; instead, their desires create instant manifestation. They have an unconditional loving presence and strive to create harmony out of every situation. Love, peace, and empowerment reign in this vibrational level. The best way to imagine this dimension is to hear this frequency through sound.

The eighth dimension (8D) is a container that holds the multiverse as we know it. The multiverse includes many universes and many timelines. This can be hard to conceptualize but is best translated through the energy of pure light. The eighth dimension is a nondual dimension that contains information of everything in the matrix of existence. All truths belong to this level of consciousness.

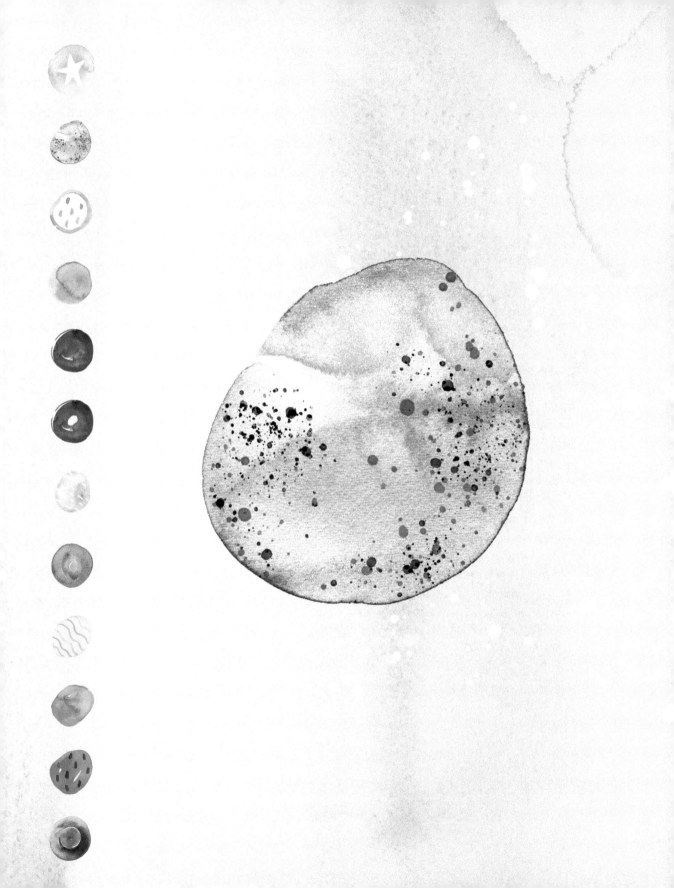

Chapter Fifteen
The 10th Chakra: Universal Gateway

The third transpersonal chakra, the universal gateway, gives you direct access to the whole Universe, the matrix that holds every reality together as we know it. This chakra most closely corresponds with the eighth dimension. Think of the eighth dimension as a library of records of everything in the Universe, containing all that is, was, and ever will be. Configurations of pure light essence flow down from this elevated plane to create sound, sacred geometry, and eventually physical form. Your universal gateway, the collective chakra, provides a portal to accessing the knowledge of the Universe in this dimension and many worlds beyond what we can imagine.

The term *Universe* normally describes our solar system with our planets, moons, asteroids, and sun. When we speak of the universal gateway, this term includes the greater Universe and all the galaxies and planets within them. There are over 200 to 300 billion galaxies in our observable Universe, and our Milky Way is but one. The Milky Way galaxy is estimated to contain 100 billion planets, making Earth an incredibly special place to be. The Universe seems to go on forever and can be an unfathomable concept for our limited human minds to comprehend. However, with this chakra available to humanity, we are ready to go beyond anything we have ever known. In terms of consciousness, this is groundbreaking.

That brings us to our next subject: the collective consciousness. This field of consciousness broadly describes all the experiences, timelines, and possibilities that have occurred, are currently taking place, or will one day manifest in the entire Universe. This field, normally held in the fourth dimension, is linked intrinsically to the eighth dimension. Both dimensions hold precious information about collective consciousness, and all this information is accessible through the universal gateway chakra. This chakra is a doorway that allows you to directly access all levels of consciousness available in the Universe and break through constraints and illusions going on within your own collective consciousness. Let's look at Earth as an example and explore how this applies to our current process of ascension.

When we are experiencing a dark age on this planet, the planet and all her inhabitants vibrate slower, and the density creates immense polarization. We are at a special time of re-remembering now. We remember a time of light, and we are entering a new Golden Age when this light is coming back to us (for more, see "The Photon Belt" on page 106). This is a time when we are beginning to shed unconscious programming that has kept us in separation mentality rather than unity consciousness. As we open up to the knowledge that this chakra is pulling in, we are better able to cut through all the false perceptions that keep us locked in limited views or unwillingly manipulated and controlled. We can perceive the whole Universe as living parts to one connected being. This oneness is a concept illuminated in detail in chapter 16, as it is represented through your eleventh chakra. It is heartfelt and peaceful, and it underlies everything we can conceive, both the seen and unseen.

Names & Meaning

The universal gateway chakra is also commonly referred to as the collective conscious chakra. In Sanskrit, the name for it is *ananta* or *anantha*, meaning "infinite, endless, limitless, or eternal." These are all beautiful ways to describe the Universe, as it is an immeasurable space without borders, edges, or boundaries. Collective consciousness refers to thought forms, ideas, programming, conditioning, and acculturation that civilizations share. Earth has a consciousness, as do all the humans inhabiting her. Your own unique consciousness possesses a perspective that feeds into the whole.

Color

The color associated with your universal gateway chakra is silver. This bandwidth is considered feminine and spiritual in nature. It is reflective and protective, as it mirrors any energy that is directed toward it. This color is associated with divinity, responsibility, truth, and redemption.

Location

The third of your transpersonal chakras is located approximately two feet to two and a half feet above the top of your head, directly situated above your stellar gateway chakra. One and a half to two arm's lengths above the head is a close approximation. The universal gateway is an etheric spiritual chakra, and it relates to the entire matrix of the Universe.

Estimated Activation

Your universal gateway is a sleeping chakra that activates once your stellar gateway chakra has been activated. This activation can occur any time after significant work has been done to clear through blockages from your galactic and Earth-side lifetimes. Most people who have done the work of unlearning (deconditioning) from the matrix will see this activation occur during this lifetime on Earth.

Senses

With an awakened tenth chakra, you will possess and expand on all other available senses, both physical and metaphysical. You will awaken to your abilities to command states of matter at will. For a physical being, this ability is quite exciting because it means manifesting desires will become easier to achieve more rapidly than ever before. This level wakes up the ability to consciously master creatorship by thought alone (and lots of practice).

Function

Your universal gateway chakra has a few primary functions; namely, it supports our collective intelligence and expansion. As beings hailing from all over the Universe, we are having a human experience, and our individual consciousness supports our personal growth. When we learn, we evolve. In the same way, our collective consciousness supports the growth of humanity as a whole. Each of our individual vibrations creates a larger collective of similar vibrational energy that holds characteristics of the sum of the parts. As humans from Earth, many of us are seeing divergent paradigms polarizing the planet right now. By connecting to your universal gateway chakra, you can better perceive the truth of reality and thereby move humanity into a higher-vibrational resonance. If we can continue to hold the collective vision of a peaceful, harmonized, unified consciousness, each of us will help shape and advance Earth in its evolution.

The universal gateway chakra unlocks mastery of matter and consciousness (and some would also include space-time). Most of us are already awakened to the fact that a sentient consciousness resides within all living things. When we expand upon this, our souls are all connected as one. What one person is experiencing is a mirror for what you are here to heal and eventually reunify with Source energy. This mastery challenges humanity to reform its ways through the heart. Through the universal gateway chakra, you can begin to understand all the layers of your heart as they apply to the collective as well as all the quantum realities you are operating within.

Simply put, heart coherence and universal understanding must begin to be a part of every interaction in order to maintain a higher frequency of a singular being. Heart consciousness and the understanding of oneness, along with the mind, are integral to our human operating system. It is always reaching out and assessing where our frequencies must be neutralized—we know that to transcend anything, neutrality is key. Neutrality doesn't mean we don't care; it means we discern wisely.

In this case, let's think about interacting with someone of a lower frequency than yourself. Instead of resisting and pushing them away, try to bring acceptance to what is coming up for you when you have an exchange with this person. This lesson is about resolving the discordant consciousness in such a way that you bring the entire consciousness into the connection of the heart, the basis for reconnection. This process brings neutral or negative energy to a higher space, and it is the best place to start in order to heal the entire human collective consciousness. When you release attachment to resistance, you open up more connection with those who hold a similar frequency to your own, thus expanding universal consciousness everywhere. This universal view aids in strengthening not only your heart coherence but also your entire chakra system.

Everything we seek to understand about this endless expanse is first created inside us. Fractal universes within universes build upon themselves, awaiting our discovery.

Archetypes

The archetypes present at this level of consciousness are the Unseen and the Shaman. Both of these concepts can be elusive to grasp because they are rather mystical in nature.

The Unseen's essence is clairvoyant guidance in the form of an ever-present energy that is indeed universal in nature. Your ancestors and all versions of your spirit rest eternally in the Unseen. This energy may come to you in many intangible forms, and its instructive presence can only be sensed. Step forward and embrace the messages you receive from the Unseen, and then add a dose of human discernment to parse wisdom from these communications. Remember, just because you can't see it doesn't mean it's not there. This may challenge your perception of reality, but as you step into a willingness to trust, you'll learn to let this archetype guide you wherever you need to go.

The Shaman is a medicinal sage, also known as the Healer. Traditionally, this archetypal energy emerges when you express willingness to work with the realms of the Unseen. The Shaman must pass through a dark night of the soul to heal personal wounds. Normally, this period reflects a time of inner crisis in which illusions are shattered and the shadow self becomes integrated. After this time is complete, you are prepared to share the healing with others collectively. Shamanic energy is also present as we heal the shadows and corrupt underpinnings of the collective on a whole. The Shaman knows that healing isn't linear, but rather it ebbs and flows as your journey expands. Remember, you are fearless, and there is nothing you will be served in this lifetime your inner shaman won't be able to handle.

Personality

Those with an active universal gateway chakra tend to be community minded and have lots of big ideas about improving the world. Rebellious by nature, these innovators challenge public policies and shun the norm. If a questionable rule or law exists, they are the first to ask, "Why?" They possess a bigger-picture awareness, which allows others to feel comfortable and inspired in their presence. This type of person is usually the one setting off a chain of awakening in their footsteps. These souls tend to be activists and leaders who organize community drives, nonprofits, and charity events or come up with resolutions to complex collective issues. They stand up for the underdog and marginalized groups while holding the vision of a brighter tomorrow. As activators of social and cultural change, they help knit together the broken pieces of humanity.

A person with an open universal gateway chakra has no trouble thinking abstractly; in fact, they love tapping into their creativity. They have a great grip on their creatorship and know that when they put their mind to something, they can effortlessly achieve their desires. These types have lightning intuition, which is translated through skillful expression. They encourage others to express themselves to achieve their highest potential, too. By consistently working at a very high level of consciousness, they influence reality and make a difference with all they do.

Deities

The ruling deities associated with your universal gateway chakra are Maya, Ma'at, Jagannath, and Lilith.

Maya, the goddess of illusion, appears in Hindu, Buddhist, and Greco-Roman traditions. Her message is simple: what appears to be real is merely part of a greater truth. It's hard for us to imagine anything outside our illusions, as we can easily be limited by our perception of reality. Call on Maya to give you clarity. Ask her to aid you in stripping away your denials and false beliefs. Everything in duality is divided by separation, which is the greatest illusion of all. To come back home, we must remember that we are all one part of the whole.

Egyptian goddess Ma'at personifies truth, justice, and cosmic order. She is the daughter of sun god Ra, and associated with Thoth, the god of wisdom and writing. Ma'at is responsible for balance and harmony on Earth and is happy to be of service now to bring peace and healing to all cycles of planetary life. Call on her to bring order to chaos and unify fractured ideas, belief systems, or laws.

Jagannath, Hindu lord of the universe, represents freedom from the cycles of birth and death. God of gods, Jagannath destroys any diseases and whatever else lies in your path. He is considered another form of Vishnu. Call on him to help you see through the material existence of the collective and be born again into the truth of the universal one.

Lilith is the final deity associated with the universal gateway chakra and is typically thought of as the goddess of independence. She works through old stories and conditioning, and her presence brings an untethering of sorts to those who may be involved in unhealthy relationships. Call on Lilith to help you claim a healthy attitude of self-worth and to courageously choose yourself again and again, no matter what.

Planets

Uranus is the ruling planet of the universal gateway chakra, representing spiritual revolution and reinvention as its core essence. This planet brings lightning transformations of electric change and epiphanies galore. Innovation and collective freedom are hallmarks of Uranus. With this energy opened up, expect upheaval in the best way possible!

Universal Gateway Exercise: Cosmic Clearing—Light Bath Meditation

Just as you would regularly wash your hands, energy hygiene is an important part of spiritual maintenance. We have a lot to do on this Earth mission to keep ourselves clear from the snares of collective fear, separation, negativities, and lower energies. Shifting your consciousness to gain personal mastery over your own vibration means you need to regularly cleanse your own field to remain a pure channel. (You can always ask for assistance in this task from your light family, angels, and guides when you need it.)

In this meditation, you will learn a simple technique you can use to clear unwanted energies from your system easily and effectively. Make sure to remove any hair accessories or head coverings before beginning this meditation to ensure that nothing is blocking your crown chakra.

Begin this meditation by lying down or sitting comfortably with your arms and legs uncrossed and with ample space over and below your head and feet. Next, say the following aloud: "I now call in my angels, guides, supporters, galactic light team, and family of light to support me in cleansing my energy field at this time. I ask that all impurities be lifted and cleared for my highest good."

Begin to picture your energy field. Remember your aura extends a few feet out around you in all directions. Just sense this for now. You may see streaks or dark spots that correspond with old programming, toxicity, or draining interactions you've come in contact with or are holding yourself. Simply recognize that this is all energy. Know that you are supported and will be receiving assistance removing anything that doesn't belong there.

Next, visualize a space in the cosmos opening above you and pure, diamond-white, shimmering starlight pouring down like rain into your auric field. Just be in a place of receiving and continue to follow your breath during this experience. Let the cosmic starlight wash away any negativities or residue from your aura. Witness your auric space clearing and shining brighter as the cleanse continues. Allow yourself to feel everything going on around you. Picture yourself bathed in Divine, cosmic, crystalline diamond light. Surrender to being in your body and feeling this space while you are detoxing. When you feel as though you are complete, close out your session by thanking the light beings and supporters that worked on you.

You may remain lying or sitting for 10 to 20 minutes or longer. Give yourself a chance to feel the new lightness and spaciousness in your auric field when you are done. You may feel like relaxing or napping afterward. Honor your body and the recovery time you need after this cleanse. Perform this exercise as often as you like for optimal energetic maintenance.

The Mandela Effect

Perhaps the most prominent example of collective consciousness affecting our reality is a phenomenon known as the Mandela effect. The theory of collective misremembering gets its name from philanthropist and political leader Nelson Mandela and the fact that many people report remembering his imprisonment and then subsequent death in the early 1980s; they claim to have watched the funeral on television. Fast-forward, and his death is announced in December 2013. (After he was released from prison alive, he went on to become the country's first post-apartheid president.) The Mandela effect, of which there are many reported instances, points to the fact that time is the great illusion of our three-dimensional reality.

With all this talk about shifting consciousness through the chakras, do you ever feel like you yourself may be "going quantum"? In fifth-dimensional realities, it's normal to view multiple outcomes at the same time. In this three-dimensional reality, we are under the premise that we are all operating in the same reality on the same timeline. But you may want to think again. As you move up and down in vibration, you begin to move up and down in the dimensional planes; therefore, you begin sliding through frames of probabilities (which all exist simultaneously layered atop one another in a quantum universe). At any given time, you could experience one reality and then shift over to the next with only your memory as a linear thread holding it all together.

So, what happens when you and a significant portion of the population remember something incorrectly? We call this misremembering, or confabulation. However, the death of Nelson Mandela in the 1980s isn't the only collective false memory. Thousands of instances have been documented with virtual inconsistences of the collective memory, which scientists and psychologists try to explain away. Many theorists conjecture that if you try to find physical proof, you won't, because the past has now changed. Memory is fallible, but the power of the collective speaks volumes. What is real? And what is just a confabulation? As we step into greater understanding of our governing matrix, we'll get to determine that for ourselves.

Chapter Sixteen
The 11th Chakra: Divine Gateway

The Divine gateway chakra is located at the pinnacle of your chakra system; it opens up and shrouds the other lower chakras like an auric umbrella. This chakra helps in complete spiritual ascension and serves as your direct connection with Source energy, or the Divine Mind. Source energy is best defined as the energy of All That Is. It is the cradle of life, the space of emptiness, and all that fills it. This energy is pure consciousness. It is a unified field that is all-knowing, all-powerful, and ever-present. Ancient religions and philosophies understood this to be God energy, yet this ever-present state is so much more. To simply label it as an omnipotent deity would not do it justice. Not only does it birth Universes into being, but the Divine Mind encompasses all realities (including those that are yet to be created).

With the activation of this chakra, your relationship with the energies beyond our known Universe becomes free-flowing and unhindered. This relationship is experienced directly as a unification and oneness with the fabric of existence. The Divine gateway chakra opens you up to exploring and knowing the deepest parts of yourself—the ecstatic motion, the excitement of your electrons, the intricacies of your heart space, the thought that transforms itself into form, and the stillness.

The Divine Mind is a well of untapped creativity that embeds itself into the very structure of All That Is. It stands to reason that when we open ourselves up to this energy, we rewire our genome to the unlimited power of our own divinity. Each one of us has a special gift, or code, to share that appears as our unique Divine spark of Source energy. You have your own special codes and resonance, yet you are a part of the greater whole of all existence.

With the opening of the Divine gateway chakra, all illusions of separation are removed and replaced with the remembrance of interconnectedness. Love is the element that binds it all together, and it is your job to remember the limitless power and potential available to you through your intention to merge with this nondual state of being. As you acknowledge and value yourself as a person, a soul, a galactic consciousness, and a collective contributor, your spirituality begins to integrate with all facets of your life—across all multiverses, timelines, and dimensions.. Your life is a gift and treasure that is fully self-actualized and activated through the opening of your Divine gateway.

Names & Meaning

The Divine gateway commonly translates to the doorway to Source energy. In Sanskrit, the name for this is *samāna*, meaning "similar," "equal," "same," "being," or "existing." Since it is believed that we were created in the image of the Divine, humans are a form of divinity unto themselves that are considered equal to Source in creatorship and sovereignty. There is nothing above this gateway and no hierarchy within this plane.

Color

The color most closely associated with your Divine gateway chakra is very pale blue. If we were to try to visualize this chakra, it would appear mostly translucent with iridescent, shimmering plasma light circulating within it. This layer represents purity, clarity, connection, Divine love, and harmonic resonance with All That Is. This bandwidth vibrates so high that it's difficult to see, touch, or hear, but we know it's there.

Location

The Divine gateway, the fourth of your transpersonal chakras, is located approximately three to four feet above the top of your head, situated directly above your universal gateway chakra. Three arms' length above the head is a good visual. This field extends above and around your entire body, much like an auric layer. It is where your personal energy ends and the world begins. This etheric spiritual chakra relates to your direct connection with Source energy.

Estimated Activation

Your Divine gateway is a sleeping chakra that activates once your universal gateway chakra has been activated. This activation can take place any time after significant work has been done to clear through blockages from all consciousness conditioning and all lifetimes. Most people who have done the work of building a connection to Source to be able to live from their heart-centered consciousness will see this activation occur during this lifetime on Earth.

Senses

With an awakened eleventh chakra, an individual will possess and expand on all other available senses, both physical and metaphysical. In addition, they will wake up to their abilities to command time at will. On Earth, humans agree to linear time, and so they run by the clock. Our experience of reality reflects this concept. However, societies do not advance because linear years pass. They advance when they align to the energy construct that supports higher vibration and awareness.

As an example, let's look at time bending. To practice this, get in the habit of not looking at the clock and imagining yourself arriving just in time. Next time you are running late for an event, rather than worrying about not arriving on time and constantly checking the clock for assurance, validate yourself internally and then do not check the clock. Instead, imagine a block of time or space opening up for you, allowing you to get to your destination with the right amount of time to spare. Be open to the magic that wants to set you free from all impossibilities, and you may just surprise yourself!

Function

Your Divine gateway chakra is most closely linked with ninth-dimensional energy. In this framework, you are the closest you can be to Source energy while remaining embodied. You are also connecting to a place that is considered the womb of creation. The womb is empty, vast, and holds unlimited potential. Think of the ninth-dimensional plane as a black hole—where everything is contained and where everything can be transcended. There are no more processes to integrate or complete at this level. This is a place where there is nowhere to go and nothing to see. It is pure Source consciousness, also known as the Void. When the first light of being popped into existence, it came from this space of nothing, and it will return to this space of nothing after it has completed its evolutionary cycles and transcended them. This plane is the beginning and the end, the Alpha and Omega. The impossible becomes possible here.

When you are functioning in unison with the Divine Mind, you become a partner with creative flow and recognize the vast container of who you are as a vessel of Divine will and love. This is a place where you can access your limitless potential. If you have progressed this far on your mission, you will likely already be aligned with your ultimate purpose. If you have struggled with connecting to your higher purpose, you can still experience the Divine gateway firsthand, although you will need to consecrate your free will to Divine will. In this way, you allow for the interplay of Divine love to guide your path. All decisions you make will inevitably be guided by the hand of truth and Divine wisdom, even if those decisions don't make sense in the moment. In this way, the Divine gateway chakra really calls on you to keep your system clear and open so that you can continue to work on a coherent level within your entire field of being for the advancement of all beings.

Your eleventh chakra allows for weaving dreams, consciously cocreating, tapping into your flow state, and experiencing Divine unconditional love all at once. This creates a life with unlimited potential, possibilities, and pathways. At this level, it is possible to stop the incarnation process if you so choose (although many enlightened beings come back as Ascended Masters to help guide others on their paths). As healers, leaders, and wayshowers, we know that we are here to inspire others to create unlimited possibilities for themselves and that serving in this collective responsibility allows us to reach our highest potential.

Archetypes

The archetypes associated with your Divine gateway chakra are the One and the Nothing. These concepts are interrelated and intrinsically linked.

The One is a field of nonduality that appears mainly as a conceptual archetype in our lives. As it is elusive, we are always striving to attain it, but it feels out of reach. It is only when we cease looking outside ourselves that we can come close to it. Our capacity to sense this precious unified space firsthand is limited but possible. We get very close when we are in a place of total neutrality, of letting go, of surrender. In terms of the archetype, this *unus mundus*—a sphere representing the unity of all existence—contains both the light and the shadow, matter and antimatter, the vastness and infinitesimally small, and all that is in between.

The Nothing archetype is like an empty box that sits on the table taking up space. Although the spaciousness can seem uncomfortable, the lesson here is not to seek to satisfy the craving to fill it up with something right away. The blank space of the Nothing invites you to have patience and hone your creative skills and action plan before manifesting your vision to life. This space is extremely powerful and representative of a time ripe with potential. Sitting through the discomfort of the space will yield rewards after all your valiant efforts.

Personality

Those who have activated their Divine gateway chakra align themselves with the highest level of consciousness possible. Their true essence is flourishing and expressed, and they have the physical, mental, emotional, and spiritual development to manage their whole being. Their level of openness, nonjudgment, equanimity, and detachment are noticeable to the world—in fact, they mainly operate from a place of nondual awareness, or ego dissolution.

When the ego dissolves, there is a loss of subjective identity. This ego death is commonly reported in psychedelic experiences as a conscious state that is achieved through the loss of the sense of Self. It's not necessary to take any psychedelics to experience the vibration of nonduality. As expected, instead of dematerializing into a whirling space-time void, ego death looks relatively benign from an outsider's perspective. Yet, inside the mind, a change has taken place that helps your mind rewire and reprogram old thought patterns and behaviors into more refined choices. A person who has crossed over into a nondual awareness can still operate in embodied duality, yet they maintain a calm centeredness of their own nondual nature throughout their experiences. This is considered engaged nondual synthesis or impartial awareness.

Personality traits here reflect a loving, accelerated vibration from a place of centered neutrality. Staying connected to humanity and continuing to participate from this state can sometimes be difficult to manage. After all, once the game has been figured out, the challenge is to continue to play as though every step is still relevant. In fact, nondual consciousness acts as a great springboard to manifest even more positive outcomes!

To live consistently in nonduality means that a person is aware of all sensory, emotional, and mental processes, but they don't identify or hold fast to them. The act of practicing being extremely present creates a conduit for accessing this zero-point state more often. Anyone who lives connected to their true nature and purpose practices opening their Divine gateway chakra. Connecting deeply to the Earth star chakra is vitally important when the eleventh chakra is open. Continual grounding will keep you from disassociating, and it will manage the coherence of your entire chakra system, ensuring your overall health and happiness as you weave through both dual and nondual states.

Deities

There is only one deity associated with the Divine gateway chakra, and it goes by many names. Sophia, Source, unity consciousness or singularity (the One), and Brahma are a few of them. Let's take a look at what each one means.

The level of the Divine gateway is closely linked with Source, or God consciousness. Religion aside, this term refers to the creator of All That Is. Rather than view this deity as an almighty presence who is greater than us, I encourage you to view Source light as an ineffable mystery that holds wisdom beyond our understanding and human knowing.

You may recognize Sophia from the soul star chakra chapter, as she can take her goddess form with different aspects that serve varied functions. Sophia Source of All That Is is the feminine aspect of the mothering energy that birthed the entire Universe. This aspect of her is recognized as the consciousness who connects you with your Divine assignments and alignments. She reminds you to practice faith before results as a key to cocreating your reality. When you call on her, you will receive beautiful synchronicities as confirmation of your courage and trust.

The One is connected to everything else; this absolute is often referred to as singularity or unity consciousness. Singularity refers to a point without dimensions. In Hinduism, this contracted point of singularity is called *nirguna* ("without attributes"). In this tradition, All That Is is known as Brahmn ("the largest and the ever enlarging"). *Nirguna Brahmn* is simultaneously a container and the contained, the fabric of existence and the structure of Universe all at once.

Planets

The Divine gateway chakra is represented by the Galactic Center of the Universe, in which nests a massive black hole. A black hole is a region of space that has collapsed in on itself due to its enormous density. Black holes were once giant stars that went through a supernova. After their collapse, no particles escape (not even radiation or light). This natural phenomenon is a complete mystery. As they cannot be observed, black holes can be thought of as elusive as the Divine creator itself. When you tap into this singularity consciousness through the stillness of your own mind, you can create worlds within worlds. From the womb of nothing comes everything.

Divine Gateway Chakra Exercise: Zero-Point Genesis Calibration Meditation

The synthesis of the Divine gateway chakra's consciousness can be summarized in one simple statement, "I AM." Saying "I AM" affirms your sovereign presence to the entire Universe. You can then begin to ask, "Who can I become?" It is out of this questioning that the nature of reality is born, polarity forms, and then all the dimensions of reality and your being spring into place. The "I AM" singularity is also known as zero-point calibration. This lifetime is an important one, meant to connect you back to all vital aspects of the totality of your being in every dimension across all quantum realities. From this space, genesis of new ideas and ways of being can emerge. Pure intention generated from your inception point rearrange and reconfigure the energy of unlimited possibilities to cocreate new realities. You can use your directives to better steer your ship once you have your zero-point dialed in.

This meditation will reconnect you to your "I AM" presence. Allow yourself a minimum of 30 minutes for this exercise. I recommend you do this meditation seated upright for the first few tries. As your vibration accelerates, your brain waves change, which can cause a feeling of dizziness, and you may feel as though you will pass out. Don't worry; this reaction is normal when accessing these levels of consciousness.

Vesica Piscis

Known as "the womb of creation," the vesica piscis is the sacred geometric pattern of creation itself. It is formed by two opposing intersecting circles of equal size. The overlapping halves merge together with a central area of union, creating a shared eye-shaped center. The shape is feminine in nature, representing mothering and genesis. The mathematics of the interlocking circles contains a powerful meaning that reflects aspects of the geometry of creation. The vesica piscis is found both in the Seed of Life shape and the Flower of Life shape all over the natural world. It is recognized as a symbol of the goddess, birth, and sensuality.

The vesica piscis is a gateway between the worlds of spirit (masculine) and matter (feminine). The mysterious junction at its center contains a potent etheric field of intention, bridging the two worlds. The vesica piscis is often seen as a representation of the Holy Trinity. The two halves must come together to create, and through this Divine alchemical union, the nonphysical manifests into reality. All things must cross through this bridge in order to be. Through the center, toroidal fields of energy begin to spin and activate around the intention in the middle. As the geometry unfolds, it turns into the Seed of Life, Flower of Life, and many more sacred symbols that hold the original intention. It is this in-between point that holds the keys to All That Is. It is from the nothing that something is born. The element of the two spheres and the eye in the middle form the three aspects of creation in every reality and in every dimension. Without the vesica piscis, neither sacred geometry nor we humans would exist.

Start by saying your intention aloud: "I call on all aspects of myself now to merge with my ever-present-now consciousness in this lifetime. I ask to be reunited to my Divine 'I AM' presence on this plane, and I request a recall of all aspects of me back to my zero-point. And so it is."

Close your eyes, breathing deeply on your inhalations and lengthening your exhalations, descending the breath. When you have followed the breath for a few minutes and settled in, focus your attention and energy on your high heart chakra. Next, visualize a diamond, pearlescent white light streaming in from three to four feet above your head, running down your transpersonal chakras and pouring through your entire body down to your feet and below you into your Earth star chakra. Once you have established a pillar of pure light, bring your focus back to your high heart.

Imagine a single star-like point at the center of your high heart and begin to breathe into it. As you expand and release your breath, see your toroidal field around your heart blossoming in a field around you, circulating energy. Grow this energy beyond your body, beyond your aura, and out as far as you can imagine the edges of the Universe might be.

Then make an intention to begin to draw in your "I AM" presence. Give yourself some time here just feeling the energy coming into your body. The energy may feel like ripples, waves, small electrical currents, buzzing, or vibrating. Spend as much time as you need energizing yourself with all of the aspects of your "I AM" presence in existence, allowing them to flow into your heart space. Notice how this makes you feel. You may choose to chant "I AM" throughout the process aloud, in your mind, or silently once or twice. This phrase acknowledges your totality and calls it in.

When you feel the energy flowing, spend a few more moments here and then call your toroidal field back in, condensing it all the way back to a single zero-point at your high heart. This point is your genesis point, as you have merged all your consciousness with your "I AM" totality. You may notice different sensations or thoughts coming to you, but try to stay in stillness. It's possible you may feel suspended here, beyond space and time—enjoy! It is your job as an observer to simply notice what, if anything, is coming to you now. New ideas have been waiting to be born from the genesis point of your "I AM" presence.

When your meditation is complete, thank all the versions of you for their willingness to reunite and continue supporting you. Journal any relevant information and insights, and then give yourself time to integrate before hopping back into your daily routine. A completely new version of you is emerging!

Conclusion: Celebrating the Chakras

The ascension quest is one of transmutation, liberation, and transcendence. Behind all the mysticism, the self-help, the waves of healing, and the heart-centered work, you are here to rediscover your soul's highest purpose. Working with the 12-chakra ascension system is an epic odyssey of remembering who you are. This model helps complement the fifth-dimensional (and beyond) being you are becoming. So please do not limit yourself to what you think you know. An open mind along with a feeling heart is all that is required here to navigate your energy and master it.

The sacred journey is a long road from who you were born as to who you are becoming. Yet the journey of self-actualization is the most crucial journey you could ever undertake. This ascension path through the chakras is not for the faint of heart. It will require you to reach beyond all you have ever known in this lifetime and into all the rest. It surpasses the individual self, as you connect to galactic quantum realities and anchor new energies deep into the heart of Gaia. It expands into the furthest reaches of space-time, into every space and every time. This adventure is a story comprised of you, humanity, and your star brothers and sisters as Earth lifts itself up into new realms. From separation to Source and back to your cosmic glory, you will overcome obstacles as you send that freedom across the Universe into every multidimensional aspect of consciousness.

With this understanding, you can use this guide as a reference tool when you are working with your own chakras or helping others with their own healing. Remember that the original chakras were actually gateways to receive Divine information through invoking goddess/god and archetypal energies. The chakras are meant to be doorways to exchange information with the world around you, and these portals are more fluid than precise in nature. Eventually, they will meld into one unified ascension column, as our DNA becomes more silica based and crystalline in nature.

I deeply encourage you to lean in and explore for yourself the fluidity and personal connection that is available to you in your own chakra system. Your system is unlike anyone else's, and no book can completely and exhaustively categorize all that is you. It is up to you to come into intimate knowing through experience. Discover what information personally resonates for you. Great benefits await you in your self-discovery journey.

As you work with your own energy, remember it is imperative to focus not only on the small and necessary details of the here and now but also on the bigger picture. This level of healing comes with the responsibility to be an active participant in the world around you through service and contribution. You can empower others to progress toward reclaiming their health because you have already walked the path. You can help them simply by sharing your journey, experience, and stories. There is always deeper knowledge and understanding to be had and shared as you uncover new spiritual processes that help you heal—and you never know what might be the gold that encourages someone else to take a leap of faith.

You are healing through lifetimes as you reconcile each healed part, and as you do, you send light to all parts of your whole through all timelines. Your body and chakras are set up as pure potential, and they wish to be in ecstatic harmonic resonance. We must listen carefully to inner wisdom if we are to acknowledge ourselves without judgment and make the changes necessary to bring ourselves into resonance and improve our lives. It takes diligence, commitment, and effort. Make space for yourself, be gentle, show compassion, and offer forgiveness to all parts of you that wish to be healed. There has never been a time in history when you were more supported. Dear one, you did not come here to play small. You are here to reclaim all of you. With a loving embrace, I bless your awakening journey.

Glossary

ACUPRESSURE: A traditional Chinese medicine technique used in healing, which utilizes meridian lines down the length of the body to stimulate qi through the body

ACUPUNCTURE: A key component of traditional Chinese medicine; a 3,000-year-old healing modality utilizing small needles inserted at specific meridian points along the body to release stagnant qi to achieve health and well-being

AMRITA: Sanskrit word for "nectar of the gods"; this concept is often used in Hindu literature to describe the potent essence of immortality (like the Greek ambrosia).

AROMATHERAPY: A healing therapy that uses essential oils from plants to directly affect the limbic system to achieve emotional, mental, and physical well-being

ARTIFICIAL ELECTROMAGNETIC FREQUENCIES (EMFs): Waves of electrical power or radiation that have been known to produce potential health risks in humans

ASCENSION: The gradual ability of the body, mind, and spirit to incorporate more light, vibrate higher, and realize their higher multidimensionality

ASTRAL PLANE/REALM: A dimension of existence outside the three-dimensional Earth plane; seven astral planes in total—three lower, which correspond to relative existence, and four higher, which ultimately ascend to the Divine Mind

AURA: The subtle body layers outside the physical body that make up the spiritual body

BREATH WORK: A healing technique in which practitioners focus attention and awareness on the breath to achieve emotional, mental, spiritual, and physical well-being

CEREMONY: A sacred observance that may include spiritual ritual, intention setting, or prayer to honor an event, occasion, or rite; often used in shamanic practices to celebrate and expand spiritual connection

COHERENCE: The state of alignment in vibration (spirit), energy (soul), and matter (DNA)

COLLECTIVE CONSCIOUSNESS: A sociological belief set that includes shared beliefs, ideas, attitudes, and knowledge that are part of a societal group; refers to a shared understanding of societal norms, so to speak

DANTIAN: An important meditative focal point located below the navel said to be used to develop the use of qi; an important point in the microcosmic orbit; loosely translated as "elixir field" or "sea of qi"; also spelled dantien

DESPACHO: A traditional shamanic ceremonial expression of gratitude, usually performed in nature with natural elements, song, and prayer to celebrate or ritualize an event, rite, or passage

DHARMIC PATH: Alignment with cosmic law and one's higher purpose

DIMENSION: A spatial principle of physics and mathematics used to describe a plane of existence and coordinates that constitute its containment

DIVINE FEMININE: The sacred, higher aspect of feminine energy that is positively and divinely expressed through receiving, allowing, nurturing, purifying, forgiving, and showing compassion

DIVINE MASCULINE: The sacred, higher aspect of masculine energy that is positively and divinely expressed through understanding, logic, reason, doing, and action, which is free from egoic control

DIVINE MIND: The Oneness, or Source energy light, that gives shape to all of creation

DUALITY: An instance of being in opposition or contrast or two aspects of something; for example, light and dark or north and south

ELEMENTS: Water, earth, air, fire, and ether (spirit), which make up the complexity of matter in all possible forms

ENERGETIC BLUEPRINT/ETHERIC TEMPLATE: The map or layout of one's energetic signature that makes up a person

EPIGENETICS: A field of study that researches what turns genes on and off by looking at factors such as phenotype (characteristics or traits) rather than genotype (genetic constitution)

FLOWER OF LIFE: A sacred geometric pattern representing the basic building blocks of all creation

GAIA: The consciousness of Mother Earth; Earth herself

GREAT AWAKENING: The Age of Aquarius and the rise of the Divine Feminine; a time of collective awareness and galactic disclosure for humanity, which began on December 21, 2012 and is occurring now on planet Earth

HIGH HEART CHAKRA: The thymus chakra, which is becoming the epicenter of chakra ascension models and heart-coherence theories; located between the throat and center of the chest near the heart

IDA: The lunar energy line that runs down the left (feminine) side of the body and the right side of the brain

KUNDALINI: A "coiled serpent" energy that rests at the base of one's spine and can be awakened to enhance personal power, sensuality, vitality, and enlightenment; also called shakti energy

LIGHT BODY: A lattice of sacred geometry in the form of light surrounding a person, supporting the health of their spiritual, mental, emotional, and physical body; radiates light energy and connects one's multidimensional self with the energies of the infinite Universe

LIGHT CODES: High-vibrational waves containing encoded information that awaken dormant aspects of one's DNA, helping bring them into alignment with their higher-self energy, often in the form of light-wave frequencies

LOGOS: A blueprint for pure Source consciousness in form, often expressing as stars

MULTIVERSE: Many versions of reality happening simultaneously, hypothesized to be a projection from other energetic realms or dimensions; holographs layered atop one another, creating grids that share energy, with no limit to how many parallel realties exist

NADIS: Small secondary channels similar to meridians that carry prana and other life-giving elements through the body; connects to the chakras on a subtle and physical level

NIRVANA: The final state of enlightenment in Buddhism, allowing freedom from all suffering, attachment of desires, effects of karma, and further incarnation cycles

NONDUALITY: Pure consciousness experiencing itself; the disappearance of opposition

NYĀSA: Energetic placements on the body that the original Hindu texts claim are spaces in which to invoke goddess/god energy

MANTRA: A sound or word used in meditation as a tool to aid concentration and break through to transcendental states of consciousness; Sanskrit for "vehicle of the mind"

MATRIX: This is a controlled environment that has set rules and unseen forces controlling it. In this case, the eighth dimension contains the matrix we live in, and nothing in our existence is beyond or outside of this "bubble." There are also smaller matrices, like the three-dimensional Earth matrix and the fifth-dimensional Earth matrix.

MAYA: The power that conceals the true meaning of spiritual reality; Sanskrit for "illusion"

MEDITATION: An ancient practice using mindful awareness practice to focus the mind and breath to train attention, achieve inner peace, and reach profound spiritual states of consciousness

MERIDIANS: The channels through which prana (life-force energy) flows; 14 major meridian lines map every organ and system in the human body

MERKABA: A vehicle formed by two interlocking tetrahedrons, which surrounds the body like an aura wrapper

MICROCOSMIC ORBIT: A technique for cultivating qi that focuses and directs life-force energy through an oval-shaped circuit down the front and up the back of the body to energize the body and stabilize the mind

OCTAVATION: Activating a higher octave of frequency (as in ascension frequencies)

PENDULUM: A tool used for divination; usually a chain with weighted pendants or crystals on the ends

PINGALA: The solar energy line that runs down the right (masculine) side of the body and the left side of the brain

POLARITY: A quality or condition that exhibits opposite properties that contrast in a dualistic nature

PRANA: Vital life-force energy, or breath

PSYCHONAUT: A person who explores activities by which altered states of consciousness are induced and utilized for spiritual purposes or the exploration of the human condition

QI/CHI: Vital life-force energy and animating force, which moves through all things; *ki* in Japanese

REFLEXOLOGY: A traditional Eastern healing modality that involves applying pressure to the hands, feet, and ears through various mapped reflex points

REIKI: A gentle, hands-on, healing-channeling modality that directs universal life-force energy into a person's body, which, in turn, helps create healing around mind/body blockages, injuries, illnesses, and more

SACRED GEOMETRY: Sacred geometric shapes, proportions, and universal patterns that help design everything in our reality and beyond; often seen in the art and architecture of ancient civilizations and said to have been passed on from neighboring cosmic visitors

SAMADHI: A state of enlightenment, or nondualistic consciousness, usually achieved through a lifetime of deep meditation and inner work

SANSKRIT: The ancient Indo-European language of India; one of the oldest known languages in the world

SCHUMANN RESONANCE: This is the resonant frequency of Earth, usually 7.83 hertz, measuring the general electromagnetic frequency of Earth's surrounding magnetic field. Due to solar activity and receiving higher light frequencies, Earth and her inhabitants vibrate higher than this rate during ascension.

STAR SEED: A person whose soul has traveled to the Earth plane from another planetary system or galactic location to help humanity in the Great Awakening

SOURCE: God consciousness; All That Is

SUBPERSONAL CHAKRA: A chakra that exists below one's physical body; the Earth star chakra, or zero chakra

SUBTLE BODY: Also known as the aura or auric field, these layers compose one's being beyond the physical layer. There are said to be seven layers that contain one's physical, mental, emotional, and spiritual blueprints.

SUSHUMNA: The channel that prana and kundalini travel and weave into one's nervous system

TRANSPERSONAL CHAKRA: A chakra that exists above the physical body—the soul star, the stellar gateway, the universal gateway, and the Divine gateway—and helps a person connect to their spiritual energies and the energies of All That Is

TOROIDAL FIELD: A revolving doughnut-shaped, three-dimensional field; located both around the heart (three feet) and entire body (six feet); exchanges subtle information between a person and their environment

VEDAS AND UPANISHADS: A body of religious texts originating in ancient India; constitutes the oldest Sanskrit literature and scriptures of Hinduism

VESICA PISCIS: A sacred geometric shape composed of two interlocking circles with an almond-shaped overlapping center; said to be the shape of the Divine Goddess and represents the union of spirit and matter as it gives birth to creation

WETIKO: A psychological effect that appears like a virus, infecting the subconscious mind of humanity; traditionally used in shamanic cultures to describe the dark side of someone's psyche

YOGA: An ancient physical, mental, and spiritual practice that expands awareness of the mind-body connection by anchoring one's awareness to their physical body through *asanas* (postures)

ZERO POINT: "I AM" singularity point that connects one back to the totality of who they really are

Chakra Chart

DiVine ✦ GATEWAY

UNIVERSAL GATEWAY

STELLAR GATEWAY

SOUL STAR

CROWN CHAKRA

THIRD EYE CHAKRA

THROAT CHAKRA

HEART CHAKRA

SOLAR PLEXUS CHAKRA

SACRAL CHAKRA

ROOT CHAKRA

EARTH STAR

Eleventh Chakra: Divine Gateway

COLOR: Translucent, pale blue

LOCATION: 3 to 4 feet above head

PLANET: Galactic Center, black hole

DEITIES: Source, Unity Consciousness, Singularity, Sophia (All That Is)

ASSOCIATIONS/REPRESENTS: Ninth dimension, Divine Mind, oneness

EMOTION: Transcendence, creativity

BODY PARTS: Outside the body

BALANCE: Nondual states of awareness, living in alignment with true nature

The transpersonal chakras are either open or closed with no underactive or overactive states.

Tenth Chakra: Universal Gateway

COLOR: Silver

LOCATION: 2 to 3 feet above head

PLANET: Uranus

DEITIES: Maya, Ma'at, Jagannath, Lilith

ASSOCIATIONS/REPRESENTS: Eighth dimension, collective consciousness, interconnectedness, freedom

EMOTION: Spiritual mastery, independence

BODY PARTS: Outside the body

BALANCE: Mass-projection awareness, matrix knowledge, breaking free of illusion

The transpersonal chakras are either open or closed with no underactive or overactive states.

Ninth Chakra: Stellar Gateway

COLOR: Gold

LOCATION: 1.5 to 2 feet above head

PLANET: Alcyone, Ophiuchus

DEITIES: Green Tara, Galactic Federation of Light (GFL)

ASSOCIATIONS/REPRESENTS: Seventh dimension, cosmic connection, star family associations

EMOTION: Explorative, adventurous, multidimensional

BODY PARTS: Outside the body

BALANCE: Consciousness unbound by space-time, galactic awareness, astral travel

The transpersonal chakras are either open or closed with no underactive or overactive states.

Eighth Chakra: Soul Star

COLOR: Pink

LOCATION: 1 foot above head

PLANET: Chiron, Saturn

DEITIES: Goddess Sophia, Isis, Horus

ASSOCIATIONS/REPRESENTS: Sixth dimension, soul purpose, spiritual development

EMOTION: Whole, complete, activated, nirvana

BODY PARTS: Outside the body

BALANCE: Soul-purpose realization, reorienting to oversoul

The transpersonal chakras are either open or closed with no underactive or overactive states.

Seventh Chakra: Crown

COLOR: Pearl white

LOCATION: Top of head

PLANET: Jupiter

DEITIES: Shiva, Saraswati, Buddha

ASSOCIATIONS/REPRESENTS: Fourth and fifth dimensions, wisdom, consciousness

EMOTION: Spiritual connection, bliss, enlightenment

BODY PARTS: Brain (upper), pituitary gland, nervous system, bones

BALANCED: Understanding, divinely guided, focused

OVERACTIVE: Materialism, headaches, jittery

UNDERACTIVE: Disconnected, depression, boredom, nervous

Sixth Chakra: Third Eye

COLOR: Indigo, violet

LOCATION: Center of forehead, between eyebrows

PLANET: Neptune

DEITIES: Vishnu, Ganesha, St. Germain

ASSOCIATIONS/REPRESENTS: Fourth and fifth dimensions, psychic seat, intuition, vision

EMOTION: Insightful, imaginative, inspired

BODY PARTS: Brain (lower), pineal gland, ears (outer), eyes, nose

BALANCED: Innerstanding (awareness), clarity

OVERACTIVE: Overthinking, vision problems

UNDERACTIVE: Self-doubt, narrow-minded, pineal gland calcification

Fifth Chakra: Throat

COLOR: Blue

LOCATION: Center of neck

PLANET: Mercury

DEITIES: Hathor, Thoth

ASSOCIATIONS/REPRESENTS: Fourth and fifth dimensions, communication, expression

EMOTION: Creative, understanding, authentic

BODY PARTS: Throat, neck, ears (inner), mouth, tongue, jaw, thyroid

BALANCED: Heard, understood, expressed, clear communicator

OVERACTIVE: Critical, stretches truth, arrogant, condescending

UNDERACTIVE: Nervous, insecure, timid, stuttering, mood disorders

Fourth Chakra: Heart

COLOR: Pink, green

LOCATION: Center of chest

PLANET: Venus

DEITIES: Jesus Christ, Krishna, Mother Mary, Quan Yin, Inanna

ASSOCIATIONS/REPRESENTS: Fourth and fifth dimensions, love, acceptance, forgiveness

EMOTION: Compassionate, loving, nurturing, peaceful

BODY PARTS: Heart, circulatory and respiratory system, thymus, vagus nerve

BALANCED: Heart-coherence, empathetic, open, vulnerable

OVERACTIVE: Stubborn, narcissistic, egotistical, jealous

UNDERACTIVE: Poor coping skills, codependency, withdrawal

Third Chakra: Solar Plexus

COLOR: Yellow

LOCATION: Belly, under rib cage, above navel

PLANET: The Sun

DEITIES: Ra, Sekhmet, Agni, Hanuman, Indra

ASSOCIATIONS/REPRESENTS: Third and fourth dimensions, personal power, vitality, will

EMOTION: Excited, confident, outgoing, courageous

BODY PARTS: Digestive system, pancreas, stomach, liver, gallbladder, bile, small intestine, metabolism

BALANCED: Motivated, connected to purpose, empowered

OVERACTIVE: Critical, judgmental, stubborn

UNDERACTIVE: Procrastination, low self-esteem, uncertainty

Second Chakra: Sacral

COLOR: Orange

LOCATION: 2 inches below navel, lower abdomen

PLANET: Moon

DEITIES: Lakshmi, Yemanja, Mary Magdalene, Mama Qocha, Poseidon, Neptune, Varuna

ASSOCIATIONS/REPRESENTS: Third dimension, emotional balance, creativity, sexuality

EMOTION: Self-reliant, adaptive, connected to sensuality, creative

BODY PARTS: Reproductive system, lymphatic systems, sacrum, hips, kidneys, bladder, uterus, ovaries, blood sugar

BALANCED: Expressive, passionate, playful, ambitious

OVERACTIVE: Manipulative, pushy, trouble letting go

UNDERACTIVE: Shy, guilty, lost, issues with desire and intimacy

First Chakra: Root

COLOR: Red

LOCATION: Base of spine, pelvic bowl

PLANET: Mars

DEITIES: Shakti, Parvati, Brahma, Bhumi

ASSOCIATIONS/REPRESENTS: Third dimension, survival, stability, primal energy

EMOTION: Grounded, stable, secure

BODY PARTS: Elimination system, skeletal system, outer sex organs, pelvis, spine, tailbone, legs

BALANCED: Independent, trusting, poised

OVERACTIVE: Domineering, greedy, bossy, jealous

UNDERACTIVE: Fearful, frustrated, issues with pelvis

Zero Chakra: Earth Star

COLOR: Brown, magenta (activated)

LOCATION: 12 inches below feet

PLANET: Earth's iron core, Pluto

DEITIES: Kali Ma, Durga, Osiris, White Buffalo Woman

ASSOCIATIONS/REPRESENTS: Deep Earth connection, grounding

EMOTION: Deep, nature-loving, humanitarian

BODY PARTS: Soles of feet

BALANCED: Two-dimensional association (microbe, plant, and mineral kingdom), connected to Gaia, harmonious, able to access innate wisdom

The subpersonal chakra is either open or closed with no underactive or overactive states.

Resources

Becoming Supernatural: How Common People Are Doing the Uncommon by Dr. Joe Dispenza

This book contains theories and science on changing your thoughts, behaviors, and energy to improve your total health and manifest in your daily life.

Chakra Balance: The Beginner's Guide to Healing Body and Mind by April Pfender

The perfect companion for anyone who is new to working with healing their chakras, this guide contains useful tips for balancing using yogic postures, crystals, essential oils, and meditation.

Crystals: How to Tap into Your Infinite Potential through the Healing Power of Crystals by Katie-Jane Wright

This is a conscious guide to accessing your inner wisdom written by a dear sister-goddess and channel, Katie-Jane. It helps you access your own greater awareness through crystal magic and meditation.

Earth Magic: Ancient Shamanic Wisdom for Healing Yourself, Others, and the Planet by Steven D. Farmer

This book contains a synthesis of shamanic practices and philosophies that help heal spiritual causes of physical and emotional illness and enhance manifestation abilities.

Eat Feel Fresh: A Contemporary, Plant-Based Ayurvedic Cookbook by Sahara Rose Ketabi

Offering a plant-based solution to balancing your system through food, this book includes alternative recipes for your dosha and a wealth of inspiration for a healthier lifestyle.

Essential Chakra Meditation: Awaken Your Healing Power with Meditation and Visualization by April Pfender

This guide to using intention and purpose to transform your mind and your body's vital energy centers is also available on Audible.

Llewellyn's Complete Book of Chakras: Your Definitive Source of Energy Center Knowledge for Health, Happiness, and Spiritual Evolution by Cyndi Dale

This well-researched compendium of timeless wisdom on the historical chakra system includes various perspectives and practices on subtle energy applications.

The Book of Shamanic Healing by Kristin Madden

This book includes techniques for understanding Earth medicine and shamanic wisdom. It offers supreme guidance on chakras, breathing, dream work, drumming, soul retrieval, and more.

The Crystalline Transmission: A Synthesis of Light (Volume III) by Katrina Raphaell

One of the first introductions to the 12-chakra system, this book presents teachings on crystalline technology and aligning with our inner light. It is a staple for New Earth wayshowers.

The Great Human Potential: Walking in One's Own Light by Tom Kenyon and Wendy Kennedy

A channeled work on the complete ascension process from two of the most well-known and respected channels we'll see in this lifetime, this book is an accessible read on our journey as creator-beings from a Pleiadian perspective.

The Sophia Code: A Living Transmission from the Sophia Dragon Tribe by Kaia Ra

This visionary sacred text will help you reclaim your sovereignty and step into Divine Feminine Christ Consciousness with revelations to activate your awareness as we launch into humanity's Great Awakening.

The Vortex: Where the Law of Attraction Assembles All Cooperative Relationships by Esther Hicks and Jerry Hicks

A channeled piece from the renowned Abraham-Hicks, this book uncovers the powerful creative vortex that has already assembled your life and everything in it you desire. It explores manifesting and provides practical tips for creating in all areas of your life.

Waking Up in 5D: A Practice Guide to Multidimensional Transformation by Maureen J. St. Germain

This book offers insightful guidance and tools on how to shift your life into higher consciousness and how to navigate quantum reality.

"The Real Story on the Chakras" by Christopher Wallis (Hareesh): hareesh.org/ blog/2016/2/5/the-real-story-on-the-chakras.

Hareesh is a Yogic-Sanskrit philosopher and practitioner with 30 years of experience studying the chakras and translating ancient sacred texts. In this definitive source for all things Tantra, he gives a modern context for chakra work as it applies to traditional practices.

References

Asur'Ana. "The Galactic Photon Belt Alignment—Part 1 of 3." Aligning with Earth. Accessed April 20, 2020. http://aligningwithearth.com/galactic-photon-belt-alignment-part-1.

Bailey, James. "Discover the Ida and Pingala Nadis." *Yoga Journal*. Last modified April 5, 2017. http://yogajournal.com/yoga-101/balancing-act-2.

Battaglia, Salvatore. *The Complete Guide to Aromatherapy*. 2nd ed. Brisbane, Australia: Perfect Potion, 2004.

Bilyeu, Tom. "How to Stay Healthy until You're 105 (It's in Your Gut) | Dr. Steven Gundry on Health Theory." May 9, 2019. YouTube video, 56:08. http://youtu.be/Uklt4zVVtS0.

Brazier, Yvette. "PTSD: What You Need to Know." *Medical News Today*. February 6, 2019. http://medicalnewstoday.com/articles/156285.php#risk-factors.

Cherry, Kendra. "The 4 Major Jungian Archetypes." *Verywell Mind*. Last modified July 17, 2019. http://verywellmind.com/what-are-jungs-4-major-archetypes-2795439.

Cromwell, Mandara. "The History of Sound Healing." *Massage Magazine*. April 1, 2015. http://massagemag.com/the-history-of-sound-healing-29245.

Dagnall, Neil, and Ken Drinkwater. "The 'Mandela Effect' and How Your Mind Is Playing Tricks on You." *The Conversation*. February 12, 2018. http://theconversation.com/the-mandela-effect-and-how-your-mind-is-playing-tricks-on-you-89544.

Dale, Cyndi. *Llewellyn's Complete Book of Chakras: Your Definitive Source of Energy Center Knowledge for Health, Happiness, and Spiritual Evolution*. Woodbury, MN: Llewellyn Publications, 2015.

Deane, Ashayana. *Voyagers II: Secrets of Amenti*. Mill Spring, NC: Granite Publishing, 2001.

Dispenza, Joe. *Becoming Supernatural: How Common People Are Doing the Uncommon*. Carlsbad, CA: Hay House, 2017.

Dunbar, Brian. "Schumann Resonance." NASA. Accessed April 20, 2020. http://nasa.gov/mission_pages/sunearth/news/gallery/schumann-resonance.html.

Energy Muse. "Crystal Meanings: The Power of Gemstones." Accessed April 20, 2020. http://energymuse.com/about-gemstones.

English, Trevor. "What Is the Schumann Resonance?" *Interesting Engineering.* October 25, 2019. http://interestingengineering.com/what-is-the-schumann-resonance.

Ernst, E., and A. White. "A Brief History of Acupuncture." *Rheumatology* 43, no. 5 (May 2004): 662–63. doi.org/10.1093/rheumatology/keg005.

Galarneau, Lisa. "A Summary of Galactic Federation Light Messages: What Our Galactic Neighbors Have to Say about Humanity." Medium. June 27, 2017. http://medium.com /planetary-liberation-front/a-summary-of-galactic-federation-of-light-messages -bcc26f1d9cb1.

Grant, Kara-Leah. "Kundalini Awakenings: Symptoms, Process, Benefits, Support & Help." *Kara-Leah* (blog). October 25, 2018. http://karaleah.com/2018/10/kundalini-awakenings -symptoms-process-benefits-support-help.

Groleau, Rick. "Imagining Other Dimensions." *NOVA: The Elegant Universe.* Accessed April 20, 2020. http://pbs.org/wgbh/nova/elegant/dimensions.html.

Howe, Linda. *How to Read the Akashic Records: Accessing the Archive of the Soul and Its Journey.* Boulder, CO: Sounds True, 2009.

Kunz, Barbara, and Kevin Kunz. *Reflexology: Health at Your Fingertips.* New York, NY: Dorling DK Publishing, 2003.

Ledwell, Natalie. "Toroidal Energetic Field? What Tha?!" *Mind Movies* (blog). Accessed April 20, 2020. http://mindmovies.com/blogroll/toroidal-energetic-field-what-tha.

Levy, Paul. "Wetiko: The Greatest Epidemic Sickness Known to Humanity." Reality Sandwich. January 3, 2011. http://realitysandwich.com/75652/greatest_epidemic.

Low, Phillip. "Overview of the Autonomic Nervous System." Merck Manual Consumer Version. Last modified April 2020. http://merckmanuals.com/home/brain,-spinal-cord, -and-nerve-disorders/autonomic-nervous-system-disorders/overview-of-the -autonomic-nervous-system.

Lucas, Stephanie. "The Seven Subtle Bodies of Multidimensional Human Consciousness." Quantum Stones. April 19, 2014. http://quantumstones.com/fostering-higher-vibrations -seven-subtle-bodies.

Miles, John R. "Improving Gut Health through Diet—A Bold Interview with Dr. Steven R. Gundry." *Bold Business.* February 21, 2019. http://boldbusiness.com/health/steve-gundry -interview-gut-health-importance.

Murphy, Andye. "What Is a Light Body?" Gaia. February 6, 2020. February 6, 2020. http://gaia.com/article/what-is-a-light-body.

Newlyn, Emma. "The 8 Limbs of Yoga Explained." EkhartYoga. Accessed April 20, 2020. http://ekhartyoga.com/articles/philosophy/the-8-limbs-of-yoga-explained.

Palmero, Elizabeth. "What Is Acupuncture?" Live Science. June 22, 2017. http://livescience.com/29494-acupuncture.html.

Pappas, Stephanie. "Oxytocin: Facts About the 'Cuddle Hormone.'" Live Science. June 4, 2015. http://livescience.com/42198-what-is-oxytocin.html.

Paul of Venus. @mtshastaspiritualtours

Prater, Douglas. *Infinity: Revolutionary Lambda Brainwave Meditation for Entering Transcendent Consciousness.* iAwake Technologies, 2017, 2 compact discs.

Psychologist World. "The Psychology of Color: Exploring Cultural Associations between Colors and Emotions." Accessed May 6, 2020. http://psychologistworld.com/perception/color.

Raphaell, Katrina. *The Crystalline Transmission: A Synthesis of Light.* Santa Fe, NM: Aurora Press, 1990.

Rigato, Lauren. "Vagal Breathing Technique." The Bodymind Centre. July 12, 2019. http://bodymindcentre.com/vagal-breathing-technique.

Rosenberg, Chana. "Body Meridians and Acu-Points Made Simple." Natural Health Zone. Accessed April 20, 2020. http://natural-health-zone.com/Body-meridians-book.html.

Sargis, Robert M. "How Your Thyroid Works." Endocrine Web. Last modified October 21, 2019. http://endocrineweb.com/conditions/thyroid/how-your-thyroid-works.

Severinsen, Stig. "Vibration Therapy." Breatheology. Accessed April 20, 2020. http:// breatheology.com/vibration-therapy.

Seymour, Tom. "Everything You Need to Know about the Vagus Nerve." *Medical News Today.* June 28, 2017. http://medicalnewstoday.com/articles/318128.php.

Siegel, Ethan. "This Is Why the Multiverse Must Exist." *Forbes.* May 15, 2019. Accessed May 6, 2020. http://forbes.com/sites/startswithabang/2019/03/15/this-is-why-the-multiverse-must-exist/#b080cdc6d086.

Swancer, Brent. "Seeing Double: Strange Cases of Bilocation." *Mysterious Universe*. January 30, 2017. http://mysteriousuniverse.org/2017/01/seeing-double-strange-cases-of-bilocation.

Vogt, Nicole. "Astronomy 110G: Introduction to Astronomy: The Expansion of the Universe." New Mexico State University. Accessed April 20, 2020. http://astronomy.nmsu.edu/nicole/teaching/ASTR110/lectures/lecture28/slide01.html.

Wallis, Christopher. "The Real Story on the Chakras." Hareesh. February 5, 2016. http://hareesh.org/blog/2016/2/5/the-real-story-on-the-chakras.

Walter, Sandra. "The Eclipse Transformations: Timelines, the Logos, Change and the Heart." *Sandra Walter Light Intel Articles* (blog). January 26, 2018. http://sandrawalter.com/the-eclipse-transformations-timelines-the-logos-change-and-the-heart.

Index

Divine gateway chakra, 195–201, 204
Divine Mind, 195–196, 198
Durga, 68

E

Earth, 69
Earth star chakra, 61–70
Egypt, 7
Element syncing, 81–82
Emotional blockages, 21–22, 50–51
Emotional Freedom Technique
    (EFT), 119
Empaths, 55
Energy, 4–5, 7–8, 18–19, 26–27, 53–54.
    See also Blockages; Subtle energy
Energy imprints, 19
Energy leakage, 20, 24–25
Epigenetics, 42
Essential oils, 41
Europe, 8

F

Feminine archetype, 78
Flower of Life, 156
Flowers, 41
Frequencies, 4–5, 10–11, 18–19, 23, 26–27.
    See also Energy; Sound therapy

G

Galactic Federation of Light, 179
Ganesha, 142
Glands. See specific chakras
Golden Age, 65, 184
Green Tara, 178

H

Hanuman, 104
Hara line, 95
Harmony, 48–49
Hathor, 130

Healer archetype, 114
Healing, 8–9, 48–49,
    See also Blockages
Healing stones, 40–41
Heart chakra, 109–120
Heart space meditation, 117, 120
Herbalism, 41
Hermetic mystery traditions, 7–8
Hinduism, 7
Horus, 167

I

Illnesses. See specific chakras
Inanna, 117
Indra, 104
Intuitives, 55
Isis, 167

J

Jagannaath, 188
Jesus Christ, 116
Jewish people, 7
Judge archetype, 140
Jung, Carl, 6, 66, 78
Jupiter, 155

K

Kali Ma, 68
Karma, 162
Kinesthetic intuitives, 55
King archetype, 101, 152
Krishna, 116
Kundalini energy, 27, 43–44

L

Lakshmi, 92
Lambda brainwave, 175–176
Law of Attraction, 20, 48
Light bath meditation, 189–190
Light/shadow balancing ritual, 93–94

Acknowledgments

The outpouring of love and support I have received over the course of writing this book truly brings tears to my eyes. As always, I'd like to acknowledge the team over at Callisto, specifically Sean Newcott and the incredible editing team that assisted in the development of this work. To my parents, George and Lu Pfender, who have encouraged me consistently since childhood to always pursue my dreams. To my little Frenchie, Skyla, who turned seven this year. She is the baddest good girl on the Westside.

I'd like to thank my close sister-teachers in the spiritual community who have shared their wisdom and channeled grace to contribute to this masterpiece: Sky Hardison (Akashic intuitive), Kimber Tiernan (ascension teacher), Ama'zjhi Dona Ho Lightsey (creator of Violet Light Alchemy), and Erika Othen (astrologer and channel). Thank you for adding a rich layer of love and support to my life and the lives of everyone you touch. Thank you to my sister-goddesses who are doing their part in healing the world: Torri Fitzgerald, Chelsea Didier, Julia Grace, Natalie Valle, Danielle Karuna, Celia Gellert, Jessy Chang, Lirany Vasquez, Zoey Sigmon Greco, Willow, Rachel Smith, Brittney Bello, Sabrina Riccio, Shakti Mayumi, Emily Thomas, Krista Williams, Tiffany P. Schmidt, Melissa Boudreau, Christine Olivia, Megan Lorelle, Sarah Anassori, and Ashley Frey. To my friends who mean so much to me: Stephanie Herrick, Danai Schulte, Kristen Williams, Jane Trieu, Danielle Franco, Sabrina Hill, Jess Moody, Sarah Tomasso, Stephanie Lemnei, Erin Kuney, Anya Christanthon, and Sue Kim. And to my brothers in light who have been such amazing supporters of me and my conscious work: Max my Lemurian brother, Paul Isaac of Venus, Ari Arcturian Isaac, Stephen Baldonado, Justin Vesci, Alain Torres, José Rosales, Eric Mellgren, Pete Orlanski, Geronimo Redfeather, and Victor Manuel.

To all the incredible humans at Unplug Meditation, including Suze, Claire, Katie, Jalina, and team—you are all the best, and I love being a part of the Meditative Revolution together! Thank you from the bottom of my heart for sharing in this incredible experience with me. You are treasured.

About the Author

April Pfender is a Reiki Master Teacher (RMT), intuitive channel, quantum healer, sound alchemist, and meditation guide practicing in Santa Monica, California, for over a decade. She is the founder of Santa Monica Healing, focusing on Reiki and quantum healing practices. April is passionate about guiding others to embrace their own multidimensionality through ascension work and activational retreat offerings, which she hosts throughout the year. As a creative passion, she has designed and developed an energetic healing jewelry line that supports the wearer through Reiki and moon-infused crystals.

This book is April's third in three years, following *Chakra Balance* and *Essential Chakra Meditation*. In addition to writing, she loves to design healing programs, workshops, and retreats with a focus on awakening, transformation, and women's empowerment. Traveling is always essential, and her passion has been visiting Mount Shasta, Joshua Tree, and Sedona as often as possible.

April is an advocate of being true to your highest self, following your daydreams, and authentic artistic expression. She believes that Reiki and meditation connect us more profoundly to ourselves, Earth, and one another. This connection lends to strengthening our vibrant conscious community, equipping us to bring more peace into the world as we rise in ascension together. Visit her website SantaMonicaHealing.com to book an in-person private appointment with her and stay updated on her public offerings.

Printed in the USA
CPSIA information can be obtained
at www.ICGtesting.com
CBHW042257300424
7724CB00003B/6

9 781647 390600